Third Language Learners

SECOND LANGUAGE ACQUISITION
Series Editor: Professor David Singleton, *Trinity College, Dublin, Ireland*

This new series will bring together titles dealing with a variety of aspects of language acquisition and processing in situations where a language or languages other than the native language is involved. Second language will thus be interpreted in its broadest possible sense. The volumes included in the series will all in their different ways offer, on the one hand, exposition and discussion of empirical findings and, on the other, some degree of theoretical reflection. In this latter connection, no particular theoretical stance will be privileged in the series; nor will any relevant perspective – sociolinguistic, psycholinguistic, neurolinguistic, etc. – be deemed out of place. The intended readership of the series will be final-year undergraduates working on second language acquisition projects, postgraduate students involved in second language acquisition research, and researchers and teachers in general whose interests include a second language acquisition component.

Other Books in the Series
Portraits of the L2 User
   Vivian Cook (ed.)
Learning to Request in a Second Language: A Study of Child Interlanguage Pragmatics
   Machiko Achiba
Effects of Second Language on the First
   Vivian Cook (ed.)
Age and the Acquisition of English as a Foreign Language
   María del Pilar García Mayo and Maria Luisa García Lecumberri (eds)
Fossilization in Adult Second Language Acquisition
   ZhaoHong Han
Silence in Second Language Learning: A Psychoanalytic Reading
   Colette A. Granger
Age, Accent and Experience in Second Language Acquisition
   Alene Moyer
Studying Speaking to Inform Second Language Learning
   Diana Boxer and Andrew D. Cohen (eds)
Language Acquisition: The Age Factor (2nd Edition)
   David Singleton and Lisa Ryan
Focus on French as a Foreign Language: Multidisciplinary Approaches
   Jean-Marc Dewaele (ed.)
Second Language Writing Systems
   Vivian Cook and Benedetta Bassetti (eds)

Other Books of Interest
Cross-linguistic Influence in Third Language Acquisition
   J. Cenoz, B. Hufeisen and U. Jessner (eds)
Trilingualism in Family, School and Community
   Charlotte Hoffmann and Jehannes Ytsma (eds)
Negotiation of Identities in Multilingual Contexts
   Aneta Pavlenko and Adrian Blackledge (eds)

For more details of these or any other of our publications, please contact:
**Multilingual Matters, Frankfurt Lodge, Clevedon Hall,
Victoria Road, Clevedon, BS21 7HH, England
http://www.multilingual-matters.com**

SECOND LANGUAGE ACQUISITION 12
Series Editor: David Singleton, *Trinity College, Dublin, Ireland*

Third Language Learners
Pragmatic Production and Awareness

Maria Pilar Safont Jordà

MULTILINGUAL MATTERS LTD
Clevedon • Buffalo • Toronto

Library of Congress Cataloging in Publication Data
Safont Jordà, Maria Pilar
Third Language Learners: Pragmatic Production and Awareness
Maria Pilar Safont Jordà.
Second Language Acquisition: 12
Includes bibliographical references and index.
1. Language and languages–Study and teaching. 2. Pragmatics. 3. Language awareness. I. Title. II. Series.
P53.J654 2005
418'.0071–dc22   2004017324

British Library Cataloguing in Publication Data
A catalogue entry for this book is available from the British Library.

ISBN 1-85359-803-8 (hbk)
ISBN 1-85359-802-X (pbk)

Multilingual Matters Ltd
UK: Frankfurt Lodge, Clevedon Hall, Victoria Road, Clevedon BS21 7HH.
USA: UTP, 2250 Military Road, Tonawanda, NY 14150, USA.
Canada: UTP, 5201 Dufferin Street, North York, Ontario M3H 5T8, Canada.

Copyright © 2005 Maria Pilar Safont Jordà.

All rights reserved. No part of this work may be reproduced in any form or by any means without permission in writing from the publisher.

Typeset by Saxon Graphics Ltd.

Contents

Acknowledgements vii

Introduction 1

Part 1: Theoretical Background
1 Third Language Acquisition 9
    Introduction 9
    Third Language Acquisition: Defining Characteristics 11
    Second versus Third Language Acquisition 14
    Bilingualism 22
    Learning a Third Language 39

2 Pragmatic Competence and Foreign Language Learning 50
    Introduction 50
    Communicative Competence 51
    The Pragmatic Component of Communicative Competence 57
    Interlanguage Pragmatics 67
    The Speech Act of Requesting 75

3 The Sociolinguistic Context: Language Learning and Use in the
    Valencian Community 85
    Introduction 85
    The Catalan Language in the Valencian Community 86
    Bilingual Education in the Valencian Community 89
    Multilingual Education in the Valencian Community 93
    Foreign Language Learning in the University Setting 95

Part 2: The Study
4 The Method 101
    Participants 101
    Data Collection Procedure 104
    Methodological Decisions Taken in the Analysis of the Data 111

5 The Role of Pragmatic Instruction in Developing Foreign
   Language Learners' Pragmatic Competence 114
   Hypothesis and Research Questions 114
   Results and Discussion..115
   Conclusions 128

6 Effects of Proficiency Level on Pragmatic Production.........................131
   Hypothesis and Research Questions 131
   Results and Discussion 132
   Conclusions 139

7 The Effects of the Task on Pragmatic Production................................140
   Hypothesis and Research Questions 140
   Results and Discussion 141
   Conclusions 151

8 The Role of Bilingualism in Pragmatic Awareness 153
   Hypotheses and Research Questions 153
   Results and Discussion 154
   Conclusions 161

9 Pragmatic Production and Awareness of Third Language
   Learners. Summarising the Findings..163

References..171

Acknowledgements

First and foremost, I would like to express my most sincere gratitude to Professor Eva Alcón, my thesis supervisor, for her comments and advice on an earlier version of the book. I would also like to highlight her patience, encouragement and support during all stages of the study described in Part 2. Without her continuous assessment, it would have been impossible to accomplish the project, since she actually instigated the study and elicited my curiosity in the field. I found evidence of her most excellent qualities both as researcher and as professor, but I would also like to stress her kind-heartedness and humane qualities. I do feel extremely obliged to her.

I would also like to thank Professor Rosa Manchón, who also supervised the study presented in Part 2, and who provided me with the most appropriate and useful commentaries. I am particularly grateful for this enriching experience in contrasting opinions, and learning how to take profit out of data.

I must also express my indebtedness to Professor Jasone Cenoz for her recommendations, support and help. I would like to stress my appreciation of her valuable assistance in gaining access to crucial resources for the first part of the book. I would also like to thank Professor Singleton and the anonymous reviewer of this collection for their most useful and valuable comments on earlier versions of the book.

Special thanks also go to Professor Maria Pilar García Mayo for her availability in assisting and providing help at all times, which I do appreciate. For providing me with useful and thoughtful comments regarding publication of this work, I'd like to thank Professor Francisco Fernández, Professor Carmen Muñoz, Professor Patricia Bou and Professor Victòria Codina.

I am very grateful to Professor Patricia Salazar for her assistance and most valuable cooperation during the instructional period, and for her reliability and forbearance. I would also like to thank Professor Maria José Esteve, Professor Mari Carmen Campoy and Professor Santiago

Posteguillo for their encouragement and moral support as well as for their constant offers of help and amiability. Thanks a lot to the Head of the Languages and Terminology Service of Jaume I University, Professor Bartomeu Prior, for his aid regarding data on the University Linguistic Policy Plan and about the status of the Catalan language in this institutional setting.

My deepest thankfulness goes to my parents, Juan Miguel and Margarita, and to my sister, Margarita, for their sincere and most reliable comfort. I also very much appreciate my boyfriend's encouraging attitude, his honesty, his comments, his invaluable aid at critical stages and also, above all, his patience.

Introduction

The birth of the European Union has increased the importance of learning foreign languages. This fact has indirectly promoted the status of the English language in our society, with the result that learning English now constitutes a necessity. Similarly, given the importance attached to language learning in our society, a concomitant interest in studying language acquisition processes has also developed. In conducting acquisitional studies, the multilingual nature of many European communities, such as those of Finland, Italy, Sweden, Austria or Spain, should be taken into account. Regarding this last country, we should point out the fact that in 1978 the Spanish Constitution was approved and Spain was recognised as a plurilingual society. Languages from each autonomous community (Basque, Galician and Catalan) are now learned at schools and universities. That is the case with Catalan in the Valencian Community, which is officially considered a bilingual area where both Catalan and Castilian are employed. This bilingual area constitutes the global framework of the present study.

The fact that most learners of English living in Europe already possess knowledge of at least two other languages has been partially neglected in second and foreign language acquisition research. The scarcity of multilingualism studies contrasts with the abundant existing research in the field of second language acquisition. Yet in the 1970s some researchers (Bain and Yu, 1980; Ben-Zeev, 1977; Ianco-Worrall, 1972) pointed to the positive impact of bilingualism on the individual's cognitive development. Subsequent research (Bialystok, 1988; Mägiste, 1984; Ringbom, 1987) has further confirmed the advantage of bilinguals over monolinguals in terms of linguistic and cognitive outcomes. These facts have given rise to a relatively young subfield in the study of language learning processes, namely that of third language acquisition.

Research in third language acquisition has addressed issues of language transfer (Hufeisen, 1991; Williams and Hammarberg, 1998) from L1 or L2 to L3, metalinguistic knowledge and creative thinking

(Lasagabaster, 1997), interactional competence (Jessner, 1999), the age factor (García-Mayo and García-Lecumberri, 2003; Muñoz, 2000) and immersion pedagogy (Bjorklund and Suni, 2000; Lyster, 1998). In fact, we may state that a growing body of investigation on third language acquisition now exists, as illustrated by the recent collection of studies provided by Cenoz and Genesee (1998), Cenoz and Jessner (2000), and Cenoz et al. (2001b). The positive results provided by third language acquisition studies that establish bilingualism as a good predictor of English language achievement (Cenoz and Valencia, 1994) argue for further investigation in this subfield in order to determine the true nature of the relationship between bilingualism and third language acquisition.

One aspect that has not received much attention in third language acquisition studies is that of the development of the learner's pragmatic competence in the target language. Fouser's (1997) study stands out as an exception. Nevertheless, Jessner (1997) posits advantages of bilinguals over monolinguals in terms of their interactional and communicative competence in the target language. For that reason, one of our main objectives relates to acknowledging the role of bilingualism in third language learners' pragmatic awareness.

In short, this book attempts to provide a bridge between two applied linguistics subfields, namely those of interlanguage pragmatics and third language acquisition studies. In the first part of the volume, and before we describe the empirical study itself, we present an overview of the theoretical background underlying the study as well as the sociolinguistic context in which the research is located. Thus, multilingual education in this community suggests/implies the existence of other multilingual education programmes in bilingual European communities. This reality has promoted research in third language acquisition and multilingualism, which will be presented in Chapter 1. In order to review research conducted within this relatively young discipline, we shall consider third language acquisition as related to but also distinguished from two other areas, namely those of second language acquisition research and bilingualism. We will first deal with defining characteristics of third language acquisition which refer to a new conception of language development (Herdina and Jessner, 2000). Individual differences, the context and the interaction between two or three languages known to the learner are seen as fosterers of the dynamism embedded in multilingual processing (Jessner, 1999). These specific characteristics of third language acquisition lead to the need to distinguish third from second language acquisition (Cenoz, 2000). Therefore, we will consider the main differences between these two applied linguistics subfields in this first chapter.

As mentioned above, we shall also consider a related discipline, that of bilingualism. We will pay special attention to that phenomenon seeing that it relates to our study in two ways. Firstly, some of the findings obtained by bilingualism studies (De Bot, 1992; Poulisse and Bongaerts, 1994) may facilitate our understanding of those processes underlying third language acquisition. Secondly, it may provide us with further information on those processing mechanisms (Hoffman, 1991; Li Wei, 2000; Volterra and Taeschner, 1978) our subjects may resort to as bilingual speakers. Finally, Chapter 1 will include previous empirical studies on the role of bilingualism in third language acquisition and use (Lasagabaster, 1997). Since the book relates third language acquisition to pragmatic competence, existing research accounting for pragmatic competence in third language use will be discussed in detail (Fouser, 1997).

Chapter 2 deals with the field of interlanguage pragmatics, and thus it focuses on language learners' pragmatic competence. This chapter will first of all include some of the most influential theories and frameworks for interlanguage pragmatists, such as existing models of communicative competence (Bachman, 1990; Canale, 1983; Celce-Murcia et al., 1995), the relevance theory (Sperber and Wilson, 1986), the politeness theory (Brown and Levinson, 1987) and the speech acts theory (Searle, 1976). Secondly, we shall present an overview of research conducted within the interlanguage pragmatics field (Kasper and Schmidt, 1996), with a focus on developmental perspectives and speech acts production (Kasper and Dahl, 1991). Since our study will specifically analyse the linguistic realisations of request acts by foreign and third language learners of English, we shall deal in particular with the speech act of requesting. A description of request linguistic formulations (Trosborg, 1995) and of peripheral modification devices (Sifianou, 1999) will also be presented, as this will constitute the basis of our analysis, which is fully described in Part 2 of the present volume.

The analysis of requestive behaviour presented in the second part of the book was conducted in the Valencian Community. This sociolinguistic context is described in Chapter 3, where we discuss language learning and use in the Valencian Community. On the one hand, an outline of that community is presented, thereby pointing to the status of Catalan and Castilian, the origin and evolution of the Catalan language in the Valencian Community and the role of bilingualism in the university setting. On the other hand, we will focus on our informants' linguistic background, particularly referring to their knowledge of English and previous learning experience. The way in which mutilingualism is tackled by educational authorities in the Valencian Community will also be dealt with in this third chapter.

Our interest in the development of pragmatic competence and awareness on the part of bilingual learners of English derives from the actual concern of foreign and second language acquisition scholars about discourse and pragmatic aspects of the target language. Recently there has been a shift from a focus on learning and using structural and lexical aspects of the target language towards a more discourse-centred perspective. Since pragmatic competence was identified as one of the main components of Bachman's communicative competence model (1990), current studies have focused on the relationship between pragmatics and second language acquisition, that is to say, on what has been termed interlanguage pragmatics. As discussed by Kasper (2000), interlanguage pragmatics research has concentrated on two main perspectives. On the one hand, scholars have focused on the learners' use of pragmatic aspects. On the other hand, some studies have focused on pragmatic development. The vast majority of research on interlanguage pragmatics has addressed second language use by comparing learners' pragmatic competence with that of native speakers of the target language (Blum-Kulka *et al.*, 1989). Topics considered within this perspective have been borrowed from studies of first language pragmatics; such is the case with speech acts, discourse sequencing and conversational management. Nevertheless, contrasting the use of pragmatic items by learners and native speakers of a given language does not seem to provide an immediate link to language acquisition, as claimed by Kasper (1996). Instead, investigation concerning pragmatic development accounts for a relationship between language acquisition processes and the pragmatic competence of the language learner. Unlike studies on L2 pragmatic use, investigation into developmental issues is rather scarce. Owing to this fact, little is known about those processes and factors implied in the pragmatic development of non-native speakers. However, scholars investigating developmental issues have provided us with some interesting assumptions.

The study[1] described in Part 2 of this book attempts to tackle some of these assumptions which relate to the role of instruction, the learners' proficiency level and the task type in the use of request acts. Furthermore, we aim at broadening the scope of research in two different areas, namely those of interlanguage pragmatics and third language acquisition. Hence, this second part of the volume includes an analysis of the use of request acts formulations and the evaluation of such use by bilingual and monolingual learners of English as a foreign (third) language. Chapter 4 is devoted to describing in detail the methodological aspects of our study; that is, the informants' characteristics, the elicitation procedures and the methodological decisions taken in the data analysis.

Chapters 5 to 8 include testing procedures, results obtained and further implications for ongoing research. Thus each chapter focuses on testing the hypotheses deriving from previous research in the interlanguage pragmatics and third language acquisition areas. Chapter 5 deals with the role of explicit instruction in foreign language learners' pragmatic production. As argued by Kasper and Rose (1999, 2002), the development of pragmatic competence will take place only if learners are immersed in the target language culture or when they receive explicit instruction on pragmatic aspects. Bardovi-Harlig and Dörnyei (1998) considered the effect of being immersed in the target language culture, and recent studies have dealt with the role of explicit and implicit instruction in the development of pragmatic competence (Barron, 2003; Rose and Kasper, 2001). Nevertheless, further empirical studies are needed to support Kasper and Rose's above-quoted assumptions (1999, 2002), particularly in foreign language learning settings. On that account, Chapter 5 deals with the role of instruction in English learners' pragmatic production.

In addition to instructional effects, studies focusing on interlanguage pragmatics development have investigated the relationship between L2 proficiency level and the acquisition of pragmatic competence (Koike, 1996). Chapter 6 examines the influence of learners' proficiency level in their use of request realisations and peripheral modification items. Researchers investigating the effects of proficiency level (Bergman and Kasper, 1993; Fouser, 1995; House, 1989; Robinson, 1992) point to a mismatch between the learners' linguistic proficiency level and their pragmatic competence in the target language. Most of these studies have dealt with subjects at advanced proficiency levels. For this reason, Kasper and Rose (1999, 2002) argue for the need to include learners at beginner proficiency levels in developmental interlanguage pragmatics studies. In an attempt to shed more light on the role of the learners' proficiency level, we have dealt with intermediate and beginner learners of English as a foreign language. This chapter analyses the influence of the learners' proficiency in their use of request acts. In order to obtain data concerning participants' requestive behaviour, different elicitation techniques are employed.

Chapter 7 deals with the role of the elicitation method used – an issue that has deserved some attention in interlanguage pragmatics (Sasaki, 1998). Findings contrasting various methods or tasks that learners were required to perform point to significant differences in learners' pragmatic behaviour. A main distinction is found between results obtained by means of oral and written task types (Beebe and Cummings, 1996). However, few studies have included more than one type of elicitation method in their analysis of pragmatic production. Because of this, there seems to be a need for resorting to various elicitation techniques in ascertaining language learners' use of pragmatic items in the target language. In view of this, we have included three different task types, namely those of a written production test, an oral production task and an awareness-raising task. The effect of each instrument on learners' performance has been examined in order to test the influence of each task type on the subjects' pragmatic performance.

Chapter 8 is devoted to analysing another aspect of the learners' pragmatic competence, that of pragmatic awareness. In so doing, a link is made with their linguistic background in order to discover differences or similarities between the monolingual and the bilingual subgroup. In this chapter we consider the extent to which pragmatic awareness may be more developed in third than in second/foreign language learners of English. Despite the fact that bilingualism effects have been taken into account in previous chapters, it is at this stage that a deeper analysis is conducted, and thus a clearer attempt is made to bridge the gap between the disciplines of interlanguage pragmatics and third language acquisition.

Finally, a concluding chapter raises the main lines of discussion and summarises results presented in previous chapters. In addition to that, Chapter 9 includes those theoretical implications deriving from the findings described in Chapters 5 to 8, as well as suggestions for further research related to the fields of interlanguage pragmatics and third language acquisition.

Note

1. Part of this study was conducted within the framework of a research project funded by Ministerio de Educación y Ciencia HUM2004-04435/FILO

Part 1
Theoretical Background

Chapter 1
Third Language Acquisition

Introduction

The status of the English language as a lingua franca in Europe has promoted the existence of multilingual education programmes in bilingual European communities. In northern European countries, English is more often employed outside the classroom context than in southern states, such as Spain. In fact, as suggested by Cenoz and Jessner (2000), it is not clear to what extent we should consider English as a foreign language in areas like Finland or Sweden. Following Berns (1990), these authors argue for a different perspective from the traditional EFL/ESL dichotomy in third language learning and use contexts. Their suggestion is to place the language in a continuum where we would find English as a foreign language at one end, and English as a second language at the other end. In this way, communities that are starting to use or have been using English in real-life contexts would place this third language halfway along this foreign to second language spectrum. From this perspective, we may assume that third language acquisition is a unique phenomenon that deserves consideration as a subfield within the global area of applied linguistics. It should then be studied in the same way as other subfields with which it bears a close relationship, such as that of second language acquisition.

The purpose of this chapter is to present an overview of research conducted in the field of third language acquisition. We will consider third language acquisition as related to but also different from two other disciplines, namely those of second language acquisition and bilingualism. As argued by Cenoz et al. (2001a), research in second language acquisition and bilingualism presents results that affect and facilitate our understanding of third language acquisition development, but there are some aspects that should be specifically dealt with. For this reason, we have subdivided the chapter into four main sections dealing with defining characteristics underlying third language acquisition, second language acquisition, bilingualism and empirical studies devoted to the analysis of third language acquisition and use in different settings. On account of the ideas expressed above, we will firstly, consider the complex nature of third language acquisition, which also applies to the term itself, as noted in the second section of this chapter. In this section, defining characteristics of third language acquisition will be dealt with, and special attention will be paid to a new approach for the study of those processes involved in the acquisition of a third language, namely that of the dynamic model for multilingualism, which has been proposed by Herdina and Jessner (2000, 2002). Individual differences, the context and the interaction between two or three languages known to the learner constitute some of the factors identified in the literature on multilingualism (Herdina and Jessner, 2002; Jessner, 1999) as promoting dynamism. A new conception of language development is then likely to arise from current empirical findings and theoretical assumptions in multilingual and third language acquisition. This new perspective will extend and support the complexity underlying third language learning raised and discussed in the third section of this chapter. We believe that focusing on the dynamic processes that take place in third language acquisition will help us account for what actually occurs in bilinguals' acquisition of a foreign language, which needs to be distinguished from second language acquisition.

For this reason, this third section aims at distinguishing third from second language acquisition. In order to present some evidence supporting such a difference, we will try to ascertain to what extent specific factors underlying third language acquisition, as pointed out by Cenoz (2000), are reflected in some of the most outstanding theories of second language acquisition. The distinction between second and third language acquisition processes will raise the issue of the complexity attributed to the acquisition of a third language. It may illustrate the idea that third language acquisition involves those factors affecting second language acquisition and also those effects deriving from the interaction between those languages known to the third language learner, who is also a bilingual speaker.

Bearing in mind the fact that our subjects are bilingual speakers learning an additional language in a foreign context, we have devoted the fourth section to bilingualism. We have dealt with this phenomenon because it relates to our study in two ways. Firstly, the inclusion and interpretation of some studies on bilingualism might facilitate our understanding of third language acquisition procedures. Secondly, it might offer some clues to acknowledge the processing mechanisms of our subjects as bilingual speakers. This section also aims at providing existing definitions of the notion of bilingual competence and the typology associated with it.

We will comment on research (Hoffman, 1991; Volterra and Taeschner, 1978) concerning the relationship between the two linguistic systems a bilingual person possesses, which may be regarded as dependent or independent. The conceptualisation of that relationship is also manifested in existing models of bilingual speech production. Taking into account the fact that our study concentrates on bilingual learners' oral production, we shall deal with existing speech production models as well as with the criticisms raised against them. Since we believe that these models should account for particular characteristics of bilingual speech, language switching will be regarded as a defining feature of bilingual speech which reflects interaction between those languages known by the bilingual person. Results from studies on language switching by third language learners (Williams and Hammarberg, 1998) will lead to the inherent complexity underlying multilingual speech.

Considering specific characteristics of our subjects and the fact that they are learning English as a third language, we will pay special attention to the role of bilingualism in third language acquisition in the fifth section. In doing so, we will also account for recent studies carried out in the field of third language acquisition. Finally, we will consider existing research that has accounted for pragmatic competence in third language use.

Third Language Acquisition: Defining Characteristics

As stated by some scholars (Fouser, 1995; Jessner, 1999), there exists a degree of terminological and conceptual confusion regarding third language acquisition. In general terms, third language acquisition denotes those languages learned after a second one, which may imply a third, fourth or fifth language (that is, Ln). Nevertheless, this conceptualisation involves a series of different L2 backgrounds (second or foreign language) and learning situations that would point not only to third but also to bilingual, or even multilingual acquisition. Following this view, terms such as bilingualism, trilingualism or multilingualism would refer to the same phenomenon. In fact, Fouser (1997: 391) states that existing definitions remain 'confusing, as terms like bilingual and multilingual are vague and controversial'. The purpose of this chapter is to present what the concept of third language acquisition entails while pointing to its main outstanding features as suggested by previous researchers in the field. Bearing this aim in mind, we shall follow Herdina and Jessner's notion (2000), which contrasts with traditional aspects characterising language learning and which has been assumed to define third language acquisition in the same way as they explained first and second language acquisition processes.

Herdina and Jessner (2000) provide a clear distinction of the terminology currently used in third language acquisition studies. According to these authors, multilingualism is to be considered as a varied phenomenon involving bilingualism and monolingualism as possible forms, but addressing mainly those languages learned after a second one. In this sense, bilinguals cannot be identified with multilinguals. These authors present representative features of third language acquisition which may involve an important change in traditional language-learning paradigms. These characteristics involve (1) *non-linearity*, (2) *language maintenance*, (3) *individual variation*, (4) *interdependence* and *quality change*. Given the aims of our study, we shall look at these particular defining features in greater detail.

Herdina and Jessner (2000) consider *non-linearity* to be one of the main characteristics of third language acquisition in an attempt to distinguish this process from that involved in acquiring a second language. In fact, language competence is viewed as a gradual process whereby learners acquire a certain degree of proficiency after some training period. This process may be fostered or slowed down by various internal and external factors affecting learners. Besides, whether the process is fast or slow, conscious or unconscious, motivating or demotivating, it is always regarded as linear by second language researchers (Nunan, 1996). However, Herdina and Jessner (2000) argue for non-linearity in multilingual processes on the basis of biological growth studies:[1]

> According to biological principles language development is seen as a dynamic process with phases of accelerated growth and retardation. The development is dependent on environmental factors and is indeterminate. (Herdina and Jessner, 2000: 87)

The retardation phase could enable us to explain language attrition in the learners' second or third language and it also seems to corroborate non-linearity as a defining feature. Considering that language learning takes place in a wide variety of both psychological and physical situations, and the fact that a non-native language requires active use to facilitate its acquisition, it is not surprising that learners who stop using that language might find it difficult to resort to their previously acquired knowledge after a certain period of time. Herdina and Jessner (2000: 91) define gradual language attrition as the opposite process to language growth. For these authors, 'lack of maintenance of a language system results in an adaptive process by which language competence is adjusted to meet the perceived communicative needs of the individual speaker'. A language needs not only to be learned but also to be maintained; otherwise the opposite process to language maintenance and growth is that of language attrition or decay. As argued by these authors, the rate of language attrition may depend on available resources providing authentic input and possibilities for output, on competition among existing linguistic systems, and on age and duration of language maintenance.

This idea leads to the identification of *language maintenance* as a second defining feature of third language acquisition. Learners have to make an effort in order to maintain their proficiency level in the languages known to them. The more languages known by an individual, the more effort is required for their maintenance. Therefore, time is just one possible cause of language attrition, but we may state that language learning, particularly in foreign language settings, needs refreshment periods to prevent attrition from taking place, as any language system needs not only to be learned but also to be maintained. Most third languages are foreign, as is the case of English in many European communities, and owing to the lack of opportunities for real practice, language attrition does occur. One example might be Spain, where learners of English complain that they spend years learning the language yet do not seem to improve greatly. In fact, it seems as though their level becomes somehow fossilised after some period of no use, or because they do not receive enough input and this is not high quality input. This may also affect subjects of the study presented in Part 2, who cannot use the language outside the classroom, thus affecting their rate of development, competence and performance in the target language.

Attrition phenomena may also be connected to *individual traits* of the learner, which concerns another defining feature of third language acquisition stated above. As complex human beings, learners might be influenced by a wide range of factors while learning a third language, thus analysing internal factors in isolation may facilitate their study, but, at the same time, it may present an unreal picture of what actually takes place in the learning process. We agree with Alcón (1997) in that these variables should be regarded from the point of view of their relation. It is also assumed that their interaction will possess a complex nature. However complex this may be, results focused on this relation might illustrate the development and progression of the linguistic system being learned. On account of these ideas, we might say that third language development could be viewed from a dynamic perspective, including variation and interaction among its defining features and influencing factors.

The interaction of specific features in third language acquisition can be explored by focusing on the existing relationships among those languages known by learners. This interdependence characterising third language learning leads us to consider learners' first, second and third languages as a whole linguistic system, which they command simultaneously. In fact, it seems more logical to consider languages known by a multilingual speaker as a whole unit than to view them as separate entities that develop in isolation.

In view of this, multilingualism cannot be interpreted as a mere quantitative change in the languages known to bilingual learners. An additional language affects the overall linguistic system of the learner, while creating new links and relationships. The whole system is restructured and new skills and learning techniques arise from learners' previous language-learning experience. In fact, we might claim that we are facing a qualitative rather than quantitative linguistic change in third language acquisition.

Considering all the ideas mentioned above, we may state that third language acquisition should be regarded as a complex phenomenon involving certain defining features, namely those of non-linearity, language maintenance and attrition, internal factors, interaction and linguistic interdependence. In line with such complexity is the idea that multilingualism should be studied from a dynamic perspective, and should also be consistent with a holistic view of bilingualism. The third language learner has a unique linguistic system which is influenced by the constant change of those relationships being established among the languages involved. Despite the specific characteristics and complexity underlying third language acquisition, as acknowledged by various scholars (Cenoz, 2000, 2003; Herdina and Jessner, 2000), it also shares certain features with other similar processes of language acquisition. Therefore, two related areas are those of second language acquisition and bilingualism. In fact, research conducted in these two subfields has probably influenced some of the current work in this young area, that of third language acquisition. Owing to this, we may focus on some aspects of bilingualism related to our purposes in the fourth section, as we are dealing not with second but with third language learners of a foreign language, who are already bilingual (Catalan/Castilian) speakers. However, we shall devote the next section to reviewing some of the most outstanding differences between second and third language acquisition in an attempt to expand the conceptualisation of third language acquisition presented above.

Second versus Third Language Acquisition

As our study concerns third language learners, it seems appropriate to account for the difference between second and third language acquisition.

The study of multilingualism is a neglected area within the general field of language acquisition. As assumed by several authors (Cenoz, 2000; Fouser, 1995), approaching language learning from a perspective different from that of a second or foreign language is quite new. In fact, as regarded by Cenoz and Genesee (1998), multilingual acquisition is often considered to be a simple variation on bilingualism and second language acquisition. In these cases, second language acquisition is used as a general term to refer to 'any language other than the first one irrespective of the type of learning environment and the number of other languages the learner might know' (Sharwood Smith, 1994: 7).

Despite this fact, scholars further criticise what has been termed the *monolingual prejudice* (Grosjean, 1982), whereby a native-like proficiency level is defined in terms of a monolingual person's proficiency in the target language. As argued by Grosjean (1985), learners' proficiency is commonly evaluated not by accounting for the learners' particular needs and usage, but from the perspective of a native-like monolingual competence. Both in the foreign and in the second language learning context, very few instances are found of second language learners who have achieved a proficiency level similar to that of a monolingual native speaker of the target language. Furthermore, as pointed out by various authors (Cenoz and Genesee, 1998; Edwards, 1994), bilinguals equally competent in their own two languages are almost non-existent. Therefore, theories of second language acquisition adopting such a monolingual bias do not seem to account for real phenomena, that is, the actual truth behind second or third language learning processes.

Among all the existing theories[2] of second language acquisition that are based on a monolingual perspective, the one that might best illustrate this idea is that of the nativisation model developed by Andersen (1983). This theory derives from Schumann's acculturation model (1978), which views second language acquisition as one further aspect of adaptation to the target language culture. Andersen also considers this cultural perspective but he incorporates a focus on internal language-processing mechanisms. According to this author, second language acquisition derives from *nativisation* and *denativisation* procedures. *Nativisation*, or assimilation, procedures relate to the learners' hypotheses in confirming the input received by their own second language system. The opposite process is that of *denativisation*, or accommodation, whereby learners try to adjust their internal interlanguage system to the target language norm. Hence the nativisation model views second language acquisition as a gradual and sequential process where attention is initially drawn to internal, and subsequently turned into external, rules. In this way, the model attributes learners' failure to achieve a native-like competence to a lack of input or lack of attention paid to that input which might be due to perceived psychological or social distance. Andersen's model (1983) has been criticised by Ellis (1995), as it does not account for the interaction between the learner and the situation. Consequently, according to Ellis, it does not consider those operations involved in the interaction between the target language input and the learner's interlanguage system.

Unlike Andersen's model (1983), Krashen's monitor model (1981, 1982) takes into account the relationship between the situation and the learner; thus, it considers the learners' internal mechanisms at work in second language acquisition as well as those situational and affective factors influencing them. Krashen's model consists of five hypotheses, namely those of the learning-acquisition hypothesis, the natural order hypothesis, the monitor hypothesis, the input hypothesis and the affective filter hypothesis. The first hypothesis mentioned above provides a distinction between learning and acquisition. The former involves a conscious awareness of language rules, as it stems from the conscious reflection on the formal properties of the target language. Acquisition takes place as a result of participating in authentic communication. Thus it refers to unconscious feelings regarding appropriateness in language use. Following this view, Krashen argues for separate storage of learned and acquired knowledge. However, this distinction has been widely criticised by scholars in the field of second language acquisition (see McLaughlin, 1978; Sharwood Smith, 1981). The natural-order hypothesis assumes that grammatical items are acquired on a predictable basis. This order will arise when the learners participate in communicative tasks. During the learners' performance in those tasks, a monitor acts as an editor before language is used. This fact reflects Krashen's monitor hypothesis, which raises the idea of the device learners resort to when editing their linguistic performance, which may be prior or posterior to production. Hence this hypothesis addresses production linked to form, not to meaning-related aspects of the target language.

Regarding comprehension, Krashen's input hypothesis leads to the idea that learners exposed to comprehensible input will acquire it in a natural way as language acquisition results from language comprehension, not production.[3] How much input is actually acquired by learners is also affected by their attitude to language learning. It is this attitude, or affective filter, in Krashen's terms (1982), that controls the quantity of input that will become comprehensible and, consequently, available for acquisition. Factors identified by Krashen (1982) and related to learners' attitude include motivation, self-confidence and anxiety. However, this author does not account for further individual differences in the acquisition process. Instead, he views variation in the rate of acquisition as being affected by the amount of comprehensible input that the affective filter may make available. Krashen's notion of variability reflects his dual conception of second language acquisition processes, which concerns two separate competencies, namely those of learning and acquisition. Because of this, the monitor theory has been widely criticised (see Bialystok, 1982, 1984; Ellis, 1984; Sharwood-Smith, 1994; Tarone, 1983).

Contrary to Krashen's claim (1982), which states that acquisition results from comprehension, Swain (1985, 1995) suggests that production is of utmost importance in acquiring a second language. According to this author, output is necessary for acquiring full competence in the target language. Furthermore, the opportunities that production provides for acquisition are described by the author in terms of the functions it performs. Swain (1995) identifies three main functions, namely those of noticing, hypothesis testing and metalinguistic reflection. As learners produce they may notice the needs they have and the knowledge they already possess that enables them to communicate effectively and efficiently. Closely linked to noticing is the second function attributed to output, that of hypothesis testing. As learners become aware of the existing gaps in their linguistic knowledge they may look for alternatives, thus making a hypothesis about linguistic structures and using such structures in testing their hypothesis. These structures may be acquired by means of this hypothesis testing process, as argued by Swain. The third function of output referred to is metalinguistic reflection. This function may be performed as learners try to solve the problems they encounter in using the language, since facing such difficulties may foster their conscious reflection about the nature of the linguistic system.

An alternative theory concerns Ellis' variable competence model (1984), which suggests that the way a language is learned reflects the way it is used. Here, variability applies to both production and comprehension processes. On the basis of this and other existing theories of second language acquisition, Ellis (1991) proposes some hypotheses which attempt to provide a more comprehensive view of the second language acquisition phenomenon. These hypotheses are grouped according to the situation in which learning takes place, the amount and quality of input the learner is exposed to, the linguistic output, learner processes and learner differences. In order to briefly review the most significant factors influencing second language acquisition, we have considered Ellis' set of hypotheses (1991) as a global framework.

The first set of hypotheses refer to situational factors that may indirectly affect the rate of acquisition and proficiency level gained. However, such situational factors might not play a significant role in the order or sequence of development. According to Ellis (1991), it can be assumed that classroom and naturalistic settings entail identical developmental sequences for second language acquisition. The learning situation will primarily influence the learner's interlanguage use just as it affects a native speakers' use of his/her mother tongue.

Another set of hypotheses describing second language acquisition (Ellis, 1991) refer to the amount and quality of the linguistic data learners are exposed to either by reading or by listening to the target language. Language input may be modified from negotiation in conversation and it may affect the order, sequence and rate of development. By the same token, the language produced by learners, that is, their linguistic output, may also affect second language development. This idea leads to hypothesis-testing procedures taking place both before and after language production, which are assumed to operate on the linguistic formulae employed by language learners. In this sense, as reported by Ellis, linguistic output does play a part in interlanguage development.

The use and construction of interlanguage by second language learners is also a central part of a third group of hypotheses referring to learner processes. According to Ellis, interlanguage development can be seen as a consequence of learners' use and acquisition of those rules underlying second language production and comprehension. Nevertheless, learner processes are also subject to learner differences. In Ellis' terms, these differences might refer to attitudinal factors (e.g. motivation and personality) and to the influence of the first language. The learners' mother tongue is regarded as an important factor affecting second language acquisition (Corder, 1978; Hatch, 1983). However, its role in the sequence of development remains doubtful, as argued by Ellis (1991). Besides, transfer effects from the learners' mother tongue should not be studied in the same way as if we were dealing with monolingual or bilingual language learners.

As noted by certain authors (Hufeisen, 1998; Jessner, 1999), third language acquisition needs to be distinguished from second language acquisition in order to account for what actually takes place in bilinguals' acquisition of a foreign language. Cenoz (2000) signals the main differences between second and third language or multilingual acquisition. These refer to: (1) the order in which languages are learned; (2) sociolinguistic factors, and (3) the psycholinguistic processes involved.

In second language acquisition, few possibilities of variation exist as far as order of acquisition is concerned: either the L2 is acquired after L1, or the two languages are learned simultaneously, which may in turn lead to bilingualism. When more than two languages are involved in the acquisitional process, those possibilities for order variation increase a great deal. The learning process of one language (e.g. L3) could be interrupted by another one (e.g. L4) during a long or short period of time owing to external causes (living in a foreign country, travelling for business and the like) or internal ones (learners' lack of motivation or interest).

The second difference between second and third language acquisition stated above refers to a set of contextual and linguistic factors influencing third language competence and performance. Cenoz (2000) subdivides such factors into those related to the context where these languages are learned and used, together with the linguistic typology and the sociocultural status of the languages involved. The context of language use implies that the L1, L2 or L3 may be used in either a natural context (being the community language) or an instructional setting (being used in class), or in both contexts, as is the case with Castilian in many Spanish communities, including our own. This would affect the L3 acquisition process, given the fact that the quality and quantity of L3 input available to the learner will influence the development of his/her oral or written skills in the target language.

The relationship between the languages being learned, as far as linguistic typology is concerned, constitutes another factor affecting third language acquisition. Languages typologically closer to the target language may facilitate its acquisition or favour code-mixing procedures. In the latter case, learners may tend to borrow terms from those languages that are typologically closer to the target language. Interestingly, as is considered by Hammarberg and Hammarberg (1993) and Williams and Hammarberg (1998), cross-linguistic influence is seen as a major source for research in third language use. These authors have particularly focused on the role of L1 and L2 in the production of a third one and results from their studies seem to attribute a default supplier role to the second language in cases where second and third languages are typologically closer. However, there are cases where the relationship between the learners' first and second language is closer than the one between their second and third language. In these cases, distance is regarded as a more powerful factor than the use of L2 as default supplier. This fact also applies to our subjects, whose first language (Catalan) is typologically more similar to their second (Castilian) than to their third language (English).

Another important factor affecting third language acquisition is the sociocultural context in which the languages are learned and used. In most multilingual and bilingual societies (if not all), languages have different privileges; that is, they are not used in the same way or for the same purposes. In fact, we find diglossic societies where the L2 is used in the media, for educational purposes and the like, while members of these societies resort to their L1 and L3 in their everyday conversations (at work, with their families and the like). This fact affects education (González, 1998). In the third chapter we will comment on the sociocultural and sociolinguistic context in which our subjects learn and have learned English and we will also pay attention to existing bilingual programmes within such contexts. As it is regarded as a specific factor affecting third language acquisition, we shall next briefly consider Nunan and Lam's description of educational programmes based on existing languages status (1998). In doing so, we will identify the type of educational programme subjects from our study presented in the second part regarding their first and second language, thus presenting a more accurate picture of their multilingual learning situation.

Nunan and Lam (1998) distinguish between dominant and non-dominant languages in multilingual societies. On the one hand, dominant languages are those that have a high or relatively high social status and political power. On the other hand, non-dominant languages lack political power and their social status is low. The latter have also been defined as minority languages. However, as argued by Nunan and Lam (1998), the term is misleading, as the fact of being a non-dominant language does not necessarily reflect the number of people that speak it or use it as a mother tongue. Taking the above assumptions and facts into account, these authors identify four educational models in what they term 'language dominance contexts'. These models are classified according to two main factors: the cultural status of the non-dominant language and its function in education. The first educational model involves language shift related to bridging programmes and transitional bilingual programmes. The non-dominant language is used as a medium for communication though not viewed as a target language, that is, a language that is to be learned. The second model includes language shift, cultural sensitivity programmes and submersion programmes for non-dominant language speakers. The non-dominant language is neither used as a vehicle nor viewed as a target language. A third model identified by Nunan and Lam (1998) is that of language maintenance involving modern, foreign and heritage language programmes. The non-dominant language is not used as a vehicle for instruction but is considered as a possible target language. Finally, the fourth model also reflects language maintenance. It involves Canadian immersion programmes, language exposure time programmes and the like. The non-dominant language is used as a means of instruction and is also viewed as a feasible target language.

We might assume that this last model would be the one that best emphasises and enhances multilingual acquisition and use. In the case of our subjects, and considering their mother tongue (Catalan) as a non-dominant language in the overall Spanish community, we can state that the fourth model quoted above reflects Catalan educational programmes. The idea of these programmes is to maintain and increase the status of Catalan in our society, which has been reduced for many years. As will be further explained (in Chapter 3), students in this region also receive some training in primary school where their second language is employed both as a means of instruction and as a target language. Later on, in high school and at university, learners are exposed to both – that is, instruction in their first and second languages. In this setting they receive instruction in English, which is considered a non-dominant language for the community, as it is not employed. Nevertheless, it is regarded as an important tool for communication within the European community. Hence the situation of our learners in this bilingual community is somewhat different from that of other monolingual communities in Spain, and also from that of other bilingual communities in the world, as is the case of Canada presented by Nunan and Lam (1998) above.

The third factor influencing third language acquisition and raised by Cenoz (2000) refers to the psycholinguistic processes involved. The successive or simultaneous acquisition of more than two languages may share some characteristics with second language processing. However, the additional language complicates internal cognitive processing by presenting a unique situation of language acquisition (Clyne, 1997). The main research areas in this respect, as reported by Cenoz (2000), have focused on early multilingualism (Harding and Riley, 1986), individual factors affecting third language acquisition (Nayak et al., 1990; Obler, 1989), the role of the proficiency level in the L1 and L2 in the acquisition of a third language (Wagner et al., 1989), and cross-linguistic influence in third language acquisition (Clyne, 1997). However, further research needs to be conducted in order to account for the differences between second and third language psycholinguistic processing. In so doing, we may discover those specific operations that particularly affect multilingual processing. Our study (see Part 2 of this volume) aims at broadening the scope of this investigation in that it considers monolingual and bilingual learners of English as a foreign and as a third language. Differences in their performance may provide us with further clues for explaining third language development.

The differences and similarities between second and third language acquisition presented in the present section have revealed the complex nature of third and multilingual acquisition and the need for further studies on psycholinguistic processing in learning a third language. In doing this, we believe that a key concept is that of bilingualism, for it is the state/background of most third language learners. Taking into account the fact that participants in our study are also bilingual speakers learning a third language, we will next consider the notions of bilingualism and bilingual competence.

Bilingualism

Bilingual competence

In the present section, our aim is both to examine current conceptualisations of bilingual competence and to present our own proposal considering the particular characteristics of our subjects, who are bilingual speakers learning a third language. For this purpose, we shall first offer a general overview of some of the most representative definitions attributed to the notion of bilingual competence, including the factors affecting it. We shall also take into account the existing variety of terms employed to describe a bilingual speaker's competence in both languages. In addition to that typology, several perspectives adopted by current research on bilinguals' competence will also be discussed. Specific issues addressed are language organisation, early language differentiation and mental representation in bilinguals.

Despite the fact that bilingualism is a worldwide reality, it is still difficult to define the phenomenon in a straightforward manner. As stated by Wei (2000), the term 'bilingual' primarily refers to the possession of two languages. However, bilingualism is a relative concept, as it refers to a complicated phenomenon that has not been clearly categorised. For this reason, there exist multiple interpretations and descriptions of a bilingual person. During the last century, linguists have referred to this dual knowledge by pointing to particular features. An early reference to bilingualism is that of Bloomfield (1933: 55–56):

> In the case where this perfect foreign-language learning is not accompanied by loss of the native language, it results in 'bilingualism', native-like control of two languages. After early childhood few people have enough muscular and nervous freedom or enough opportunity and leisure to reach perfection in a foreign language; yet bilingualism of this kind is commoner than one might suppose, both

in cases like those of our immigrants and as a result of travel, foreign study, or similar association. Of course, one cannot define a degree of perfection at which a good foreign speaker becomes a bilingual: the distinction is relative.

Here the author raises certain doubts regarding the bilingual person's proficiency level in both languages. Bloomfield (1933) particularly addresses the second language being learned, as he explicitly refers to foreign speakers being somehow immersed in the target-language culture. He also points to the idea that children have more chance of becoming bilingual or learning other languages than adults do. However, at this time no empirical findings existed regarding bilingual language processing.

The first empirical studies focusing on bilingual subjects were carried out in the 1960s. Weinreich (1968), considered as a founder of research on bilingualism, provides the following concise definition of the phenomenon: 'the practice of alternately using two languages will be called bilingualism, and the person involved, bilingual' (Weinreich, 1968: 1). On the basis of this definition, a bilingual person is one who uses two languages irrespective of his/her command, the linguistic skills (speaking, listening, reading or writing) mastered or the context in which the languages are used. This conceptualisation may involve a certain degree of ambiguity, as it does not provide defining features that distinguish monolingual from bilingual processing, except for the use of two languages in the case of the bilingual person.

Another description of the bilingual phenomenon is provided by Mackey (1970: 555):

It seems obvious that if we are to study the phenomenon of bilingualism, we are forced to consider it as something entirely relative. We must moreover include the use not only of two languages, but of any number of languages. We shall therefore consider bilingualism as the alternate use of two or more languages by the same individual.

According to Hoffman (1991), none of the above definitions accounts for the situations in which languages are used, or for the particular requirements of the language selected. For this reason, the author suggests certain considerations that should be taken into account when describing bilingualism. This phenomenon compels certain methodological and theoretical constraints in its study, as there are social, psychological and chance factors affecting a bilingual speaker's behaviour. Hence we may assume that any generalisation attributed to the concept of bilingual competence would posit difficulties in its empirical validation. In fact, current existing definitions refer only to a particular group of bilingual speakers who are under similar circumstances. One example of these specialised definitions is the one provided by Skutnabb-Kangas (1984: 90):

> A bilingual speaker is someone who is able to function in two (or more) languages, either in monolingual or bilingual communities, in accordance with the sociocultural demands made of an individual's communicative and cognitive competence by these communities or by the individual herself, at the same level as native speakers, and who is able positively to identify with both (or all) language groups (and cultures) or parts of them.

In this particular case, the author refers to immigrants and minority children, that is, she is considering a specific group while describing bilingualism. Following Hoffman (1991), we also believe that focusing on a specific bilingual community is probably the best option in attempting to describe bilingual competence, as it may enable us to conduct research and validate our description on the basis of empirical findings. In fact, this is the approach used in the study presented in this volume, where we focus on a particular group of bilingual speakers using their first and second languages in a bilingual community. Bialystok (2001) also follows such a perspective as she tackles cognitive development of bilingual children by analysing specific cases.

There are certain factors that should also be considered in investigating bilingual speakers. Hoffman (1991: 31) identifies the following:

(1) *Language development*. This makes reference to language attrition or maintenance regarding the first or second language.
(2) *The order in which the languages have been acquired*. We find cases where languages are learned either simultaneously or successively, at early stages in our life or when we are adults.
(3) *The proficiency level* attained in these languages. Being bilingual does not necessarily mean having a perfect command of both languages. In fact, a wide degree of variation in attainment has been reported in the literature (see below).
(4) *Particular characteristics of the situation* in which each language is used, that is with whom, when, and what first or second language is employed.
(5) *The attitudes towards the languages or towards being bilingual*. Existing theories of second language acquisition (Cenoz and Valencia, 1994; Crookall and Oxford, 1988; Dörnyei and Csizér, 1998; Gardner, 1985; Schumann, 1978) assume that attitudes towards the language

being learned or towards the learning situation might affect second language processing. By the same token it might be assumed, as Hoffman (1991) does, that attitudes towards the bilingual speaker's first or second language might influence not only its development but also its use.

(6) *Pressures due to motivational, social or psychological factors.* As stated by Dörnyei (1994), motivation is to be regarded as an eclectic construct that integrates characteristics from the learners themselves, the language and the learning situation, thus including the teacher, the course and the context. The author reported on motivation in second language acquisition. However, we believe that these characteristics may also be applicable to bilingual acquisition.

(7) *Environmental circumstances surrounding the bilingual speaker.* Bilingualism has been studied from a sociolinguistic point of view in many minority language societies, as determining its use and maintenance (Auer, 1997).

(8) *The degree of familiarity with the two cultures.* Whether or not the two languages known by the bilingual person belong to the culture where s/he is immersed is also considered as a differential feature in his/her language development.

To those factors mentioned above we may also add the degree of competence in the two languages on the part of the subjects. In the literature on bilingualism a whole array of terms have been used to describe the bilingual speaker regarding various degrees of competence in both languages. Following Li Wei (2000: 6–7), these terms are summarised in Table 1.1.

This table shows ambiguity and confusion as far as bilingual competence is concerned, given the various notions used to describe the same phenomenon (e.g. successive and consecutive bilingual). In general terms, being bilingual relates to the knowledge of two different linguistic systems. Interaction between these two systems, language organisation[4] and language processing are key concepts which have promoted much of the existing research. Two approaches aim at studying language organisation in the bilingual's brain, the main difference lying in the subjects studied.

On the one hand, scholars have studied aphasic bilinguals, that is, people who have suffered from brain damage due to an accident or illness and who then find difficulties in using their languages. Investigation in this field addresses the issue of discovering any recovery or loss distinction between the two languages known to the speaker. Case studies[5] to date

Table 1.1 Types of bilingual competence

Additive bilingual	Someone whose two languages combine in a complementary and enriched fashion.
Ascendant bilingual	Someone whose ability to function in a second language is developing owing to increased use.
Balanced bilingual	Someone whose mastery of two languages is roughly equivalent. (Also termed *ambilingual*, *equilingual* and *symmetrical bilingual*.)
Compound bilingual	Someone whose two languages are learned at the same time, often in the same context.
Coordinate bilingual	Someone whose two languages are learned in distinctively separate contexts.
Covert bilingual	Someone who conceals his or her knowledge of a given language owing to an attitudinal disposition.
Diagonal bilingual	Someone who is bilingual in a non-standard language or a dialect and an unrelated standard language
Dominant bilingual	Someone with a greater proficiency in one of his or her languages and who uses it significantly more than the other language(s).
Dormant bilingual	Someone who has emigrated to a foreign country for a considerable time period and has little opportunity to keep the first language actively in use.
Early bilingual	Someone who has acquired two languages early in childhood.
Functional bilingual	Someone who can operate in two languages with or without full fluency for the task at hand.
Horizontal bilingual	Someone who is bilingual in two languages which have a similar or equal status.
Incipient bilingual	Someone at the early stages of bilingual acquisition where one language is not fully developed.
Late bilingual	Someone who has become bilingual after childhood. (Also termed *achieved bilingual*.)
Maximal bilingual	Someone with near native control of two or more languages.
Minimal bilingual	Someone with only a few words and phrases in a second language.
Natural bilingual	Someone who has not undergone any specific training and who is often not in a position to translate or interpret with facility between two languages. (Also termed *primary bilingual*.)
Productive bilingual	Someone who not only understands but also speaks and possibly writes in two or more languages.

Table 1.1 *continued*

Receptive bilingual	Someone who understands a second language, in either its spoken or written form, or both, but does not necessarily speak or write it. (Also termed *asymmetrical bilingual, passive bilingual* and *semilingual*.)
Recessive bilingual	Someone who begins to feel some difficulty in either understanding or expressing him or herself with ease owing to lack of use.
Secondary bilingual	Someone whose second language has been added to a first language via instruction.
Semilingual	Someone with insufficient knowledge of either language.
Simultaneous bilingual	Someone whose two languages are present from the onset of speech.
Subordinate bilingual	Someone who exhibits interference in his or her language usage by reducing the patterns of the second language to those of the first.
Subtractive bilingual	Someone whose second language is acquired at the expense of the aptitudes already acquired in the first language.
Successive bilingual	Someone whose second language is added at some stage after the first has begun to develop. (Also termed *consecutive bilingual*.)
Vertical bilingual	Someone who is bilingual in a standard language and a distinct but related language or dialect.

have shown no conclusive findings. According to Grosjean (1982), different types of recovery have been found, namely those of 'antagonistic' (one language regresses while the other progresses), 'mixed' (languages remain mixed), and 'successive' restitution (one language is not restored until the other one progresses completely). No study has accounted for the linguistic command of the speaker before suffering from aphasia, and only those subjects with spectacular illnesses were analysed.

On the other hand, scholars such as Genesee *et al.* (1978) and Galloway (1980), studying normal bilinguals, have attempted to decipher languages organisation in the bilingual's brain by means of specific tasks performance. These studies have focused on what has been termed *language lateralisation*. The brain's left hemisphere is commonly associated with linguistic activity while the right hemisphere is related to visuospatial processing. This idea has been assumed as a standard pattern for brain organisation (Andrews, 1977; Galloway and Krashen, 1980; McGlone, 1978). There exist controversial views in the literature on bilingual cerebral lateralisation. The focus of current conflicting views has to do with whether or not there is greater right-hemisphere participation in bilinguals than in monolinguals; that is to say, whether language processing is different in bilinguals and monolinguals. Paradis (1990) finds no differences in any of the two groups, and concludes that left-hemisphere participation in bilingual and monolingual language processing is identical. Other scholars (Albanèse, 1985; Sussman et al., 1982) suggest a greater left-hemisphere engagement in monolinguals than in bilinguals, while a third group (Gordon and Weide, 1983; Vaid, 1983) sustains that lateralisation is different in terms of the languages being used. Nevertheless, according to Obler et al. (2000), a wide variety of variables need to be taken into account when interpreting results deriving from research on bilingual lateralisation. Obler et al. point to (1) variables pertaining to the bilingual subjects themselves (gender, age, L2 proficiency level), as well as (2) methodological aspects of the research in the area (methodological approaches adopted, practice effects observed and reliability measures used). In fact, the issue of tasks and instruments measuring language processing and cerebral activity is complex enough to claim that there exists a certain amount of evidence that points to higher/lower right-hemisphere participation. So far, no mechanism has been able to measure cognitive processes, and bilingual lateralisation is not an exceptional case.

Within those cognitive processes associated with bilinguals' competence, a different perspective from that of language organisation related to brain participation has also been adopted, namely that of early language differentiation. In this case the focus lies on bilinguals' development in the two languages rather than on brain participation in language use. Therefore, authors concentrating on the early stages of bilingualism attempt to provide a theoretical framework that explains cognitive processing taking place during bilingual development. Two main hypotheses have been put forward, namely the *Unitary Language System Hypothesis* and the *Independent Development Hypothesis*. The former refers to the bilingual child's use of a common system that gradually becomes separated. This hypothesis is based on Volterra and Taeschner's (1978) three-stage model. According to these authors, in a first stage the child has a common lexical system for both languages. In a second stage, s/he distinguishes lexical items between both languages but syntactic characteristics are common to the two languages. The final stage involves separation of lexical and syntactic elements in the languages known to the child.

The second hypothesis stated above (Independent Development Hypothesis) refers to the ability to differentiate two linguistic systems (Bergman, 1976; Padilla and Liebman, 1975). Empirical studies have attempted to validate this hypothesis by examining whether their subjects illustrated an initial distinction between their two linguistic systems (de Houwer, 1990; Genesee, 1989; Meisel, 1986). On the one hand, Meisel's study (1987) demonstrates that young bilingual children use first and second language syntactic constructions even more consistently than monolingual children do. On the other hand, de Houwer (1990) claims that her findings represent evidence for the Separate Development Hypothesis. Despite the fact that findings from these studies may offer no conclusive evidence on early differentiation, results seem to contradict Volterra and Taeschner's (1978) three-stage model and lead to a potential awareness of two linguistic systems.

Genesee (1989) criticises existing studies by stating that, in order to make the case for early language differentiation, researchers should have focused on the context. In fact, according to this author, only those results showing bilingual children's use of both languages in all contexts of communication would validate the Independent Development Hypothesis. According to Hoffman (1991), present studies seem to favour the Independent Hypothesis, although further research should focus on other aspects, such as the one mentioned by Genesee (1989) above, in order to validate the theory. On the basis of this idea, the author suggests the following factors influencing language choice in adults and children. These relate to 'the person engaged in the speech event, the setting or situation, the purpose of the interaction, the topic and the linguistic proficiency level in both languages' (Hoffman, 1991: 91–92). Hoffman argues in favour of the independent development hypothesis as shown by her definition of bilingual language acquisition (Hoffmann, 1991: 92–93):

> Bilingual language acquisition involves developing an awareness of two distinct systems, acquiring their features and learning to keep them apart. Becoming bilingual implies making choices between two languages, following rules that are laid down by the environment or that the individual has decided upon by himself.

A related area to language development in bilinguals, also connected with bilingual cognitive processing, is that of the storage or mental representation of linguistic knowledge. As in studies dealing with bilingual linguistic development, researchers studying the representation of languages have adopted two different positions. On the one hand, the Separate or Independence Hypothesis states that bilinguals keep their two languages in two different storage systems where the means of connection is that of a translation process. On the other hand, the Shared Storage or Interdependence hypothesis points to a single storage system with two different input and output channels. Current empirical findings support both hypotheses (Heredia and McLaughlin, 1992; Hummel, 1993; Paivio, 1991). For this reason, Baker (1996) advocates a model that integrates both the Independence and the Interdependence Hypothesis. According to this author, the bilingual speaker keeps three separate systems which are interconnected: a first language system, a second language system and a non-verbal image system. These systems are also linked to the individual's first and second language experience and to his/her background knowledge. These previous experiences are connected to his/her first, second and image systems by means of a filter containing senses (i.e. touching, hearing, seeing, smelling and tasting). Each system is responsible for the output produced, whether it be in the first language, second language or non-verbal. Nevertheless, the output is produced on the basis of the existing interconnections among the systems and the individual's previous experience. Therefore, on the basis of Paivio and Desrochers (1991), Baker (1996) describes a model for bilingual storage that contains both dependent and independent systems.

In fact, actual theories (Matsumi, 1994) emphasise the idea that both separate and connected aspects of bilingual mental representations should be included in a descriptive model of bilingual cognitive processing. Within this group of theories attempting to explain processing cognitive mechanisms, we find speech processing models. These are going to be dealt with next because of their relevance for the study to be presented in the second part of this volume, where we study bilinguals' use of a third language.

Models for bilingual speech processing mechanisms

Existing models of speech production have focused on monolinguals' language use (Dell, 1986; Mackey, 1967); however, there have also been some attempts to incorporate bilinguals' processing in speech production (de Bot and Schreuder, 1993; Green, 1986). This section aims at describing some of the most influential speech production models from both a monolingual (Levelt, 1989) and a bilingual perspective (de Bot, 1992; Poulisse and Bongaerts, 1994) in the field of language acquisition. We will also refer to some criticisms raised by these models and will comment on the model that in our opinion would best illustrate the use of a third language by a bilingual person.

Levelt (1989) proposed a model aimed at describing adults' spontaneous speech production. This model was based on previous empirical psycholinguistic research (Dell, 1986; Garrett, 1975; Kempen and

Hoenkamp, 1987) which focused on observation of speech errors and experimental data. As illustrated by Figure 1.1, the model consists of various components that represent either declarative or procedural knowledge. The former refers to encyclopaedic knowledge, that is, background knowledge, while the latter relates to those processing mechanisms required in the act of producing the language. Encyclopedic knowledge includes information about the world, scripts, frames and the like, and a lexicon includes lemmas and forms, that is, semantic and morphological characteristics of terms, which are used in both production and reception mechanisms.

Regarding processing components, Levelt presents a 'conceptualiser', a 'formulator', an 'articulator' and a 'comprehension system'. The former involves the selection and organisation of relevant information which

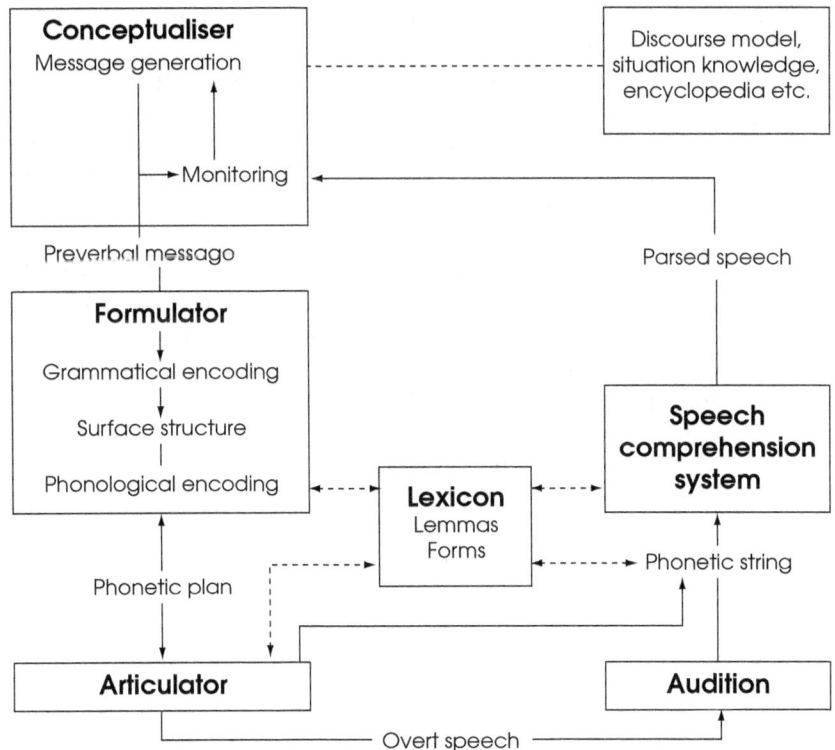

Figure 1.1 Levelt's speech production model (From Levelt, 1989: Figure 1.1)

confirms the speaker's intention in generating the message. A pre-verbal message is originated at this stage and this will be grammatically and phonologically encoded in the formulator. This component converts the speaker's plan into lexical units, thereby differentiating between lemmas and forms. Semantic activation involves conceptual properties as well as grammatical, pragmatic and syntactic features of the selected lexical item. Hence the speaker first decides on the concept and considers characteristics of its use in a particular context and its relationship with other items, thereby referring to aspects such as tense, aspect, mood, collocations and the like. Afterwards a particular form is provided for this unit, taking into account its phonological and morphological properties. As shown in Figure 1.1, the surface structure formation compels grammatical and phonological encoding. This part is connected to the lexicon which includes information on lemmas and forms. The formulator turns the speaker's intention into a phonetic plan which may be internally checked by the speech-comprehension system. This provides the speaker with feedback, which may help her/him reformulate the original message articulation or phonetic plan.

This phonetic plan is converted into actual speech in the articulator, which provides the speaker's message with actual sounds, thereby including features referring to the point (i.e. central, frontal, back), the manner of articulation (i.e. plosive, labiodental, palatal and the like), and the intonation and pitch, among others. The articulator is connected to the auditory component, which in turn leads to the speech comprehension system. The latter guides oral speech just as it provided feedback to the original phonetic plan before being produced. At this stage the whole message may be reformulated as the speech production system is connected to monitoring in the conceptualiser; thus the speaker may decide to modify either its original intention or other aspects of the message encoding and further production.

Speech production in this model takes place gradually, that is, it starts on the left and ends on the right side of the framework displayed in Figure 1.1, although we may view it as a whole cycle where all components are connected in a certain way. The model assumes that several language chunks are sequenced by new ones while the former chunks are produced. Therefore, activation of all components is parallel to sequenced chunks of language in the mind of a speaker. Speech production follows an order which allows for the simultaneous or parallel activation of all components in the production system. For instance, while the articulator is producing a lexical unit, the conceptualiser is selecting from among different concepts that will follow the unit being produced. As stated by de Bot (1992), processing is then viewed as automatic.

Levelt's model (1989) has been used in subsequent research[6] concerning second and foreign language production. Despite the fact that this model has been rather influential on studies on oral communication and interaction, it has also been criticised for not considering other instances of oral communication, such as the case of bilingual speech production. In this respect, de Bot (1992) points to some additional features the model should include in order to account for bilingual production. According to this author, it should illustrate the fact that two language systems may be used either jointly or separately. This makes reference to phenomena such as code-switching (Auer, 1997; Kellerman and Sharwood Smith, 1986), cross-linguistic influence (Faerch and Kasper, 1989; Poulisse, 1993) or language interference (Ringbom, 1987). Besides, the model should also account for the different degree of competence the bilingual person may have in the two languages. As previously mentioned, several types of bilingual competence are identified in the literature, ranging from balanced to early bilingualism. Another aspect raised by de Bot (1992) implies the possibility of representing knowledge of more than two languages where interaction among those languages should not pose any problem.

Bearing in mind the above modifications on Levelt's (1989) original framework, de Bot (1992) presents his own model for bilingual speech production. The main adjustment in Levelt's model refers to the activation or non-activation of the languages known to the speaker and what stage in the process refers to the selection of one or another language. Following Green (1986), de Bot (1992) assumes that there are various levels of activation, namely those of the languages being selected, activated or dormant. The latter imply the non-activation of the language during the whole production process. The main difference between those languages being activated and those being selected is that the former is chosen and processed parallel to the selected language, but it is not articulated. This idea signals out the simultaneous activation of both first and second language in the knowledge component and consequently in the conceptualiser, while establishing two parallel phonetic plans that will be converted into speech plans in the formulator. However, only the speech plan of the selected language will be articulated and produced. De Bot's (1992) adjustments may be illustrated as follows.

As shown by Figure 1.2, it is not clear how the languages can be activated in parallel in the pre-verbal message and phonetic plan and then be separated in overt speech. In de Bot's view, a bilingual speaker who wishes to express a thought in his/her mother tongue activates grammatical and phonological characteristics for both the first and the second language, so s/he provides the intended message with a first and a second

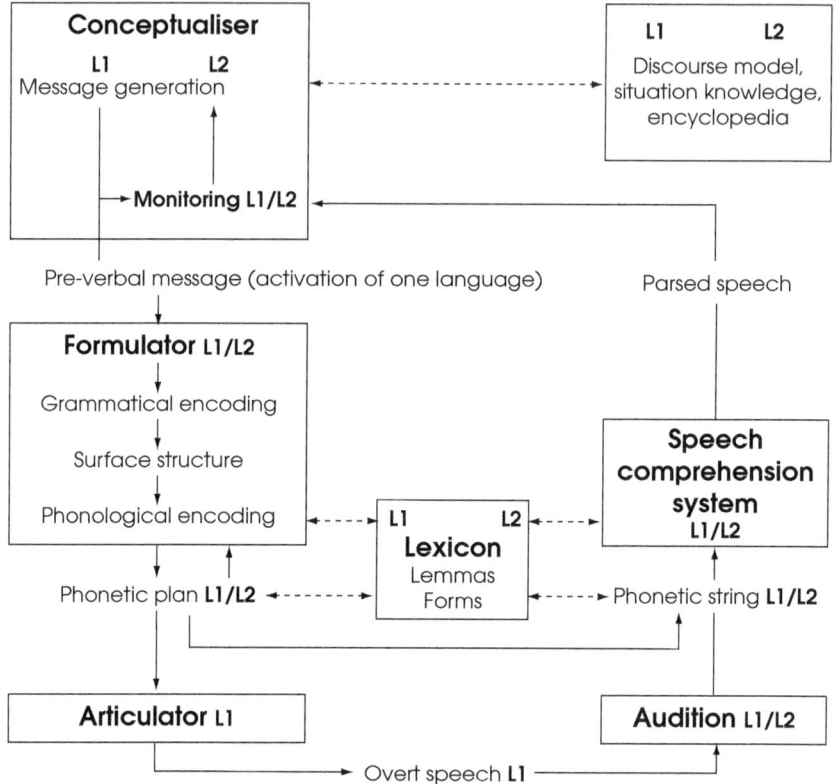

Figure 1.2 de Bot's (1992) adaptation of Levelt's (1989) speech production model

language surface structure. At the end, only the phonetic plan involving the first language is converted into normal speech. Furthermore, the sequence of events in this model, that is, the fact that all components remain activated while the message is being produced, makes it rather difficult to understand the specific role of certain components, particularly those involved in the phonetic plan and the phonetic string or parsed speech. In fact, the function of those components taking part in the phonetic plan and phonetic string, namely, formulator, speech comprehension system, and audition, will be three or fourfold rather than twofold, as suggested in Levelt's original model (1989). Nevertheless, the components' parallel activation would explain cross-linguistic phenomena to a certain extent. In this respect, de Bot (1992) states that problems referring to the selection of a particular lexical unit needed to express a concept may lead the speaker to choose another lexical unit from his/her mother tongue. In so doing, the first language should be activated and this would take place in the formulator and lexicon components. This simplified version of de Bot's reasoning (1992) in favour of the two languages' activation does not seem to explain the difference between intentional and unintentional language switches as far as processing mechanisms are concerned. Although cross-linguistic phenomena are referred to in this model by the speaker's selection of one or another lexical item from his/her first language, the parallel activation of the two languages would only account for intentional language switches, i.e. not considering slips of the tongue or hesitators, which are also termed 'unintentional switches'.

Poulisse and Bongaerts (1994) have also criticised Levelt's model (1989) for lack of clarity and lack of economy in terms of processing effort. According to these authors, the parallel activation of two speech plans and their subsequent formulation is not clear if we consider that the pre-verbal message only involves one particular language. Besides, it is uneconomical to have different languages activated in parallel, as there exists a possibility for knowledge of more than two languages to be represented in the model. Hence, in the case of a polyglot knowing five different languages, these should all be activated simultaneously in his/her language-processing system. It is difficult not to assume that the activation of five linguistic systems would not pose any problem at least in terms of processing speed, as was assumed by de Bot (1992).

On the basis of their criticism, Poulisse and Bongaerts (1994) propose that lexical items from different languages should be regarded as part of a common conceptual core and that information on language choice is then added to the pre-verbal message in the form of a language component. This language component is responsible for the activation of one or another language. Hence, language is another feature for selection while generating the message. Contrary to de Bot's framework (1992), this new model enables the activation of lemmas that correspond to one language while preventing the other from being activated. In this way, extra processing effort is diminished, as there is no need for double or triple morphosyntactic or lexical retrieval. Furthermore, Poulisse and Bongaerts' model (1994) is supported by previous studies on slips of the tongue in second language-switching. Hence, unlike other previous models, it can account for unintentional as well as for intentional language-switching, which are considered the defining features of bilingual speech.

Considering second language learners as unbalanced bilingual speakers, Poulisse (1997) proposes four main characteristics that should be taken into account when developing a model of second language production. This author mentions the facts that L2 knowledge is not complete, L2 production includes hesitators and shorter sentences, L2 speech may illustrate some characteristics of the L1 by means of intentional or unintentional switches, and advanced speakers may keep the two languages apart as balanced bilinguals do. These four characteristics of second language users may also be applied to third language use, although some more adjustments may be needed in order to fully describe the interaction among those languages known to the third language learner, who in the case of our participants is also a bilingual person. Following other scholars (Grosjean, 1985; Jessner, 1997), we believe that bilingualism is not to be viewed as the mere sum of two linguistic systems but rather as a holistic system involving competence in two languages. Bearing this idea in mind, a model of bilingual speech production should account for the interaction between those languages known by the speaker, and that would be the case with Poulisse and Bongaerts' (1994) proposal mentioned above. This holistic view of bilingualism may help us interpret differences in language use between monolingual and bilingual subjects in our study. It is from this perspective that we shall consider variation in the learners' pragmatic performance. Specific characteristics of bilinguals' language use, such as that of language contact, are also relevant to our study, as learners' linguistic production constitutes the sample data for our analysis.

Features of bilingual speech

There are certain features characterising bilingual speech which reflect interaction between those languages known by the bilingual person. A salient feature that is increasingly receiving considerable attention is that of language switches. We will focus on this phenomenon, not only because it is the one that best illustrates the difference between monolingual and bilingual speech production, but also because of its relevance for the study of third language acquisition. Hence, the third language learner's behaviour reflects competence in two languages. Bilinguals' knowledge of two languages is manifested in their oral production when these linguistic systems interact with each other.

Language switches arising from linguistic interaction have been studied from three main perspectives: sociolinguistic, conversational and psycholinguistic. Most of the literature on language switches derives from the sociolinguistic approach, which reflects patterns of social variation and identity (Auer, 1997; Gumperz, 1971; McClure, 1977). This sociolinguistic approach differs from the psycholinguistic or conversational perspectives in the nature of its investigation. Sociolinguistic researchers adopt a more ethnographic approach than do psycholinguistics or conversation analysts, who tend to focus on experimental studies. Rampton (1999) also points out this difference when he states that second language acquisition research, which would reflect a psycholinguistic perspective, is concerned with learning; thus, it does not account for socialising processes. Manchón (2001) offers a detailed revision on language switches with a focus on language-learning by adopting a psycholinguistic perspective. The author deals with transfer as a language-use strategy and analyses the role of learners' L1 in foreign language production. The studies that adopt this psycholinguistic perspective, in contrast to the work done in sociolinguistics, do not focus on minority languages. Instead, greater attention is paid to dominant cultures. In line with these ideas, Franceschini (1999) distinguishes the term 'code-switching', derived from sociolinguistics and conversation analysis, from that of 'interlanguage', which stems from a psycholinguistic perspective. According to this author, code-switching and interlanguage share some features, as they are both produced in a particular sociocultural situation and are not stable in nature. However, code-switching relates to group norms and functions, and it expresses group identity.

Considering the distinction made above between the disciplines studying language switches, it is the psycholinguistic perspective that most interests us because it refers to processing and cognitive mechanisms in bilingual production and development (Clyne, 1987). This psycholinguistic approach embraces those studies that have analysed the interlanguage of bilingual and multilingual learners. For this reason, we shall offer a brief overview of the research conducted on the basis of this approach.

Psycholinguistic studies addressing language-switching have characterised these shifts as being either intentional or unintentional. Intentional switching relates to those mechanisms the language learner employs to overcome difficulties in using the target language. Such is the case of generalisation (e.g. *vehicle* for *car*) or morphological creativity (e.g. to *ironise*). This is the approach adopted in studies dealing with borrowing, language-mixing and the use of compensatory strategies (Faerch and Kasper, 1983; Kasper and Kellerman, 1997; Kellerman, 1977; Poulisse, 1993; Poulisse and Schils, 1989). Besides, unintentional language-switching involves those studies focusing on slips of the tongue, self-repair, the use of fillers and the like. We shall now consider results from two particular studies on intentional and unintentional language-switching, namely those of Poulisse and Bongaerts (1994) and Williams and Hammarberg (1998), since they examine the production of monolingual (in the case of the former), and bilingual learners of a third language (in the case of the latter study). Therefore, participants in these studies described below share some degree of similarity with the subjects of our own study, who may also be considered to be monolingual and bilingual learners of an additional language.

Unintentional language switches have recently received more attention. Poulisse and Bongaerts (1994) examined non-intentional language switches in second language learners of different proficiency levels. Their subjects were Dutch learners of English, who were distributed into three groups according to their proficiency level in the target language. They were required to perform a story-retelling task, an interview with a native speaker and a picture-description task. The authors identified unintentional switches on the basis of hesitation phenomena and intonation. Results from their investigation show that learners at a lower proficiency level with little exposure to the target language produced most switches. The authors also point out that function words were more often involved in this type of switch than were content words. This finding seems to support the idea that there exist different kinds of language switches in second language production.

On the basis of the above-mentioned study, Williams and Hammarberg (1998) carried out a longitudinal study in order to ascertain the different roles of their subject's first and second languages in the production of a third one. The participant in this study was an adult learner of Swedish whose mother tongue was British English and whose second language was German; she also knew French and Italian. Data was taken from interviews between the participant and one of the researchers, who was a native speaker of Swedish and whose second languages were English, German and French. In fact, the participant in the study was Sarah Williams, one of its authors. After analysing their data on the basis of various categories that illustrated intentional as well as unintentional language switches, the authors attributed a *default supplier role* to the subject's second language and an *instrumental role* to the first one. Other studies involving more than one subject (Clyne, 1997; Dewaele, 1998) present evidence which supports Williams and Hammarberg's assumptions regarding the default supplier role performed by the second language. However, the first language did not play the same role in all the studies quoted above. In this sense, Williams and Hammarberg's findings (1998) were partially contradicted.

In our opinion, this fact illustrates the idea, also raised by Williams and Hammarberg (1998), that language-switching becomes a complex phenomenon when the learner is bilingual and the target language is not a second but a third one. In fact, this issue leads to the high degree of complexity involved in multilingual education. Further research must provide an answer to the following questions that await an answer: (1) How do the learners' first and second languages influence L3 production? (2) To what extent will learners' linguistic and cultural background affect L3 production? (Williams and Hammarberg, 1998).

The study presented in the second part of this book will not focus on language-switching as the main object of study; instead, it will consider L3 pragmatic competence. However, since participants in the study are both monolingual and bilingual learners of a third language, we will try to provide an answer to the questions quoted above, which raise the idea of cross-cultural transfer in L3 use and thereby focus on politeness issues. In this section we have described two studies of language-switching that illustrate monolinguals' (Poulisse and Bongaerts, 1994) and bilinguals' (Williams and Hammarberg, 1998) use of an additional language. We believe that differences between first and second languages in the use of a third one present evidence for distinguishing between second and third language use, and they also justify the need for further research on multilingual education. Studies conducted so far that adopt this perspective and which also relate to our own study are described in the following section of this chapter.

Learning a Third Language

The effect of bilingualism in third language acquisition

As has already been mentioned in previous sections, third language acquisition is not the same as second language acquisition, nor can it be viewed as the mere sum of linguistic systems. Following the holistic view of bilingualism presented before, we can state that third language acquisition involves widening the linguistic system of an individual both quantitatively and, above all, qualitatively. This section aims at reporting on the influence of bilingualism in the acquisition of English as a third language. For this purpose, we shall comment on those skills that are responsible for the linguistic development of a third language, as acknowledged by Herdina and Jessner (2000). The advantages of bilingualism in learning an additional language concerning cognitive development will also be dealt with; we shall particularly consider metalinguistic awareness and creative thinking as indicators of cognitive processing. Finally, we will present the definition of multilingual proficiency provided by Jessner (1999), which connects both linguistic and cognitive development in third language acquisition.

Learning a third or further language involves the development of certain skills that relate to *learning, management* and *maintenance* processes (Herdina and Jessner, 2000). *Language-learning* skills refer to cognitive aspects of language-learning. As shown by certain studies (Hufeisen, 1998; Jessner, 1999), having undergone a previous learning process in a second or foreign language will facilitate development of a further language. *Language-management* skills are defined by Herdina and Jessner (2000: 93) as 'the multilingual art of balancing communicative requirements with language resources'. Following this definition, we may assume that learning an additional language helps to develop not only internal processing mechanisms, but also the use of this language. The third group of skills stated above is that connected to *language maintenance*. This implies an extra effort on the part of multilingual people to maintain and develop the languages known by them.

Studies conducted on the above-quoted skills, particularly those referring to learning (Hufeisen, 1998; Jessner, 1999), seem to indicate that knowing a second language fosters development of a third one. This idea also relates to the role of bilingualism in learning a third language. For the last 30 years, research on bilingualism has shown that bilingualism may entail certain advantages in terms of cognitive development. As reported by Jessner (1997), several studies have shown that bilinguals have cognitive superiority over monolinguals in acquiring a third language (Bialystok, 1991; Hamers and Blanc, 1989; Lambert, 1977). This author emphasises results deriving from measuring certain cognitive skills, namely those of *creative thinking* and *metalinguistic awareness*.

Various studies demonstrate a higher degree of creative thinking in bilingual than in monolingual subjects (Álvarez, 1984; Koulos, 1986; Ricciardelli, 1992). Creativity involves fluency in producing a wide range of ideas, flexibility in showing different types of ideas and originality in denoting uncommon thoughts (Torrance, 1966). However, as argued by Lasagabaster (1997), further research is needed to actually ascertain a direct correlation between bilingualism and creativity in using a third language.

Lasagabaster (1997) has also studied the effect of bilingualism on metalinguistic awareness in acquiring a third language. Metalinguistic awareness has been defined as follows:

It is the ability to think flexibly and abstractly about the language; it refers to an awareness of the formal linguistic features of language and ability to reflect thereupon. Metalinguistic awareness allows the individual to step back from the comprehension or production of an utterance in order to consider the linguistic form and structure underlying the meaning of the utterance. To be metalinguistically aware, then, is to know how to approach and solve certain types of problems which themselves demand certain cognitive and linguistic skills. (Malakoff, 1992: 518)

Bialystok (1988, 2001) presents evidence of the advantage that bilingual children have over monolingual ones in terms of their metalinguistic awareness. According to this author, higher levels of bilingualism correlate with higher achievement in the ability of thinking about the language. We may assume that such an idea might relate to bilinguals' skill in evaluating appropriateness in language use, thus leading to pragmatic aspects, which is one of the concerns of the study presented in this book. However, we should point out the fact that Bialystok deals mainly with children who are bilingual and use two languages, whereas our focus is on bilinguals using a third language (i.e. English) in a foreign setting; therefore research accounting for such a perspective is also very relevant for our purposes. To that end, we have also considered authors dealing with third language learning and its relationship with metalingustic awareness, such as Jessner (1999) and Lasagabaster (1997).

Results from Lasagabaster's (1997) research points to an advantage for bilingual subjects (Castilian and Euskera) over monolingual ones (Castilian) in acquiring English as a third language. On the basis of the above definition and considering results from Lasagabaster's (1997) study, we may assume that bilinguals solve production or comprehension problems more efficiently than monolinguals do. In fact, as argued by Jessner (1999), metalinguistic awareness is considered a key component in language-learning and it may be regarded as a crucial issue in third language acquisition. It involves an important degree of dynamism in multilingual competence, as the growth in language experience fosters individuals' learning outcomes, and it is also subjected to distinct individual variables (Cummins, 1991; Jessner, 1997). Following this view, Herdina and Jessner (2002) suggest a dynamic model of multilingualism where the progression and attrition at an individual level and the complex interaction between those factors affecting language acquisition are reflected. According to Jessner (1999), this model is based on a holistic conception of multilingualism (Larse-Freeman, 1997) which opposes static or linear models in traditional paradigms. Linear models assumed multilingual competence to be the sum of knowledge of more than one linguistic system, but interaction among these systems and individual differences were not considered. On the basis of that dynamic view stated above, Jessner (1999: 207) describes multilingual proficiency as 'the results of the effects both on the language system and the cognitive system due to the perceived communicative needs of the multilingual which are subject to change'. Bearing this notion in mind, research on multilingualism should focus on variability because it is regarded as a key factor in multilingual processing. Hence we may state that further research is needed concerning the advantages of bilinguals over monolinguals in third language acquisition and use, paying attention to both individual and situational variables involving multilingual processing. In so doing, we should consider those aspects already dealt with by previous studies on third language acquisition.

Studies focusing on third language acquisition

Empirical studies dealing with third and multilingual language acquisition have experienced considerable growth. Scholars have focused on the role of previously learned languages in language production (cf. studies of language-switching, Williams and Hammarberg, 1998) and on the presumed advantages of bilinguals over monolinguals in learning an additional language (Bild and Swain, 1989; Cenoz, 1991; Cenoz and Genesee, 1998; Eisenstein, 1980). We shall now consider those studies that have tried to ascertain the differences between monolinguals' and bilinguals' acquisition of a second (in the case of the former), and a third language (in the case of bilingual speakers). Despite the fact that L3 acquisition research is still in its infancy, various studies have been conducted, particularly within the European setting, that focus on the acquisition of English by bilingual speakers (Byram and Leman, 1990; Hoffman, 1998). Special attention will be drawn to research conducted in Spain, since certain sociolinguistic aspects, such as the fact that the first language does not enjoy the same status as the second one, may be shared and their results may have further relevance for our own study.

As shown by Cenoz and Jessner's volume (2000), recent research conducted within the European setting tackles sociolinguistic, psycholinguistic and educational aspects of third language acquisition. Research adopting a sociolinguistic perspective addresses the status of English as a lingua franca in Europe (James, 2000; Viereck, 1996). Since we shall deal with the role of bilingualism in using a third language, we are interested in psycholinguistic and educational investigations.

Scholars have attempted to identify characteristics of third language acquisition processing (Cenoz and Genesee, 1998; Hufeisen and Lindemann, 1998) by pointing to subjects from different linguistic backgrounds; Kecskés and Papp (2000) focus on Hungarian subjects and Schönpflug (2000) on Polish/German learners of English, and Bouvy (2000) addresses French-speaking Dutch and German/English learners in Belgium. As argued by Cenoz and Jessner (2000) and illustrated in their volume, research adopting an educational perspective has been carried out in three main European areas, namely Finland (Björklund, 2000), Friesland in The Netherlands (Ystma, 2000), and Spain (Lasagabaster, 1997; Muñoz, 2000). All the studies quoted above report the positive effects of bilingualism in third language acquisition. Other variables analysed in these studies, which also show influential effects on the subjects' performance, are motivation, intelligence, exposure to the English language, and age.

On the basis of results derived from research into the acquisition of English as a third language within the European context, Cenoz and Jessner (2000: 257) propose some directives for further research, specified as follows: (1) the effect of the spread of English on other minority languages at the linguistic, sociolinguistic and psychological levels; (2) the examination of the linguistic characteristics (phonetic, mophological, syntactic and pragmatic) of non-native speakers of English in Europe; (3) the role of L1 and L2 in various aspects of third language acquisition, and (4) the role of metalinguistic awareness in L3 development. The study presented in Part 2 aims at addressing some of the above-quoted needs, as it will particularly focus on non-native speakers of English within a bilingual community (Catalan/Castilian), whose mother tongue (Catalan) is a minority language in their speech community (the Valencian Community). This study also attempts to discover differential effects of being monolingual or bilingual on using English as a third language, thereby focusing on the participants' pragmatic production and metapragmatic awareness. As we will focus on Spain as an example of a multilingual context (Turrell, 2000), and given the need for further research that enables comparison between non-native learners of English as a third language (Cenoz and Jessner, 2000), we shall next describe recent studies adopting an educational and psycholinguistic perspective within the Spanish context. Studies presented are thus those of Cenoz and Valencia (1994) and Lasagabaster (2000), who concentrate on the Basque Country, and Muñoz (2000) and Sanz (2000), who deal with the

Catalonian sociolinguistic situation. We would like to stress that the reason we focus on the studies quoted above also relates to the fact that participants in all these studies share the same second language as our participants, namely Castilian. Furthermore, limitations on learning and using the mother tongue in these communities have been affected by general social and political conditions which also influenced the context in which our study has been developed (see Chapter 3 for a full description).

Cenoz and Valencia's (1994) study aims at ascertaining the positive effects of bilingualism on learning a third language. Participants in the study were 260 students attending six schools in the Basque Country. They were monolingual (Castilian) and bilingual (Euskera/Castilian) speakers learning English as a third language, who were aged between 17 and 19 years old. These authors also examined the effect of the variables of intelligence, age, motivation and exposure by means of various tests and questionnaires (i.e. Otis-Lennon Test, questionnaire on attitudes and motivation, sociocultural questionnaire). The students also took English-language tests in order to measure their proficiency in the target language. The tests and questionnaires were distributed in two two-hour sessions and some days later each student participated in an oral interview, which was recorded in order to evaluate their oral proficiency in English. As suggested by these authors, their empirical findings should lead one to consider the beneficial effect of bilingualism for achieving an optimal degree of multilingual competence. Regarding the variables analysed, high scores on motivation, intelligence and exposure to the English language were associated with higher achievement in that language. Younger learners also performed better than older ones. However, attitudes and sociocultural variables did not affect subjects' performance in the English language. The interaction between the effect of these variables and bilingualism showed no significant variance. Therefore, the effect of bilingualism was obtained independently from the influence of other variables. As quoted above, bilingualism turned out to be a good predictor for the acquisition of English as a third language.

Lasagabaster (2000) also focuses on the Basque-Country context as a bilingual community. In this study, the author attempts to determine the levels of competence in Castilian, Basque and English of students in several bilingual educational programmes, which vary in terms of the language of instruction (i.e. either Euskera or Castilian) and the amount of tuition received in any of these two languages. Participants were 252 students aged from 10 to 14 years. The subjects' competence in Basque and

Castilian was measured by means of standardised tests (Galbahe tests) created by the Department of Education in the Basque Government, while their competence in English was measured via a vocabulary, a grammar, a reading, a listening, a writing and a speaking test. Results from this study suggest that subjects with a good command of the two languages of that community, Basque and Castilian (i.e. balanced bilinguals), possessed a higher proficiency level in English. Therefore, a beneficial effect of bilingualism on learning English as a third language was found. Furthermore, as argued by Lasagabaster (2000), the presence of three languages in the curriculum did not posit any negative effects; instead, these languages may be seen as promoters of metalinguistic competence (Lasagabaster, 1998), as illustrated by the bilinguals' higher degree of competence in the target language.

Another study suggesting positive consequences of bilingualism is that of Muñoz (2000). This author studied subjects from another bilingual Spanish region, that of Catalonia. Muñoz also considered the role of knowing two languages, Catalan and Castilian, in the acquisition of English, with the focus being on the age factor. Subjects were divided into three groups according to their age. The first group consisted of 256 schoolchildren aged 19, the second group included 286 schoolchildren aged 12, and the third group involved 296 secondary-education students aged 17. In order to measure their linguistic competence in the three languages, Catalan, Castilian and English, participants were administered a series of tests, two Catalan and Castilian tests and four English tests. The Catalan and Castilian tests consisted of a dictation and a cloze test, while the English tests included a dictation, a cloze test, a multiple-choice grammar test and a listening comprehension test. In line with Lasagabaster's (2000) results quoted above, Muñoz's empirical findings (2000) suggest that learners showing a good competence in Catalan and Castilian, i.e. bilingual subjects, show a higher level of English proficiency than monolingual ones. Regarding the age factor, the author focused on the 10-year-old and 12-year-old groups, as they had the same hours of instruction. Findings reveal that the older group performed better on the dictation, cloze and multiple-choice test, whereas no differences were found in their listening comprehension performance. For this reason, Muñoz (2000) argues for the need to account for those aspects of the target language in which younger learners may perform better than older ones.

Focusing on this same region, that of Catalonia, Sanz (2000) analyses the effect of bilingual immersion programmes in high school compared to monolingual programmes in the acquisition of English as a third language. This author adopts a cognitive perspective in dealing with factors such as motivation, intelligence and sociolinguistic status. Participants in the study were 201 students (77 monolinguals and 124 bilinguals), and they completed the following tests and questionnaires in two 50-minute sessions: Raven's progressive matrices test (Foulds and Raven, 1950), the vocabulary and structure sections of the CELT English proficiency test (Harris and Palmer, 1970), and a questionnaire including personal information, intelligence-measuring items (from Foulds and Raven, 1950), exposure to English, motivation to learn English (from Cenoz, 1991), and attitudes towards the British and American populations. Results from this study are in line with Cenoz and Valencia's (1994) findings quoted above on the higher performance achieved by students engaged in immersion programmes and who are learning a third language. Therefore, this study also demonstrates the positive and facilitative role of bilingualism in learning an additional language. Sanz (2000) proposes some suggestions for further research in the field of third language acquisition which relate to the effects of variables such as age, order of acquisition, knowledge and use of the L1 and L2 on L3 acquisition.

Considering current research, we are able to assume that bilingual learners will acquire an additional language faster and more efficiently. Cognitive and individual factors have been studied to a certain extent. Nevertheless, features of language use have not received much attention, particularly those dealing with third language learners' interactional competence, as discussed in the following section.

Studies on third language use focusing on pragmatic features

Current research on third language acquisition that focuses on cognitive and developmental processes has pointed out the advantage of bilinguals over monolinguals, as described by Lambert's hypothesis (1990: 212):

> Only further research will tell us how this advantage, assuming it is a reliable phenomenon, actually works. Perhaps it is a matter of bilinguals being better able to store information; perhaps it is a greater separation of linguistic symbols from their referents or the ability to separate word meaning from word sound; perhaps it is the contrasts of linguistic systems that bilinguals continually make that aid them in the development of general conceptual thought. My own working hypothesis is that bilingualism provides a person with a

comparative, three-dimensional insight into language, a type of stereolinguistic optic on communication that the monolingual rarely experiences.

This hypothesis is partly supported by previous research on communicative sensitivity, which can be defined as the ability to meet the listener's needs in communication exchanges and, thus, might be regarded as one feature of pragmatic competence. Genesee *et al.* (1975) carried out an experiment with bilingual and monolingual children. Subjects described a game to two people, one of whom was blind. Results showed that bilingual speakers were more sensitive than monolingual ones where interpersonal skills were concerned. According to Oskaar (1990), interactional competence, including sensitivity to the listener among other features, can be described as the ability to transfer sociocultural norms. This definition also implies pragmatic issues of the languages known by the bilingual or multilingual speaker. Jessner (1997) also points to the advantage of bilinguals over monolinguals regarding their interactional competence, that is, their ability to communicate with others, to perform and interpret communicative actions on the basis of the sociocultural and sociolinguistic norms of a particular speech community. In fact, as argued by this author, bilinguals show a higher degree of development in pragmatic competence than monolingual speakers. Nevertheless, very little research has been devoted to date to investigating pragmatic competence in third language learners.

Fouser's research (1997) focuses on the pragmatic transfer of an adult Korean advanced learner of Japanese as a third language in manipulating various speech levels and honorifics in Japanese. Participants in this study were a 27-year-old Korean/English speaker learning Japanese as a third language at an advanced level, and a native speaker of Japanese aged 24, who acted as a native-speaker informant. In order to elicit the use of honorifics and collect relevant data from the subjects, they were asked to complete a Japanese C-Test, a translation task, a Discourse Completion Test, a Discourse Evaluation Test, a short writing task, and a language-learning-experience questionnaire. Both participants also held a retrospective interview with the researcher. The use of various elicitation techniques aimed at obtaining information on their global proficiency level, pragmatic production, affective and cognitive variables and metapragmatic knowledge. The hypothesis of this study was based on perceived language-distance effects in target language production, which have also been dealt with by Kellerman (1991) and Cenoz (2000). Therefore, the author predicted that language transfer would occur from the language perceived as closest (Korean) to the target language (Japanese). Fouser's prediction was supported by the results, which pointed out the overruling effect of perceived language distance in pragmatic transfer. Subjects resorted to their first language (Korean) regarding pragmatic features of the target language (Japanese). The influence of the second language (English) was not clearly seen. On the basis of these results the author posits a mismatch between advanced learners' linguistic and pragmatic competence. However, as stated by Fouser (1997), individual variables might also have promoted the results. The author also raises the idea that cognitive variables and differences in formal education and metapragmatic knowledge might have affected the learners' output.

Following Fouser's (1997) assumptions, we also believe that further research should consider other variables that may influence bilingual learners' pragmatic competence in a third language. Investigation should then account for the complex nature of multilingualism on the one hand, and for particular characteristics of pragmatic development on the other. Both pragmatic production and comprehension deserve future investigation, as do other cognitive and affective variables that have already been considered in current research, such as the age factor, metalinguistic creativity, and proficiency effects (Lasagabaster, 1997; Muñoz, 2000). Despite the growing body of research on interlanguage pragmatics on the one hand (Barron, 2003; Kasper and Rose, 1999, 2002; Rose and Kasper, 2001), and a recent interest in third language acquisition, on the other (Cenoz and Jessner, 2000; Cenoz and Hoffmann, 2003; Cenoz et al., 2001), few studies have addressed these two research areas. Following this view, we have carried out our study presented in Part 2, which concerns pragmatic competence of third language learners in a bilingual foreign language setting. Hence we focus on multilingual production of specific pragmatic realisations, namely those of requests. Bearing in mind the relevance of interlanguage pragmatics for our study, we shall devote the next chapter to the analysis of pragmatic competence in foreign language learning.

Notes

1. The authors quote Waddington's (1977) and van Geert's (1994) assumptions on biological growth
2. Among others we may quote Schumann's (1978) Acculturation Model of second language learning, which refers to the learners' adaptation to the second language culture, and Giles and Byrne's (1982) Accommodation Theory which relates to acquisition being held in a group situation, since they illustrate monolingual-oriented perspectives.

3. As reported by Skehan (1988: 11): 'Krashen (1982) proposed that comprehensible input is the deriving force for interlanguage development and change, and that the effects of such change carry over to influence production, that is, one learns to speak by listening, a claim which is interesting because of its counter-intuitive nature'.
4. Language organisation refers to the way in which language is stored and structured in the individual's mind.
5. Most reported studies referred to in the literature are those of Paradis (1977, 1980), Albert and Obler (1978) and Paradis and Lecours (1979).
6. Poulisse (1993) presents a framework for communication strategy use on the basis of Levelt's model (1989).

Chapter 2
Pragmatic Competence and Foreign Language Learning

Introduction

The purpose of this chapter is to present an overview of research conducted to date in the field of interlanguage pragmatics, since our study deals with the pragmatic competence of foreign language learners. We shall first present some influential theoretical background on which most studies are based. We will deal in particular with the notion of 'communicative competence' and existing models stemming from second language acquisition research, namely those of Canale and Swain (1980) and Canale (1983), Bachman (1990) and Celce-Murcia *et al.* (1995). In so doing, special attention will be paid to the pragmatic component. Bearing in mind the fact that analyses of second language learners' production have adopted theories and paradigms from first-language pragmatics, the third section of this chapter will describe the three main theories that have influenced studies on second language learners' pragmatic performance. Thus we will consider the applicability of Relevance Theory (Sperber and Wilson, 1986) to acquisition studies (Foster-Cohen, 2000) and Politeness Theory (Brown and Levinson, 1987), as well as criticisms made of it from the perspectives of language-learning and speech acts theory (Searle, 1976).

The third section presents an overview of interlanguage pragmatics research focusing on speech acts production. Some scholars have already presented detailed compilations of research conducted within the interlanguage pragmatics subfield, namely Kasper and Schmidt (1996), Bardovi-Harlig (1999, 2001), Kasper and Rose (1999, 2002), Kasper (2000, 2001) and Rose and Kasper (2001). Following these reviews, we will consider those studies conducted from both a cross-sectional and a developmental perspective. This part will set out the instructional issues affecting the production and recognition of speech acts (Kasper and Dahl, 1991), and will list the ascertained needs that should be tackled by further studies, some of which will be addressed by our study. As we are dealing with foreign language learners' production and recognition of requests, the fourth section will specifically deal with the speech act of requesting. A description of request linguistic realisations following Trosborg (1995) will illustrate the basis of our analysis. Studies on the use of requests by foreign language learners will also be addressed, as they relate to our main focus of concern, which is the analysis of request production and awareness on the part of Catalan/Castilian learners of English.

Communicative Competence

The notion of communicative competence arose from those criticisms raised against the Chomskyan notion of linguistic competence (1965). Scholars from various fields (linguistics, psychology, sociology and anthropology) argued against the absence of aspects related to language use in the concept of linguistic competence, for it merely described an ideal grammatical knowledge shared by native speakers of a given language. Hymes (1972) first suggested that Chomsky's notion of linguistic competence should be replaced by that of communicative competence in order to include social and referential aspects of the language. Nevertheless, the term 'communicative competence' would involve much more than the mere extension of linguistic competence. According to Cenoz (1996), it also implies a qualitative change and a different approach to the study of language use, since communicative competence is a dynamic concept which depends on the interlocutors' negotiation of meaning. Thus the construct involves the interplay of several variables (i.e. relationship between interlocutors, intention in producing message, hearer's interpretation).

The construct of communicative competence has been particularly influential in the field of second language acquisition, as it has a direct relationship with the communicative approach to language teaching. For this reason, some scholars in the field of second language acquisition have attempted to describe the construct by identifying its various components. The most representative and significant models that have arisen within the field of second language acquisition are those of Canale and Swain (1980), Bachman (1990) and Celce-Murcia et al. (1995).

The model by Canale and Swain (1980) and Canale (1983) distinguished between four main subcomponents of the concept of communicative competence, as shown by Figure 2.1.

Grammatical competence consists of knowledge about lexis, morphological rules, syntax, phonology and semantics. It refers to the knowledge required in order to distinguish grammatical from ungrammatical sentences and to produce language accurately. The second component, sociolinguistic

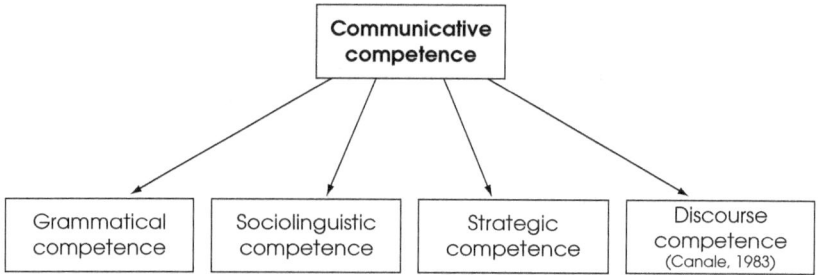

Figure 2.1 Canale and Swain (1980) and Canale's (1983) model of communicative competence

competence, relates to two norms: norms of use and norms of discourse. In this sense, it addresses the speakers' ability to understand and interpret the social meaning of utterances, taking into account situational and contextual factors of language use. Strategic competence entails the speakers' capacity to overcome problems in communicating or to reinforce his/her communicative intention. It then relates to the appropriate use of verbal and nonverbal communication strategies. Finally, discourse competence is defined as the ability to combine linguistic forms in the production and interpretation of unified oral or written texts. This last subcomponent was later added by Canale (1983) to Canale and Swain's original model (1980). This author distinguished discourse from sociolinguistic competence by stating that the last one would refer only to sociocultural norms, while discourse competence would include formal cohesion and semantic coherence. Canale and Swain's (1980) and Canale's (1983) framework has been rather influential on studies of second language use (Tarone, 1980), although it is also subject to certain criticisms. Cenoz points out the lack of a description of those mechanisms operating in strategic competence, and, according to Alcón (2000b), although the model helps us acknowledge those abilities necessary for the acquisition of a second language, it does not specify the existing relationship among its constituents. We agree with Alcón (2000b) about the absence of an explicit connection among its subcomponents, and we also believe that further development and more detailed description of each component would be necessary to fully develop what the notion of communicative competence actually involves.

Bachman (1990) presents a more detailed description of the construct of communicative competence in her proposed framework. This model was first designed in view of language-testing and evaluation considerations, and it might be illustrated as follows:

Pragmatic Competence

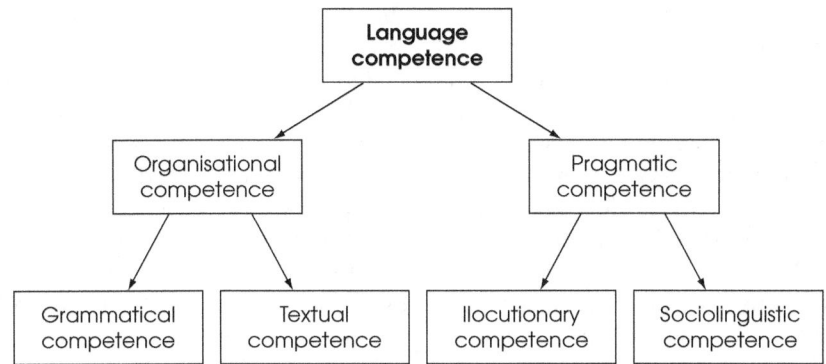

Figure 2.2 Bachman's model of communicative competence

As shown by Figure 2.2, Bachman (1990) distinguishes between organisational and pragmatic competence. The former refers to those abilities involved in the production and identification of grammatical and ungrammatical sentences, and also in understanding their meaning and in ordering them to form texts. These abilities are subdivided into grammatical and textual competence. Grammatical competence involves knowledge of vocabulary, morphology, syntax and phonology or graphology. It then relates to the choice of words, forms and organisation in utterances to illustrate speakers' intentions. The second ability relates to textual competence, which involves knowledge of the existing norms for joining sentences in order to form a text that is cohesive and coherent. Textual competence addresses the rhetorical organisation of a text as well as its effect on the language user. According to Bachman (1990), this competence also involves those conventions structuring oral discourse. We may thus assume that organisational competence deals with those norms associated with the creation and interpretation of utterances, sentences or texts.

A second component of Bachman's (1990) model refers to the relationship between the language and the language users, namely that of pragmatic competence. Bachman (1990) provides a description of the pragmatic component on the basis of van Dijk's (1977) work. In this sense, pragmatics is understood as dealing with the relationships between utterances and the acts performed through these utterances on the one hand, and as the features of the context that promote appropriate language use on the other. The former conceptualisation concerns the illocutionary force, whereas the latter, which relates to the context, involves those sociolinguistic conventions that are related to language use. Therefore, the pragmatic component in

Bachman's model is made up of two subcomponents, those of illocutionary and sociolinguistic competence. Illocutionary competence is defined in terms of Searle's (1969) speech acts and Halliday's (1973) language functions, since it involves the relationship between the utterances and the speakers' intentions specified in them. Sociolinguistic competence refers to sensitivity to differences in variety and register and to the ability of interpreting cultural references. This sociolinguistic subcomponent bears certain similarities to Canale and Swain's (1980) sociolinguistic competence mentioned before.

Bachman's (1990) model has been rather influential on studies concerned with the development and use of pragmatic aspects in a second or foreign language, as it identifies pragmatic competence as one of the main components of communicative competence. Hence it points out the idea that communicative competence can not only be achieved by improving learners' grammatical knowledge, but also concerns the development of other competencies such as the textual and pragmatic ones. However, like Canale and Swain's (1980) framework, this model of communicative competence does not seem to specify the existing relationship among its components and subcomponents. According to Alcón (2000b), only Celce-Murcia *et al.*'s (1995) model accounts for the connection between all constituents of the concept of communicative competence.

Celce-Murcia *et al.*'s (1995) framework of communicative competence differs from the two previously described models in its conceptualisation of discourse competence, since it does not stand as an isolated subcomponent, but depends on three further constituents, namely those of sociolinguistic, linguistic and actional competence. This might be best illustrated as follows:

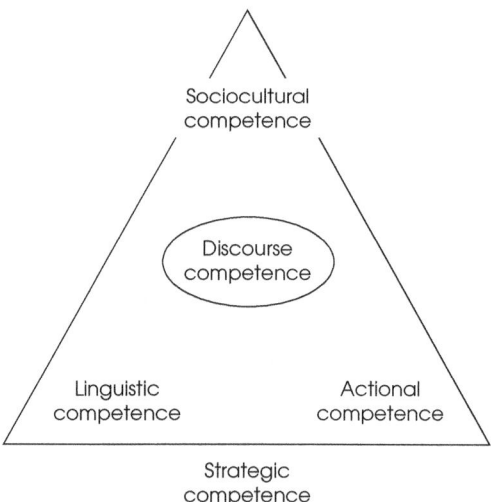

Figure 2.3 Celce-Murcia *et al.*'s communicative competence framework

As shown in Figure 2.3, the model comprises five constituents: linguistic competence; actional, competence; sociocultural competence; discourse competence and strategic competence, which are interrelated. Linguistic competence would correspond to Canale and Swain's (1980) grammatical competence, but it does not refer only to grammatical abilities, as it also involves knowledge of the distinct layers of a linguistic system, thus including sentence patterns, morphological inflections, lexis, phonological and orthographic systems. The actional component would be included in Canale and Swain's (1980) sociocultural component and also in Bachman's (1990) pragmatic competence, since it refers to the knowledge of language functions and speech acts sets in interpreting and showing speakers' intentions by means of linguistic forms. The third constituent, sociocultural competence, is related to Canale's (1983) sociocultural competence and to Bachman's (1990) sociolinguistic competence, as it addresses the issue of expressing messages appropriately according to the cultural and social conventions of the context in which it is produced. Therefore, as stated by Celce-Murcia *et al.* (1995: 24), sociolinguistic competence can be affected by social, contextual, stylistic, cultural and non-verbal communicative factors. The central component in Celce-Murcia *et al.*'s proposal is that of discourse competence, which, as shown in Figure 2.3, also bears a close relationship to the three components described before, namely linguistic, actional and sociocultural competence. The subcomponents of discourse competence are cohesion, deixis, coherence, genre structure and conversational structure. All these features will also depend on the speakers' knowledge of the linguistic system, his/her interpretation and intended meaning in producing a message, and the appropriateness of that message to a particular context or situation.

All four subcomponents named so far are influenced by the last constituent within the framework, i.e. strategic competence. Celce-Murcia *et al.* conceptualise strategic competence as the knowledge and use of communication strategies. Despite the fact that these strategies have traditionally been related to problem-solving in communication, the authors believe that they should also include attempts to improve communicative effectiveness. Bearing this conceptualisation in mind, strategic competence consists of five main strategies, namely those of avoidance, achievement, time-gaining, self-monitoring and interactional strategies. According to Celce-Murcia *et al.*, this part of their model could be further extended to include other strategies involved in foreign language learning and use. This further development is carried out by Alcón (2000b) in her proposal for a model of communicative competence (see Table 2.1 overleaf), which has been developed on the basis of Celce-Murcia *et al.*'s (1995) framework.

Table 2.1 Suggested model of communicative competence

Discourse competence	Linguistic competence Textual competence Pragmatic competence
Psychomotor skills and competencies	Listening Speaking Reading Writing
Strategic competence	Communication strategies Learning strategies

Source: Alcón (2000b: 238)

Alcón's (2000b) framework consists of three main components, namely discourse competence, psychomotor abilities and competencies and strategic competence. As in the case of Celce-Murcia *et al.*'s (1995) model, discourse competence is understood to be a central component constituted by three other subcomponents, those of linguistic, textual and pragmatic competencies. Linguistic competence, as in Celce-Murcia *et al.*'s model, refers to knowledge of all aspects of the linguistic system, including lexis, phonology, orthography, morphology and grammar. Textual and pragmatic competencies relate to those processes involved in the creation and interpretation of discourse, thus bearing a relationship with Bachman's pragmatic component and Celce-Murcia *et al.*'s actional and sociocultural constituents. As noted by Alcón (2000b), discourse competence is influenced by those psychomotor abilities of listening, speaking, reading and writing, which are needed in using the language for communication purposes. The last component in Alcón's model, strategic competence, includes both communication and learning strategies, which may be identified in psychomotor abilities and also affect discourse competence. Therefore, all components in this model are interrelated and they explain those conditions affecting and promoting appropriate and effective foreign and second language use.

As far as we are concerned, identifying the constituents of communicative competence should not lead to a mere listing of competencies, as in the case of Canale and Swain's (1980) framework, nor should it posit any doubt about the interrelationship among all constituents, as Bachman's (1995) model does. On the one hand, a model of this sort should be explanatory enough to account for all competencies involved in its operation. In so doing, it would help us to ascertain how to foster foreign language learners' communicative competence. On the other hand, it should also present the kind of relationship that exists among its constituents and its effect on the learners' overall communicative process. These two criteria might be illustrated in Alcón's proposed model (2000b), which serves as a basis for explaining oral discourse competence in the foreign language classroom. As we are also dealing with foreign language learners' oral discourse competence, this model would also provide the most appropriate framework for our study. However, given the fact that we shall analyse pragmatic aspects, it may be noteworthy to pay more attention to the pragmatic component by reviewing the literature on pragmatics in second language acquisition research.

The Pragmatic Components of Communicative Competence

As has been previously mentioned, in this chapter our aim is to provide an overview of the pragmatic component of communicative competence from the perspective of second language acquisition research. We will consider those theories and paradigms that have influenced research in the field. For this reason, relevance, politeness and speech-act theories will be examined/explored. When dealing with relevance theory we shall consider Foster-Cohen's (2000) assumptions on the applicability of this principle in second language acquisition research, as well as its adoption by certain studies in this field (Carroll, 1995). Politeness issues (Brown and Levinson, 1987) will also be tackled, as our study is concerned with learners' production of speech acts. Consequently, an overview of the literature on speech acts (Searle, 1976) will also be provided in this section.

Relevance theory

Despite the fact that relevance theory was intended to describe native speakers' interpretation processes in communication, it has also influenced the work of certain scholars in the field of second language acquisition who focus on comprehension mechanisms (Foster-Cohen, 1994; Ross, 1997; Rost, 1990). One of the areas that has adopted relevance theory is that of interlanguage pragmatics of speech-act production and comprehension (Kasper and Blum-Kulka, 1993). We shall next present a general outline of relevance theory, focusing on those aspects related to second language acquisition processes.

Relevance theory was conceptualised in the light of Grice's maxim of relevance (1975) and the criticisms made of it by Sperber and Wilson (1986). Nevertheless, there is one aspect common to both these principles, which is that of the distinction between informative and communicative speaker's intentions. The former will be achieved only if the hearer is aware of the speaker's intention. The main differences between Grice's and Sperber and Wilson's paradigms concern inferential processing conditions in human beings. Grice (1975) points to some established rules that guide human behaviour: those of truth, relevance, clarity and informativeness. Conversely, Sperber and Wilson (1986) argue against the existence of established norms; instead, these authors argue for those conditions operating in human cognition. Relevance is defined in terms of cognitive effort and contextual effects. An utterance may then be said to be irrelevant if it involves too much cognitive processing or if there are no significant contextual effects. Additionally, the hearer may stop cognitive processing when the interpretation of the speaker's message involves significant contextual effects. These effects will take place when there is an enlargement of the hearer's representation of the world by means of deduction or inferential processes. The deductive device and the notion of manifestness are central aspects in relevance theory, as they attempt to describe human comprehension systems. According to Sperber and Wilson (1995), the hearer will be able to infer only what is manifest to him from the speaker's message, that is, what he can perceive and what will lead to a shared cognitive environment between speaker and hearer. This common cognitive environment includes the required contextual information that enables communication.

According to Foster-Cohen (2000), interactions between non-native speakers could also illustrate this idea. In fact, the author states that the pragmatics of native speakers' comprehension systems may also work with non-native speakers. The only difference would relate to the type of input provided and the results obtained, but it would still be relevance-oriented. This idea would lead to second language acquisition studies that focus on learners' hypothesis formation deriving from the kind of input they may be exposed to (Gass and Madden, 1985). Foster-Cohen (2000) sees a direct application of relevance theory to learners' use of the deductive device in order to modify their linguistic representation on the basis of their prior knowledge, the nature of input and other individual factors. In this respect, the idea of learners' awareness in language use would also be connected to relevance theory. In our opinion, thinking-aloud protocols or learners' evaluation of the discourse generated would illustrate the role of the deductive device in second language comprehension systems. Furthermore, following Foster-Cohen's (2000) assumptions, the role of contextual effects in the second language learning context also leads one to focus on form studies adopting an interactional perspective, where learners' attention may be drawn to form as input for acquisition (Alcón, 1997; Fotos, 1997; García Mayo, 2001).

As illustrated above, relevance theory is linked to second language acquisition processes, and further research on the basis of this pragmatic theory would probably help to explain second language inferencing and comprehension processes. Despite the importance of identifying inferential mechanisms in learners' awareness and understanding of the target language, we must also consider the importance of the production system and the rules or conditions underlying it. These conditions involve the particular context of language use affecting linguistic choice. As we are dealing with foreign language learners' use of directive speech acts, it may be worth exploring politeness issues that would also be embedded within the pragmatic component of communicative competence.

Politeness principle

In this section we offer an overview of the politeness principle from the second language acquisition perspective. We will consider Brown and Levinson's politeness principle (1987) as far as it affects current research on interlanguage pragmatics, which is the main topic of our study. Criticisms raised against this principle will also be dealt with as long as they relate to language-learning processes. We will particularly consider Turner's (1996) and Meier's (1997) assumptions, since they may provide us with an overall picture of politeness theory, its criticism and its effect on second language learning and teaching.

Brown and Levinson's (1987) politeness theory attempted to explain existing deviations from Grice's (1975) cooperative principle in language use. According to Brown and Levinson (1987), the reason why interlocutors may not follow Gricean rules in communication (e.g. be informative, be brief, be relevant, be true) involves their willingness to communicate politely, and the main goal of this kind of communication is the collective preservation of 'face'. In fact, a core concept in politeness theory is that of face, which distinguishes positive from negative face. The former involves the desire to be liked and to keep all that one possesses, while negative face relates to the wish to maintain one's territory unimpeded. This twofold notion of face (positive and negative) implies a certain departure from Grice's norms if the communicative act entails any risk to the addressee's face. In fact, a speaker may not be brief if their message implies an invasion of their interlocutor's territory (e.g. 'Would you be so kind as to do this for me, please?'). A third assumption refers to the achievement of the participants' goal by choosing the most appropriate means. The 'calculation of face' work is done by considering three main aspects, namely those of social distance, relative power and degree of imposition. As claimed by Brown and Levinson (1987), the sum of these three aspects provides the exact amount of 'face work' to be developed by participants.

Brown and Levinson's (1987) theory has attracted different criticisms. Slugoski and Turnbull (1988) state that politeness theory does not consider the existence of variables other than those of social distance, power relationship or degree of imposition. They particularly point to the role of affect, and argue for its addition to the politeness model. On the same lines, Watts *et al.* (1992) argue against the lack of a clearly defined relationship between those acknowledged variables in Brown and Levinson's model stated above. For these authors, the three variables that help calculate the amount of face work developed by participants bear a close interdependence. In fact, as reported by Meier (1997), no definition of politeness theory is provided in Brown and Levinson's politeness principle (1987). This author also criticises the universality underlying face wants, since requirements in this respect are culture-bound, and thus cannot be identical. Another aspect that has received much criticism concerns the proposed classification of face-work strategies, which may be illustrated as follows:

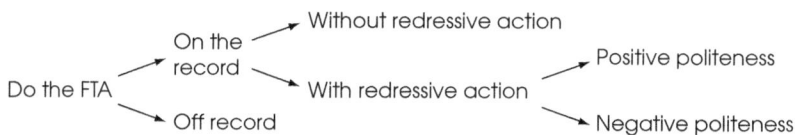

Figure 2.4 Face work strategies from Brown and Levinson (1987: 69)

As shown in Figure 2.4 above, silence appears as the most polite strategy, while speaking directly on record is not considered to be polite. This classification of face-work strategies follows a directness-to-politeness scale in which indirect expressions are assumed to be the most polite. Nevertheless, this hierarchy has not been validated by most of the studies investigating politeness phenomena in different linguistic communities. In fact, Blum-Kulka and Sheffer (1993) distinguished between conventionally and unconventionally indirect strategies in their study of the perception of politeness and indirectness of English and Hebrew speakers. According to Blum-Kulka and Sheffer (1993), politeness is associated with conventional indirectness, while unconventional indirectness involves a higher degree of imposition for the addressee, since s/he has to infer the intended meaning. Therefore, from Blum-Kulka's results, it might be assumed that Brown and Levinson's politeness scale does not represent universal polite behaviour, as the authors suggest. The universal nature attributed to politeness theory has also been regarded as denoting ethnocentrism (Meier, 1997), since speakers of whole speech communities produce direct yet still polite utterances. Indeed, one example is the Spanish-speaking community, on which our study is based, where the use of imperatives does not necessarily imply impolite behaviour.

In the light of the problems associated with politeness theory, other alternative principles or perspectives have arisen. Leech (1980) regards politeness as a whole construct encompassing an undetermined number of rules such as those of tact, approbation, generosity or modesty. Sperber and Wilson's (1986, 1995) relevance theory is also viewed as an alternative model for pragmatic inference (see Jary, 1998). However, as far as we are concerned, none of them seems to address the overall communicative act. Instead, they focus on one of the participants, the speaker's sociolinguistic considerations in the case of politeness theory, and the hearer's inferencing processes in the relevance theory. Furthermore, as stated by Turner (1996), studies dealing with politeness have focused on the morphosyntactic structures. This fact is reflected in current textbooks and ELT materials (Alcón and Tricker, 2000) dealing with politeness and pragmatic issues in a second or foreign language learning situation. In Turner's view (1996), politeness effects should be considered as deriving from the interaction between semantic structure and context. The fact that the latter is not experienced in the same way by all people may also affect language learning and teaching. Following this line, Meier (1997) considers that the utmost regard should be paid to the context in his proposal of a working definition of politeness for second and foreign language pedagogy, which concerns the notion of appropriateness. This notion is situation-dependent and it allows for a distinction between what is formal or informal for particular cultures. Therefore, Meier (1997) argues for an anthropological approach which leads to awareness-raising procedures of perceived roles of dominance, power or rights. As stated by the author, this awareness-raising process has two main aspects. On the one hand, it focuses on the existence of evaluations of appropriateness across cultures and on learners' interpretations of politeness aspects on the basis of their own linguistic and cultural systems. On the other hand, attention to contextual features may enable learners to choose from among various linguistic strategies in negotiating effective communication. Meier's proposal involves a dynamic approach whereby learners gain insight into the cultural factors underlying contextual features. This cultural approach, in the author's opinion, is crucial to the teaching and learning of speech acts in the second language classroom.

Existing studies on speech-acts production by second language learners first focused on research conducted in the field of pragmatics. Thus in the next section we deal with speech-act theory by paying special attention to suggested classifications of speech-acts. In fact, these proposed taxonomies and subsequent modifications constitute a basic tool for analysing speech-acts behaviour in second language acquisition contexts.

Speech-act theory

We shall first focus on Searle's (1976) proposal of a classification of speech-acts. Secondly, modifications and criticisms raised against Searle's taxonomy and provided by scholars belonging to the pragmatics field, such as Wunderlich (1980), Thomas (1995) and Cruse (2000), will also be dealt with.

Searle (1976) classifies illocutionary speech-acts in five groups, namely those of *representatives, directives, commissives, expressives* and *declarations*. *Representatives* are an attempt to describe the world and the 'world to match the words' (Searle, 1976: 3). When the speaker tries to get the hearer to commit to some future course of action we are dealing with *directives*. According to Searle, directives are attempts to make the world match the words. In the case of *commissives*, the speaker commits himself to some future course of action, while the purpose of using *expressives* is to show the speaker's psychological state of mind regarding his/her attitude to some prior action or state of affairs. Finally, *declarations* require extralinguistic institutions for their performance (e.g. appointing a new director).

Searle's classification has been adopted and adapted by other authors. Haverkate (1984) provides a definition of exhortative speech acts on the basis of Searle's conceptualisation. In Haverkate's (1984) view, directive speech acts are those where the speaker wants the hearer to do something. These acts are characterised as being either impositive or non-impositive. The former group includes the most threatening acts, those of requesting, pleading and ordering; whereas non-impositive directives include suggestions and instructions. Cruse (2000) also adapts Searle's (1969) classification to his suggested taxonomy of performative verbs, which include assertives, directives, commissives, expressives and declaratives. According to the author, the following verbs are examples of assertives: state, suggest, boast, complain, report and warn. Directives comprise verbs such as order, command, request, beg, beseech, advise, warn (to), recommend, ask and ask (to). Commissives involve promising, vowing, offering, contracting and threatening, while expressives include verbs such as thank, congratulate, condole, praise, blame, forgive and pardon. Finally, within declaratives we find performatives such as resign, dismiss, divorce, christen, name, open, sentence, consecrate, bid or declare. From this typology, we may state that Cruse (2000) concentrates on what he terms 'grammatical performativity', that is, the particular ways in which a language can indicate illocutionary force. Hence a semantic view of speech-acts behaviour is implied. The illocutionary force of a language is encoded at both a lexical and a structural level. Explicit performativity, according to the author, is expressed by means of performative verbs, which follow the above-quoted taxonomy, and by certain grammatical structures, such as declaratives, interrogatives, imperatives and exclamations.

Nevertheless, Searle's classification has also received some criticism regarding both the actual classification and the author's view on the overgeneralisation of the rules governing speech-act behaviour. According to Wunderlich (1980), Searle's attempts to classify speech acts is not really convincing. For this author, commissives should be regarded as reactions to directives rather than as speech acts in themselves. By the same token, Wunderlich (1980) claims that questions should be considered as a sole speech act, instead of as a subtype of directives. A third criticism points to other speech acts that are not illustrated in Searle's taxonomy, such as warnings, advice, proposals and offers. On the basis of these ideas, Wunderlich (1980) proposes four main criteria for a classification of speech acts:

(1) Grammatical markers, including the interrogative mood (erotetic speech acts), the imperative type (directive speech acts), declarative mood (representative speech acts), and specific performative formulas (declarative speech acts).
(2) The type of propositional content and the illocutionary outcome. As these two aspects are closely related, a separate classification for each type is not feasible.
(3) Their function, i.e. whether speech acts represent an initiating or a reacting move.
(4) Occurrence in everyday conversations, natural or primary speech acts, or institutional or secondary speech acts.

As stated by Wunderlich (1980), the main classes of speech acts should be defined within the semantics of grammatical mood, since some speech acts are grammatically marked (e.g. questions), others require specific formulae, and most share semantic characteristics. All possible concretions on the type and subtype or realisations of speech acts will be an issue of pragmatics. However, certain speech acts will only be treated at pragmatic level, such as warnings or pieces of advice. For this author, these two acts are only differentiated either by the use of particular words or because advice predicts an event that bears negative consequences.

Leech (1983) also argues against Searle's (1976) proposed speech-acts classification because of its 'formal' character. Leech's perspective (1983) is more functional, since he is also interested in the meaning of speech-act verbs as a key to knowing how people talk about illocutionary acts, rather than as a key to the nature of these same acts. Leech presents a functional classification including convivial (thanking and apologising) and competitive (complaining, requesting and correcting) speech-acts.

The overgeneralisation of rules governing speech-acts behaviour in Searle's proposal has also raised some opposing views. Thomas (1995) criticises the fact that Searle treats speech-acts as if they were clearly defined categories with clear-cut boundaries. For this first author, the boundaries between commanding, inviting, ordering, requesting and asking are often blurred. In fact, an identical speech-act or linguistic realisation may cover a range of slightly different phenomena, as illustrated by the distinct strategies that may realise it. As reported by Thomas (1995), two distinct speech acts may overlap in certain cases and this should be considered as a common fact illustrating pragmatic language use. In fact, as argued by Thomas (1995: 105) 'it is a mistake to sacrifice the potential to exploit all the potential richness of meaning of speech acts for the sake of a tidy system of rules'. Nevertheless, this author also assumes that certain criteria exist for a classification of speech acts. Unlike Searle's (1976) taxonomy, which merely considers formal aspects, Thomas regards functional, psychological and affective factors. Additionally, one should also consider whether a given speech act is culturally specific or context-specific, and to what extent participants' interaction affects the realisation of speech acts. On the basis of these ideas, Thomas points to Searle's failure in providing specific arbitrary rules governing speech-acts behaviour. Instead, the author advocates the term 'regulative principle', given the context-specific nature of speech-acts realisation.

We concur with Thomas in the idea that speech-acts are not governed by arbitrary rules. These acts are motivated, as they result from the interaction between the speaker's intention in producing a given act (request, compliment, promise) and other pragmatic factors, such as the context in which they occur. Bearing this idea in mind, efforts by researchers to provide a complete and ordered taxonomy of speech acts and its corresponding realisations seem unfeasible. However, if our aim is to analyse and implement speech-acts use and understanding in the foreign language classroom, we should consider certain pragmatic patterns in a systemised way. In the next section we present our own proposal for fostering pragmatic competence in the foreign language classroom.

A proposal for fostering pragmatic competence in the foreign language classroom

In the previous sections of this chapter we have presented an overview of some of the most significant aspects affecting pragmatic competence (relevance, politeness and speech-acts theories), from the perspective of both existing theories and the criticisms raised against them. The purpose of this section is to present our proposal for the promotion of pragmatic competence in classroom settings.

Contrary to Boxer and Pickering's (1995) assumptions about the unrequired teaching of sociopragmatic aspects in a foreign language setting, we believe that these features are of the utmost importance in these particular language learning contexts. Unlike second language learners, subjects learning a foreign language do not have many opportunities to be exposed to natural and authentic language use. If we do not provide them with sufficient sociocultural and sociolinguistic information, we are increasing their difficulty in understanding and producing politeness issues in the target language. Therefore, we would argue for a focus on comprehension of pragmatic information in the target language, as well as on fostering pragmatic production in the language classroom. With regard to comprehension, the learners' deductive devices may be aroused so that they can adapt their linguistic and pragmalinguistic representation of the target language according to their background knowledge (Foster-Cohen, 2000). Pragmatic production may focus on appropriateness, thus paying attention to both propositional content, on the one hand, and cultural effects (Meier, 1997), on the other.

Considering the identification and use of speech acts in the classroom, we have argued for the need to have access to more or less systematised pragmatic patterns. Nevertheless, this does not mean that we should focus merely on traditional form-focused typologies, as has been the case with most previous studies in interlanguage pragmatics (Blum-Kulka *et al.*, 1989). Instead, we should consider findings from previous studies in the field of second language acquisition and interlanguage pragmatics and apply them to particular aspects of the situation we are dealing with, such as contextual features, participants' relationship and motivation. Our proposal is based on three major tenets of pragmatic theory, including relevance theory, politeness issues, and the speech-acts paradigm and its applicability to second language acquisition. It may be best described in terms of the following assumptions:

(1) There is a need to teach sociopragmatic aspects of the target language in a foreign setting with a focus on comprehension and production.
(2) Comprehension of pragmatic items might be achieved by fostering learners' connections between their previous pragmalinguistic information (in both their L1 and the TL) and the new pragmatic information they may be provided with.
(3) Learners' pragmatic production should be guided in terms of appropriateness and cultural effects.
(4) The need for providing systematised pragmatic patterns in identifying and using specific speech acts should be based on findings from research in interlanguage pragmatics and foreign-language acquisition.

We believe that pragmatic competence should be fostered in the foreign-language classroom, taking into account the fact that it is one of the main components of the global construct of communicative competence. Hence, production and comprehension of the sociocultural norms underlying target-language use should be considered, as is shown in Figure 2.5.

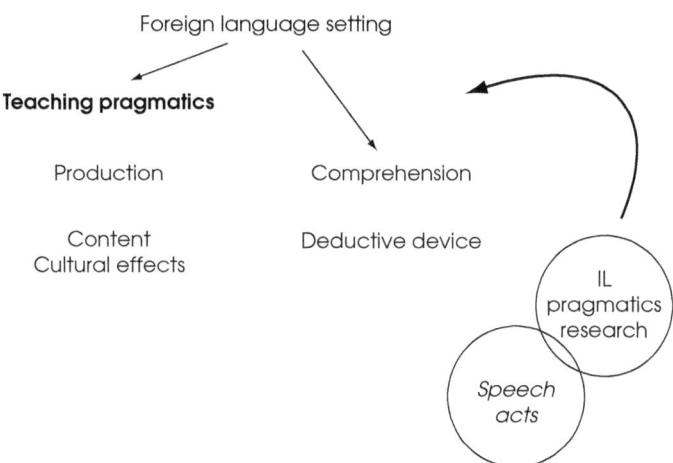

Figure 2.5 Suggested proposal for the promotion of pragmatic competence in an EFL setting based on Searle (1980), Sperber and Wilson (1987), Brown and Levinson (1987), Thomas (1995), Meier (1997) and Foster-Cohen (2000)

We have attempted to include some of the existing theories of pragmatic behaviour in a global framework for the promotion of pragmatic competence in the foreign language context. Nevertheless, it should be further extended in order to account for underlying processes in foreign-language pragmatic development. For this purpose, in the following section we will focus on research carried out in the field of interlanguage pragmatics.

Interlanguage Pragmatics

Interlanguage pragmatics is a relatively new subfield within the second language acquisition research area. It is concerned with the pragmatic competence and performance of second and foreign language learners; thus, studies in this field focus on the non-native speaker's use and acquisition of pragmatic knowledge in/of the target language. The first studies appeared almost 30 years ago in North America (Borkin and Reinhart, 1978) and Europe (Hackman, 1977). From that moment, scholars have focused on speech-act performance by learners of a second language. One of the most influential works in this field is that of Blum-Kulka *et al.* (1989), who attempted to discern variation in speech-acts production by individuals from different linguistic backgrounds. In general terms, results from their study showed that language learners, as well as native speakers, made use of different linguistic realisations for various situations. However, language learners did not always consider the appropriateness of certain routines for particular contexts. The mismatch of second language learners' grammatical and pragmatic competence has frequently been pointed out (Blum-Kulka, 1996), and this fact has aroused interest in the study of pragmatic competence by second language acquisition researchers.

As discussed in the first section of the present chapter, the inclusion of pragmatic competence as a main component of communicative competence in Bachman's (1990) model has probably made more explicit the need to acquire pragmatic knowledge in order to communicate efficiently in the target language. Most studies in interlanguage pragmatics to date have considered non-native speakers' use of speech-acts, thereby adopting perspectives and theories from investigation on first-language use. For this reason, it is not surprising that the focus of interlanguage pragmatics has followed existing trends from first-language pragmatics rather than from the second language acquisition field. This fact is illustrated by the wide amount of research projects examining speech-act use compared to the quantity of studies on the acquisition of pragmatic aspects of the target language. In the next two subsections we present an overview of research carried out with a focus on speech-acts use, on the one hand, and on its development, on the other. We believe that this account of current studies within the field of interlanguage pragmatics may help us explain the relevance of our own study in the field of second language acquisition.

Studies on speech-act use: Cross-cultural perspectives

We have already mentioned Blum-Kulka et al.'s (1989) project on cross-cultural differences between native and non-native speakers' use of requests and apologies. This project entailed the collection of specific linguistic realisations by means of a discourse completion test. Learners used the target language in order to write down incomplete exchanges that elicited linguistic realisations of requests or apologies. This project has provided many valuable insights into the differences and similarities of speech-act use by native and non-native speakers from distinct cultural backgrounds. It raised the issue of the 'waffle phenomenon' or verbosity in language learners, and that of the transfer of certain first-language pragmatic norms into the second language (e.g. the case of imperative use by Spanish speakers). Other authors have conducted studies on speech-act production on the basis of the Cross-Cultural Speech Act Research Project named above.

Eisenstein and Bodman (1993) examined expressions of gratitude used by native and non-native speakers of American English from different linguistic backgrounds. Their results reported differences at sociopragmatic and pragmalinguistic levels: the former referred to situations that elicited thanking behaviour, while pragmalinguistic differences involved the use of specific linguistic formulae. Non-native speakers showed certain difficulties in adjusting more complex linguistic forms to certain contexts. Expressions and perceptions of gratitude appeared to be culture-bound in the case of language learners' performance. In a later study, Eisenstein et al. (1996) focused on gratitude expressions produced by native and non-native speakers of American English, and found sociocultural effects on the learners' performance. In fact, the use of certain types of greeting appeared to be particularly problematic for learners because of their cultural background. In this sense, the findings from this study show the presence of pragmatic transfer regarding conventionalised forms.

Cross-cultural effects are also reported in Nelson et al.'s (1996) study on complimenting. These authors examined American and Egyptian subjects' use of compliment responses by means of interviews, in which the subjects were asked to list the last compliments they had made, observed or received. Differences in the subjects' performances revealed that American compliments were shorter, that Egyptians used more comparatives, and that gender played a role in paying compliments. It was also noted that limited routines exist in American and Egyptian compliments, although patterns were not equivalent. Therefore, cultural differences were also displayed in the subjects' performance.

Other speech acts that have received attention in cross-cultural studies are those of apology and complaint (see Olshtain and Cohen, 1983, and Holmes, 1989). Olshtain and Weinbach (1993) analysed and compared the production of apologies and complaints by intermediate and advanced learners of Hebrew with that of native speakers by means of production questionnaires. According to these authors, non-native speakers produced longer stretches of discourse and their selection of particular formulae was influenced by the social distance of the interlocutors. As occurred in Eisenstein and Bodman's (1993) study quoted above, learners displayed a high degree of variability in their responses, but linguistic formulae did not follow appropriateness criteria. Therefore we may say that both studies point to the following aspects: learners lacked control over pragmatic conventions underlying the use of apologies and complaints; and learners produce more speech than native speakers do in general terms.

English learners' use of complaints is also analysed by Murphy and Neu (1996). These authors sought to determine American native speakers' evaluation of learners' output. For this purpose, Murphy and Neu (1996) employed an oral discourse-completion test, which elicited complaints realisations, and a questionnaire on acceptability judgements. This instrument was employed in order to collect native speakers' evaluation of learners' performance, since American speakers listened to responses produced by Korean speakers in situations that required the use of complaints (i.e. oral completion tests). These responses involved the use of criticisms rather than complaints. Findings showed that cultural issues can affect a given speech-act production to the extent that a completely distinct act is used. For identical situations, different speech acts were employed by subjects from different cultural backgrounds. Hence we can state that the use of speech acts by language learners is strongly influenced by their sociolinguistic context, that is, by the situational and contextual norms underlying language use in their own speech communities.

Considering the studies quoted above, which have adopted a cross-cultural perspective, we can state that cultural interference does play a role in the production of particular speech acts. Most studies aimed at describing learners' output as opposed to native speakers' use, and, in some cases, there was also the possibility of comparing learners from different linguistic backgrounds. Following Goldschmidt (1996), we find those studies most valuable for the information provided on speech-act forms, functions and patterns as related to the target-language culture and the role of other cultural backgrounds on their perception and use. However, as noted by Kasper (1996), studies of speech-act use by nonnative speakers have addressed issues borrowed from the pragmatics field and not from a learning perspective. Therefore, there seems to be a need for more developmental studies on L2 pragmatic acquisition. This existing need has already been addressed by scholars in the field of interlanguage pragmatics, as is illustrated in the following subsection.

Developmental perspectives

Compared to the existing body of research carried out on the use of speech acts, developmental studies still have to meet certain requirements in order to provide a complete view of L2 pragmatic processing. During the 1990s various researchers adopted this perspective and established the basis for ongoing investigation in interlanguage pragmatics. Following Kasper and Schmidt (1996), we will distinguish between cross-sectional and longitudinal studies focusing on acquisitional development.

Most cross-sectional studies have accounted for speech-act production and recognition of subjects at different proficiency levels. These pseudolongitudinal studies have dealt with refusals (Houck and Gass, 1996; Robinson, 1992; Takahashi and Beebe, 1987), apologies (Maeshiba *et al.*, 1996; Trosborg, 1987, 1995), requests (Hassall, 1997; Hill, 1997; Takahashi and DuFon, 1989), greetings (Omar, 1991) and compliments (Rose, 1998, 2000). Participants in these studies had different nationalities (Danish, Japanese, Cantonese and English) and were learning English as a second or foreign language, with the exception of Hassall's (1997) and Omar's (1991) participants, who were English speakers learning Bahasa Indonesian and Kiswahili, respectively. The elicitation techniques employed by scholars in cross-sectional studies include discourse completion tests, role-plays, rating scales and cartoon oral production tasks. It should also be noted that few studies have employed more than one of these instruments. Regarding the results, most studies point to proficiency effects on second or foreign language pragmatic production and development. Takahashi and DuFon's subjects (1989) showed a preference for direct requests as their proficiency level increased, while Trosborg (1987) also noted that learners expanded their repertoire of apology realisations in line with their proficiency level. Another proficiency effect raised by other studies is that of pragmatic transfer. Maeshiba *et al.* (1996) observed that even lower-level learners tended to provide fewer direct refusal realisations, which the authors interpreted as an instance of transfer from their mother tongue. However,

Takahashi (1996) reported that the learners' proficiency level had little influence on their performance. In fact, both intermediate and advanced learners resorted to their first language in producing request acts.

Pragmatic development may also be influenced by the length of stay in the target-language country. Omar (1991) reported on the positive role of being immersed in the target culture in the use of more appropriate greeting routines. A connection could then be drawn between cultural immersion and pragmatic development. Considering the studies mentioned above, we can state that cross-sectional research on speech-act realisation has taken into account proficiency effects, the influence of the learners' first language and the length of stay in the target-language community. Nevertheless, certain drawbacks are also associated with these studies. As argued by Kasper and Schimdt (1996), and also by Kasper and Rose (1999, 2002) in their literature review on acquisition-oriented interlanguage pragmatics research, cross-sectional or pseudo-longitudinal studies have not shown developmental stages that help us acknowledge processing issues. In fact, none of the existing studies to date have accounted for learners at a beginner level, and their research design has merely focused on elicitation techniques that require at least an intermediate proficiency level in the target language.

The lack of information on developmental stages deriving from cross-sectional studies can be overcome by longitudinal investigations. In the field of interlanguage pragmatics, few longitudinal research projects have been carried out concerning speech-act realisation and development, but their results are worth mentioning. Speech acts investigated in these studies are those of requests (Ellis, 1992, 1997; Schmidt, 1983), suggestions and rejections (Bardovi-Harlig and Hartford, 1993), and thanking and apologies (Cohen, 1997). Schmidt (1983) and Ellis (1992, 1997) focused on the early pragmatic development of beginner learners of English as a second language. Schmidt (1983) carried out a three-year study of an adult non-native speaker's acquisition and use of request formulas in an English-speaking community, namely that of Hawaii. The subject of the study was a Japanese speaker living in Hawaii. After three years, his request realisations were more elaborate and his performance also denoted an increase in his tendency to employ imperatives. However, as reported by Schmidt (1983), some non-native characteristics still remained. Data for this study was obtained by means of recordings and observations of authentic discourse. Ellis (1992, 1997) also made use of authentic discourse, although the author analysed two English learners' request production in a classroom setting. The participants were aged 10 and 11 and their performance revealed three developmental stages in request production. Firstly, the learners' productions showed illocutionary intentions but not social or linguistical appropriateness. Secondly, the participants started making use of certain routines and mitigators (e.g. 'please'); and, finally, they showed more variation in request strategies' use and politeness aspects.

A different speech act was analysed in Bardovi-Harlig and Hartford's (1993) study, which focused on the production of suggestions and rejections by English learners in advising sessions. Participants in this study were 16 advanced ESL learners and data consisted of their interaction with native speakers, which was recorded and transcribed. Although their competence increased over time, according to the authors, they did not learn how to mitigate their realisation formula. These findings may be attributed to the lack of focus on the linguistic expressions employed, seeing that the advisors commented only on the suitability of the speech acts employed by non-native speakers. In our opinion, another relevant outcome of this study relies on the taxonomy employed by Bardovi-Harlig and Hartford in analysing their data, since it offers an alternative perspective for the study of speech-act use in particular settings. The authors based their interpretation on the maxim of congruence (see Bardovi-Harlig and Hartford, 1990), which predicts speech-act realisations produced by participants depending on the role allocated to them in a given situation. In this sense, participants should be congruent with their role in performing these acts, as stated by the maxim of congruence (Bardovi-Harlig and Hartford, 1993: 281): 'make your contribution congruent with your status'. This maxim is best described on the basis of six status-preserving strategies as reported by Bardovi-Harlig and Hartford (1993: 281): '(1) appear congruent, use the form of a congruent speech act where possible; (2) mark your contribution linguistically, use mitigators; (3) do not begin with a non-congruent contribution; (4) avoid frequent non-congruent turns; (5) be brief; (6) use appropriate content'. On the basis of this maxim, the authors distinguish between those acts assumed to be produced by teachers and those presumably realised by students in the classroom setting. We believe that this distribution can also be applied to other situations, and it may help us both identify appropriateness in speech-act behaviour and teach appropriateness in the second and foreign language classroom.

An example of the need to implement the teaching of speech-act appropriateness in the foreign language classroom is given by Cohen's study (1996). This author focused on himself as a foreign-language learner of Japanese. Data was collected by means of a learning diary during one semester in which a first-year Japanese course took place. Cohen learned some formulae to produce requests, thanking expressions and apologies, but his results by the end of the course did not fully meet his expectations in terms of pragmatic development. According to the author, the teacher's role, opportunities for practice outside the classroom and a structural syllabus might have influenced his final result.

Other scholars have further analysed the role of instruction in performing particular speech acts, as well as the effect of explicit and implicit instruction (Fuyuka et al., 1998; Fuyuka and Clark, 2001; House, 1996; Rose and Ng, 2001; Takahashi, 2001; Tateyama et al., 1997). Explicit instruction focused on description, explanation, discussion of pragmatic features, and practice. Results from these studies point to a positive improvement in the learners' pragmatic competence after the instructional process. In fact, according to Kasper (1997), there is little evidence for aspects of pragmatic competence that resist development through teaching. A recent study by Norris and Ortega (2000), synthesising the role of instruction in interlanguage pragmatics, denotes a clear advantage of explicit over implicit instruction. Teaching pragmatic items explicitly has been undertaken by means of two different task types, awareness-raising and activities providing communicative practice. The former involves learners in observing pragmatic aspects of the target language from both oral and written discourse, while the latter imply group interaction, where learners take part in role-play and simulation activities. Olshtain and Cohen (1990), in their study on the effect of instruction in developing the pragmatic competence of Hebrew learners of English as a foreign language, found that certain aspects of speech-act behaviour could be taught in the foreign-language context, namely those of downgrading, situational features and realisation differences. As reported by Cohen (1996), further work on speech-act instruction should also consider what pragmatic information is available to learners in foreign-language contexts and examine ways of exploiting it in the classroom. The author particularly points to multimedia software as a useful tool for displaying sociocultural and sociolinguistic contexts in which speech-act use may be observed. Kasper (2000) also sees the need for acknowledging the extent to which attention to pragmatic forms enhances acquisition development even beyond instruction. The author particularly points to Yoshimi's (2001) results on the effect of focusing on interactional task demands in developing pragmatic competence since, as reported by Yoshimi, the learners' knowledge of the interactional functions of certain pragmatic features (i.e. Japanese discourse markers *n desu, n desu kedo, n desu ne*) was fostered by means of classroom interaction. However, according to Kasper (2000), the type of interventions that may promote this development should be further examined.

In this subsection we have attempted to present a general view of current issues underlying investigation on speech-act development in second and foreign language contexts. Existing reviews of research on L2 pragmatic development (see Bardovi-Harlig, 1999; Kasper, 2000; Kasper and Rose, 1999 and Kasper and Schmidt, 1996) illustrate the increasing interest among interlanguage pragmatists in second-language pragmatic development and the growing body of studies that focus on this issue. These reviews have also provided their own research agendas, which point out current needs and ideas to be tackled in further studies. Bardovi-Harlig (1999) highlights the need for integrating studies on grammatical development with those focusing on pragmatic acquisition in order to ascertain the exact nature of the relationship between linguistic and pragmatic competence. In this respect, Kasper and Rose (1999) state that future studies should provide a much more detailed linguistic and pragmalinguistic analysis. These authors, on the basis of Kasper and Schmidt's (1996) guidelines, also argue for investigating the way in which principles of second language learning affect second-language pragmatic development. They particularly point to issues such as that of noticing (Schmidt, 1983; Swain, 1995), focus on form (Doughty and Williams, 1998), and whether comprehension precedes production, and also to mechanisms involved in pragmatic developmental stages which would be studied from a cognitive and interactional perspective in second language acquisition.

From a sociocultural perspective, Kasper and Rose (1999) point to the part played by individual differences in pragmatic development. Gender, age, type of input, motivation and attitudes, learner's personality and first-language influence all seem to play a role in interlanguage pragmatic development. In fact, a vast field of possibilities needs further exploration in order to actually account for the acquisition of pragmatic competence. All the authors quoted above have highlighted two main issues that need to be explored in future developmental studies. On the one hand, these authors argue for expanding populations to beginner-level learners, and, on the other, they argue for a wider range of instruments and elicitation techniques that should better combine written and oral methods, and could also consider more ethnographic data. The study described in the second part of this volume attempts to meet some of the existing needs by including beginner-level learners and by making use of both oral and written elicitation techniques. We also try to shed light on the role of individual differences through the study of the learners' linguistic and sociolinguistic background. However, as noted by scholars in the field of interlanguage pragmatics (Meier, 1997), we also need a systematic classification of those acts that are analysed in our study. For this reason, we next present a detailed description of the speech act we focus on, namely that of requesting.

The Speech Act of Requesting

The study focuses on the speech act of requesting. As mentioned in the second section of this chapter, requests are those illocutionary acts belonging to Searle's category of directives. As reported by this author, 'these are attempts by the speaker to get the hearer to do something. They may be very modest attempts as when I invite you to do it, or they may be very fierce attempts as when I insist that you do it' (Searle, 1979: 13). Therefore, request acts are performed by the speaker in order to engage the hearer in some future course of action that coincides with the speaker's goal. In this sense these are pre-event acts, which anticipate the desired or expected action, as opposed to apologies, which constitute post-event acts. Asking somebody to do something for your own purposes bears an impositive nature which may then be regarded as an intrusion into the interlocutor's territory. Using Brown and Levinson's (1987) terminology, requests are characterised by their 'face-threatening' nature. In fact, some authors prefer to group these acts under the term 'impositive acts' (Green, 1975; Leech, 1983), rather than that of directives. However, we agree with Sifianou (1999) that requests do not always place an imposition on the hearer, although they frequently direct him/her to perform some action; thus, the term directive would be preferred. Sifianou also points out that request acts show the existing social relationship between participants, as these last ones may choose the element that will be placed in prominent position when performing the request: (1) the speaker *Can I close the door?*, (2) the addressee *Can you close the door?*, (3) both speaker and addressee *Could we close the door?*, and (4) the action *Would it be possible to close the door?* These features are taken into account by Trosborg (1995) in her suggested classification of request formulations, which we describe in the following subsection.

Request realisations

There are many different linguistic forms that can convey a request act. This act is made up of two main parts: the core or head of the request, which performs the function of requesting, and its peripherical elements, which mitigate or aggravate the force of the request. Focusing on the core of a request unit, Sifianou (1999) distinguishes between interrogatives, imperatives, declaratives, negatives and elliptical forms as possible linguistic realisations. Therefore, this author focuses on the construction or structure of the request core. As it offers no contradiction to Sifianou's proposal (1999), for the purposes of our study we shall focus on Trosborg's

(1995) taxonomy of request strategies, as far as the head part is concerned, since it is based on Austin's (1962) and Searle's (1969) theories, Brown and Levinson's (1987) reformulations and Blum-Kulka and Olshtain's (1984) adaptations. This classification of request-act realisations is constituted by three main categories which illustrate the indirectness to politeness continuum suggested by Brown and Levinson (1987), as mentioned in the earlier subsection on the Politeness Principle. Despite the criticism raised against that relationship, it has been demonstrated by research in interlanguage pragmatics (Blum-Kulka, 1991) that no speech community lacked that directness-to-indirectness scale. Furthermore, since we are dealing with English as the target language and this indirectness scale has been associated with an anglocentric view of politeness (Meier, 1997), we believe it is still useful for our purposes, as it illustrates English pragmatic performance. Request head categories in Trosborg's (1995) suggested classification comprise indirect, conventionally indirect and direct request strategies. This distinction is also considered by Sifianou (1999) in her treatment of indirectness in requesting behaviour. Like Trosborg (1995), this author differentiates between pragmatic and structural indirectness. The former is realised mainly by means of declaratives of the sort of *It's rather hot in here*, and it corresponds to Brown and Levinson's off-record strategies (1987), also called hints. In contrast, structural indirectness involves a wider variety of forms, such as interrogatives, declaratives or negatives, as in *Would you open the window?* or *I would like to ask you to open the window*, since this type of indirectness (or on-record strategies, Brown and Levinson, 1987) relies heavily on form.

Indirect request strategies (or pragmatic indirect strategies in Sifianou's (1999) terms are examples of opaque expressions employed by the requester when opting for not showing his/her intention explicitly. These vague expressions are assumed to be interpreted by the hearer as utterances conveying an additional content to that expressed by their surface structure. For instance, when using the expression *It's hot in here, isn't it?*, the requester would actually be asking his interlocutor to open a window or to turn off the heater. Bearing the nature of these expressions in mind, the speaker should know the other person to the extent of having information about his/her background knowledge in order to predict the possibility of achieving his/her own objectives by means of hints. Another important factor that would allow the speaker to predict potential outcomes deriving from his/her request relates to the routinised experience in using these hints within a specific social group or between two individuals.

Other strategy types in which the speaker's intention is made explicit are those termed 'conventionally indirect', which correspond to Sifianou's structural indirect strategies (1999). By means of these formulations the requester specifies his/her goal while considering the threatening nature of their request. Trosborg (1995) distinguishes between hearer-oriented and speaker-oriented strategies. The former refer to the hearer's ability and willingness to perform the action requested. This subcategory is constituted by expressions of ability, willingness and permission and suggestory formulae. Ability substrategies usually take the form of a question and they include the modal verbs 'can', 'could' or 'may', as in the expression 'Could you please tell me the time?'. In utterances where the speaker refers to the hearer's willingness to do an action, we find propositions such as the following:

(1) Would you hurry up?
(2) Will you do that for me?
(3) I'd appreciate it if you would tell me about it that later.
(4) I'd be grateful if you wouldn't mind photocopying this document.

The requester may also ask permission of his/her interlocutor when making the request, as in 'Can I borrow your pencil?'; or s/he may make use of suggestory formulae for the same purpose, as in 'How about lending me your pencil?'. According to Trosborg (1995), by resorting to suggestions the speaker may test his/her interlocutor's willingness to cooperate while softening his/her own intention. The second category of conventionally indirect request formulations focuses on the speaker and it comprises two main subcategories, namely those of wishes and desires. The former imply polite ways in which the speaker addresses his intention to modify the hearer's behaviour for his/her own benefit (e.g. 'I would like to borrow your computer'); while desires and demands refer to more direct ways of addressing the hearer, thus lowering the degree of politeness implied (e.g. 'I need your computer'). Resorting to speaker-oriented strategies increases the directness level in performing the request, as it makes the speaker's intention more explicit. However, these formulations are not as explicit as those found in the direct-requests category.

Direct-request realisations involve the requester in expressing his illocutionary intent by means of performatives, imperative or obligation statements. Obligation is signalled by means of certain modals that attribute a certain authority to the speaker over the hearer (e.g. 'You must finish this task'). Besides, performative verbs like 'ask', 'request', 'demand' or 'order' convey the speaker's intent in making the request. As is the case with obligation statements, performatives are rather direct and authoritative and the level of politeness varies depending on the propositional content of the expression chosen. For instance, the utterance 'I ask you to lend me your car' would be more polite than 'I order you to lend me your car'. Finally, imperatives or elliptical phrases would compose the most direct and impolite forms of addressing a request. For this reason, they are modified by means of downgraders such as 'please' or 'will you?' in order to soften their impositive nature.

Mitigators are also used in other requests with the purpose of varying politeness levels and decreasing threatening conditions. As noted above, they constitute the second part of a request act, that of the peripheral elements, as noted before. These elements involve a certain modification of the head or core of the speech act and have a notable importance when dealing with requests. Both Trosborg (1995) and Sifianou (1999) analyse modification in requesting. However, we believe that Sifianou's (1999) classification of these peripheral elements best applies to our analysis, since it is based on similar classifications proposed by Edmondson (1981), House and Kasper (1981) and Blum-Kulka and Olshtain (1984). In addition to that, as happened with the classification of request strategies, Sifianou's (1999) classification of modification devices involves no contradiction with Trosborg's (1995) description.

Sifianou (1999) distinguishes between external and internal modification in request realisations. Internal modification may be performed by means of openers, hedges and fillers, while external modification is realised by what the author terms 'commitment-seeking devices' and 'reinforcing devices', as illustrated in Table 2.2.

The above classification considers openers as one instance of internal modification. According to Sifianou, these are opening words and expressions that look for the addressee's cooperation. They can either initiate the request or appear at the end, as in the following examples:

(1) Do you think you can close that window?
(2) Can you close that window, do you think?

The use of openers in English is highly conventionalised, as they are regarded as pragmatic features involving a certain degree of formality. These devices may then soften the impositive nature of request acts for they highlight the addressee's collaboration. Hedges are also viewed as features decreasing the threatening character of request behaviour. However, Sifianou (1999), in an attempt to account for languages other than English, distinguishes between softeners and intensifiers, although the latter are less often employed in English since they aggravate the impositive character of the act and are thus considered to be

Table 2.2 Classification of peripheral elements in request realisation

Internal modification	Openers	Softeners	Diminutives
			Miscellaneous
	Hedges		Tag questions
	Fillers	Intensifiers	
		Hesitators	
		Cajolers	
		Appealers	
		Attention-getters	
External modification	Commitment-seeking devices		
	Reinforcing devices	Grounders	
		Disarmers	
		Expanders	
		Please	

Source: Sifianou (1999: 159)

instances of impolite behaviour (e.g. come here *at once!*). Yet softeners are more often employed in English request acts and these include other subtypes, such as diminutives, tag questions and a variety of fixed expressions. Diminutives are not frequently employed in English, particularly diminutive suffixes (e.g. doggy), except when talking to children. As reported by Sifianou (1999: 167), 'the use of diminutives is related to intimacy, group membership and familiarity'; thus, they are not employed in cases where there are status differences. In contrast to the use of diminutives in English, tag questions are very often employed in request realisations, since these items restrict the possible consequences of the speaker's request and protect him/her from a potential refusal on the part of the hearer. Examples of tag questions in requests are as follows:

(3) Pass me the salt, will you?
(4) You could bring that file, couldn't you?

As stated above, some fixed expressions are also employed in softening the request act, including terms like *a moment* or *a second* and some adverbs such as *just, possibly, perhaps* and *sort of*:

(5) Will you possibly send this letter for me?
(6) Can you just phone Mr. Smith?

(7) Could you perhaps come to my office for a moment?

A second subgroup denoting internal modification is that of fillers, which are those lexical items used by the speaker in order to complete the gaps occurring during the interaction. This subgroup involves hesitators, cajolers, appealers and attention-getters, as illustrated in Table 2.2. Hesitation devices denote a certain degree of insecurity on the part of the speaker in performing the request act. For this reason, s/he makes use of repetition or synonym expressions (e.g. *could you....could you... perhaps you could inform me about that meeting later*). Cajolers are addressee-oriented devices that aim at clarifying the intention of the speaker in asking for the cooperation of the hearer in the request move. Instances of cajolers in English are expressions like *you know, you see* or *I mean*. Other addressee-oriented items are appealers, which seek a sort of compromise on part of the hearer. The terms most often employed for this purpose are *OK* and *right*, as reported by Sifianou (1999). In order to attract the hearer's attention, the speaker may resort to attention-getters, which include formulaic entreaties (e.g. *excuse me*), formulaic greetings (e.g. *hello*) and imperative constructions with perception verbs (e.g. *Listen...*).

The second type of request head modification is external modification, which includes some optional clauses that soften the threatening or impositive nature of the request head. Sifianou (1999) distinguishes between commitment-seeking and reinforcing devices. The former group corresponds to Edmondson's pre-exchanges (1981); that is, initiation moves that focus to the speaker's assurance of fulfilment before making the request:

(8) Can I ask you a question?
(9) Could you do me a favour?

Sifianou (1999) subdivides reinforcing devices into *grounders, disarmers, expanders* and *please*. According to the author, these devices have a dual function, for they mitigate the force of the request and they may also intensify its impact. Grounders may exemplify this double function, since they are clauses that either precede or follow a request act and which may provide an explanation or threaten the hearer:

(10) Could you switch off the light? *I have a terrible headache.*
(11) Can you be here on time? *Otherwise we will talk seriously about your lateness.*

Example (10) illustrates an explanation that softens the impositive nature of the request, while Example (11) denotes a threat to the hearer and thus intensifies the force of the act. Focusing on the addressee, 'disarmers', as the name indicates, are intended to limit the hearer's possibilities for refusal to perform the requested action. Typical examples of English disarmers include 'if' clauses (e.g. *If you have the time*, could you please type this letter for me?), although declaratives can also be used (e.g. *I wouldn't like to bother you*, but could you type this letter for me?). The speaker may also opt for repetition of the request move in order to increase its effect on the hearer. Sifianou (1999) refers to this possibility as the use of expanders, because when repeating or providing synonym expressions for the request act, the speaker is expanding his/her intention:

(12) *Could you come to the party?* We'll have a good time. Please, *come*.

A final instance of external modification proposed by Sifianou (1999), and which is very common in English requests, involves the use of the particle *please*. Given its multifunctionality, it is treated separately as a sole entity that softens the force of the request and which may appear at the beginning or end of the request move, isolated when the social distance is high or low, and, as stated by Ervin-Tripp (1976), in direct, indirect or conventionally indirect realisations. However, House (1989) states that *please* cannot be employed with opaque (i.e. indirect) strategies, since it would mark the utterance as a request and result in a contradiction. According to Searle (1975), *please* may be regarded as the most conventional form for requests in English:

(13) Please pass me the bread.
(14) Could you please look for the report?
(15) I wonder whether you could tell me what happened yesterday, please?
(16) A: Could you photocopy that for me?
     B: Sure!
     A: Please.

As shown in the above examples, *please* is very frequently used in various request realisations. Despite the actual presence of *please* and other modifiers in request acts, most research in interlanguage pragmatics has focused on strategies involved in the request head act. In the following subsection we shall present some of the studies that have examined foreign language learners' use of requests, and which, as does our study, also aimed at denoting differences in the production of these acts.

Studies on request production by foreign language learners

Trosborg's (1995) taxonomy described above has been used in studies investigating second and foreign language learners' production and assessment of request acts. In fact, this author made use of this classification in her study, which contrasted the use by (1) native speakers of Danish, (2) native speakers of English, and (3) English learners of requests in a role-play task including 10 request situations. Regarding strategy use, all the learners showed a preference for strategies belonging to the conventionally indirect type. However, their realisations varied from those of native speakers in terms of utterance modification (e.g. use of mitigators or supporting moves). Learners at lower levels made less use of hints than more advanced learners and English native speakers did. The author attributes these findings to the lexical and grammatical difficulty implied in performing hints. Direct strategies were also less frequently employed by both learners and native speakers. Trosborg (1995) reports on the underuse of direct formulae on the part of beginner and intermediate learners compared to the use of direct strategies by native English speakers. Different results were obtained by House and Kasper (1981) and Blum-Kulka (1983), who dealt with German and Hebrew participants. In these studies learners always resorted to direct strategies more frequently than did native speakers of the target language. As reported by Trosborg (1995), this apparent controversy in her findings might be associated with the social parameters involved in the situations, with L1 influence and with the task type that elicited the use of requests in all these studies. On the one hand, social parameters in Trosborg's (1995) study varied in terms of dominance and social distance, since interlocutors were assigned the roles of authoritative figures, strangers and friends in the oral role-play task they were required to perform. On the other hand, House and Kasper (1987) elicited requests by means of a closed discourse-completion test (written), which included the dominance parameter (i.e. authoritative roles) in most situations and only a few situations which illustrated degrees of familiarity, that is, strangers' or friends' roles.

House and Kasper's subjects (1987) were faced with situations in which authoritative roles needed to be displayed, thus eliciting the use of imperatives or obligation realisations. The fact that these participants were engaged in a written task that included response moves in all situations and the absence of an interlocutor might also have affected the learners' possibilities for selecting a wider range of strategy types, since the degree of imposition of the request act might not have been perceived as prominently as in oral face-to-face encounters.

The overuse of direct strategy types is also reported in Hill's (1997) study, which focused on the analysis of request strategies employed by Japanese learners of English as a foreign language. This author found that learners at different proficiency levels overused direct strategy types. Nevertheless, as their level increased, learners used conventionally indirect strategies more frequently, particularly those belonging to the willingness subtype. In this way, learners' development denoted an approximation to the target-language norms. These findings are in line with Ellis' (1994) results concerning the pragmatic development of two participants in terms of request production. These subjects first resorted to imperatives belonging to the direct category and, as their proficiency level increased, they started making use of conventionally indirect strategies of the ability type. From the above-quoted studies, we may assume that the choice of request realisations is influenced by the situation, the elicitation method used in the study and the proficiency level of the participants.

Nevertheless, taking into account the differences between Trosborg's (1995) and House and Kasper's (1987) findings in terms of the subjects' strategy selection, there seems to be a need for studies implementing various elicitation techniques in order to fully contrast the effect of these instruments on request-acts behaviour. Studies dealing with request production have focused on learners at different proficiency levels, but more studies are needed that account for beginner learners (Kasper and Rose, 1999). Given that, with the exception of Trosborg (1995), most studies have focused on second language learners (the Cross-Cultural Speech Acts Project, Blum-Kulka et al., 1989), there is a need for research on foreign language learners.

For these reasons, we have focused on learners of English in a foreign context, as is the case in most European communities, and we have examined beginner and intermediate learners' request performance in both written and oral tasks. Another issue that requires further investigation is the role of individual differences in pragmatic development. On that account, we have particularly focused on our subjects' linguistic background. We have dealt with bilingual speakers learning a third language, which is an issue that has not been fully researched in the field of interlanguage pragmatics. We believe that accounting for third language learners' pragmatic production and awareness may expand the scope of the research on the acquisition of pragmatic competence. The study described in the second part of this book thus attempts to illustrate the particular case of a bilingual community exposed to foreign language instruction and which may share some characteristics with other speech communities in the European Union or in various foreign language contexts.

In the following chapter we further analyse specific characteristics of that bilingual community in which third language acquisition takes place, and which has served as the sociolinguistic framework for our analysis concerning the pragmatic competence of foreign language learners of English.

Chapter 3
The Sociolinguistic Context: Language Learning and Use in the Valencian Community

Introduction

The first aim of the present chapter is to offer a sociolinguistic description of the community in which the informants of our study live. We believe it is worth outlining the status of the languages known to them, and noting particular characteristics of their mother tongue that also relate to the sociolinguistic context in which it is used. For this purpose, we shall first comment on the origin and evolution of the Catalan language in the Valencian Community, drawing special attention to periods when the language was suppressed and to its standardisation. These facts are assumed to have affected the present status of the language and they have also had an impact on the current Valencian educational system, which will be discussed in the second section, where we shall present existing programmes promoting Catalan language learning and use in primary and secondary education. Additionally, the role of bilingualism at the university level will also be dealt with, and we shall specifically consider the university setting in the Valencian Community, particularly that of Castelló region, for it is the institution in which our subjects study.

The second aim of the chapter is to offer further information on our informants' linguistic background. In this respect, we shall refer to their knowledge of other languages that are not usually employed in their community, i.e. those termed foreign languages, but which are nevertheless part of their linguistic repertoire. We will focus on English, since in the present study we are examining the learners' production of this foreign language. For this reason, we are interested in our learners' previous English-language learning experience, as described in the third section of this chapter. We will also deal with the way in which multilingualism is fostered by educational authorities and other institutions in the Valencian

Community. Among these institutions we find Jaume I University (Castelló – Spain), which considers multilingualism to be an important objective promoted by specific divisions and departments. In the fourth section, we will describe the way in which this institution has tackled the current social demand regarding English language knowledge. Unlike other universities in the Valencian Community, Jaume I University has implemented English as a compulsory subject in all BA degrees and diplomas. By the same token, the Languages and Terminology Service (*Servei de Llengües i Terminologia*) offers complementary training in this foreign language, together with certain grants that provide students with opportunities to use and learn the target language in an English-speaking country.

The interest of Jaume I University in foreign language learning is also illustrated by the research conducted in this field by scholars belonging to that institution. These research projects have considered various features involved in foreign language learning and use. However, as noted in the fourth section of this chapter, none of them has tackled bilingualism as a determinant factor in foreign language use. In this sense, we can state that our study will somewhat broaden the scope of previous research. In fact, most research on Catalan-Castilian bilingual learners of English has considered the Catalonian region, but, as will be illustrated in the following section, the sociolinguistic characteristics of Catalonia and the Valencian Community are not identical.

The Catalan Language in the Valencian Community

The main purpose of this section is the description of Catalan language use in the Valencian Community. We shall focus on the origin of that language in our community and we will also deal with problems faced by individuals in maintaining the language. In doing this, we shall present specific sociolinguistic characteristics of this language in our region which are to be distinguished from conditions underlying its use in either of the other two communities named below, those of the Balearic Islands and Catalonia. A brief overview of the past may also help us understand the present status of the language, which concerns the context in which our study has been conducted.

At present, more than 7 million people around the world speak Catalan as their mother tongue. We find Catalan speakers in Catalonia, Andorra, the 'Franja' in Aragon, the French Roussillon, l'Alguer in Sardinia, the Balearic Islands and the Valencian Community. In Spain there are three main areas where Catalan is spoken: the Balearic Islands; Catalonia and the Valencian Community.

The Catalan language developed in the later period of the Roman Empire from a variant of Latin spoken in the northern and eastern parts of the Pyrenees. As a Romance language, it bears many similarities to the Castilian language that is spoken in all Spanish territory. The constant contact with Castilian is particularly manifested in those regions where both languages, Catalan and Castilian, are used. However, the history of the Catalan language and its evolution in these areas (Catalonia, the Balearic Islands and the Valencian Community) is different, as shown by the existing dialectal varieties.

The origin of the Catalan language in the territories now known as the Valencian Community dates back to the 13th century and the arrival of King James I. At that time, Valencian society used the language for administrative, political, cultural, economic and social purposes. The Catalan language was then a common instrument that connected the Valencian region to Catalonia and the Balearic Islands. This privileged status of the language continued until the 16th century, when castilianisation of the territory gradually increased. Upper social classes started adopting Castilian as a sign of prestige linked to the Castilian crown. In the 17th century, with the triumph of Philip V, the use of the Castilian language was expanded to all territories belonging to his empire, which included the Valencian region. The dominance of Castilian over Catalan would continue during the 18th and 19th centuries. However, Catalan was still used by people in towns and rural areas and in informal everyday conversation. In the 19th century two contradictory factors arose, namely the literary recovery of Catalan and the growth in the social prestige attributed to the Castilian language. This latter language was spread mainly by means of education, at schools, and also by its use in the administrative and economic activity of that territory. In contrast, the Catalan language was used by the upper classes in Catalonia as a sign of their identity, which reflected the important industrial advances made by the territory which were not shared by the Valencian region.

The literary movement in Valencia quoted above, known as the *Reinaixença*, gave rise to fundamental changes to the Catalan language in the 20th century. In fact, the standardisation and orthographical normalisation of Catalan took place in that period. At the beginning of the 20th century, under the First Spanish Republic, an organised Valencianist political movement paralleled the increased literary production in Catalan and the creation of the *Societat Castellonenca de Cultura* (Castelló Cultural Society) in 1919. The fact that the use of the Catalan language had long been reduced to oral encounters had promoted high dialectal variability, which required urgent grammatical normalisation. Bearing this purpose in mind, intellectuals concerned about the language met in 1932 in Castelló and produced a document known as 'Les Normes de Castelló', which contained certain orthographical and grammatical codes. These norms were influenced by certain spelling rules previously approved by *Institut d'Estudis Catalans* (Catalan Studies Institute) in 1913 and by a former Catalan grammar, namely Pompeu Fabra's *Gramàtica Normativa de la Llengua Catalana (Normative Grammar of the Catalan Language)*, both of them developed in Catalonia.

As suggested by certain historical facts mentioned above, in the Valencian territory the Catalan language has often been considered to be inferior to Castilian. In contrast to the social status of the language in Catalonia at the end of the 19th and beginning of the 20th centuries, Catalan was mainly spoken in towns and rural areas, whereas Castilian was seen as a prestigious language. However, possibilities for using the language after its total normalisation and standardisation would soon diminish in both communities. The dictatorship period in Spain, which lasted for 40 years, from 1936 to 1976, also involved the non-official and unadvised use of the Valencians' and Catalans' mother tongue. During this time, Castilian was the only official language of the Spanish state and Catalan, together with other languages such as Basque and Galician, was totally forbidden and used only in very limited settings (i.e. in the family and in rural areas). This was a determining factor for the supremacy of Castilian over Catalan in the Valencian Community.

The superiority of Castilian influenced educational policies in the Valencian Community during and for some years after the dictatorship. All school subjects were taught in Castilian and students could not read or write in their mother tongue. The only language employed by the mass media was Castilian, despite the fact that most inhabitants used Catalan in the street. Therefore, we may say that its use was reduced to informal oral encounters. Some time after the death of the dictator, with the birth of the Spanish Constitution, Catalan was recognised as another language used in some regions of Spain. Nevertheless, there was and still seems to be some disagreement over the name of the language, that is, whether it should be Catalan or Valencian, as the former seems to imply the Catalonian region for some Valencians. In this book we have referred to the language as Catalan, in accordance with previous research in the third-language acquisition field (Muñoz, 2000; Sanz, 2000), where knowledge of this same language was examined. In this way we attempt to point out that it is the same language as that spoken in Catalonia, but in a different sociolinguistic context. We shall refer to the language as Valencian only when quoting certain institutions' and political authorities' rules or norms.

Given the purpose of this study, we shall not deal with the importance of the name, but rather focus on the language itself and its use in education.

From the birth of the Spanish Constitution in 1976, when all languages spoken in Spanish regions were recognised as official within their own particular communities, there has been an increasing tendency to maintain Catalan and to spread its use in both informal and formal settings. In 1982, the *Estatut d'Autonomia* in the Valencian Community proclaimed the existence of *Valencian* and Castilian as official languages in this community, and the right of every inhabitant to use and learn them. As a consequence, it was the responsibility of the autonomous government to guarantee the learning and use of both languages. The *Estatut d'Autonomia* gave rise to the regulation and use of the Valencian language by the *Llei d'ús i ensenyament del Valencià* in 1983, under which the incorporation of the Valencian language in education was made compulsory. This law addresses the issue of the obligatory knowledge of Valencian/Catalan for both teachers and students, in oral as well as written production. From that time, various laws and rules have attempted to regularise the inclusion of the Catalan language in the Valencian Community educational system by means of various bilingual educational programmes. These programmes affect mainly primary but also compulsory secondary-school curricula. As we are dealing with bilingual subjects who have received instruction on the basis of these bilingual programmes, we shall describe them in the following sections.

Bilingual Education in the Valencian Community

As stated above, this section sets out to describe existing bilingual programmes in the Valencian Community in order to define the sociolinguistic and previous educational context of our bilingual subjects. For this reason, we shall firstly comment on the legislation guiding these programmes, and we will further present the defining characteristics of each educational model. Finally, we shall consider bilingualism in the university setting, particularly that of Jaume I University at Castelló, which is the institution our subjects belong to. This aspect will help us acknowledge the amount of exposure to the Catalan language in specific degree courses, as well as the use and promotion of that language in the university setting.

In 1990 a nationwide modification of the Spanish educational system took place which also affected autonomous communities. This modification is commonly known as LOGSE (*Llei d'Ordenació General del Sistema Educatiu* – Law for the General Regularisation of the Educational System).

Under this law, certain issues affecting bilingual education in the Valencian Community have been tackled in subsequent years, as curricula for primary and secondary education have been redefined from 1992 to 1997. The main goal for all bilingual education models is to guarantee that students obtain a good command of Castilian and Catalan by the end of their compulsory educational period, which includes primary and part of secondary education. In the first stage of the implementation of these curricula modifications, a bilingual model was applied in schools, namely that of the Progressive Incorporation Programme or PIP (*Programa d'Incorporació Progressiva*). According to this programme, some school subjects would be taught in Catalan and others in Castilian. However, the programme received criticism from certain regions in the Valencian Community whose first language is Castilian. For this reason, and after examining the results of the PIP incorporation, two other programmes were developed in order to include the sociolinguistic situations of all inhabitants in the Valencian Community. These programmes are known as the PIL (*Programa d'Immersió Lingüística* or Linguistic Immersion Programme) and the PEV (*Programa d'Ensenyament en Valencià* or Valencian Training Programme).

The first programme above, PIL, addresses non-Valencian-speaking areas in the Community, most of them located in areas fairly close to Castilian-speaking communities. The PIL programme is assumed to be a transitional step towards bilingualism. In the early stages of education adopting the PIL programme, learners receive instruction in Castilian and only one subject is taught in Catalan. In subsequent years the number of subjects taught in Catalan progressively increases until for most school subjects Catalan is a vehicle of instruction, except of course for Castilian language and literature. In this way bilingualism is then ensured, and the main goal of the new educational system is reached.

Besides this, a second programme has also been developed for Catalan-speaking regions, which is the case of most areas in the community. This model is best known as the PEV (*Programa d'Ensenyament en Valencià* or 'Valencian' Teaching Programme), and it includes the use of Valencian as a vehicle for instruction from the early stages of primary education. The Castilian language is employed only in the instruction referring to this language, its literature or its history. Therefore, we may say that this model involves 90% of instruction in Catalan, whereas only 10% includes Castilian, which may correspond to the learners' second language.

The above description of the PIP, PIL and PEV models is based on the guidelines provided by the autonomous government in terms of their recommended application. According to the *Conselleria d'Educació i Ciència* – division of the autonomous government that deals with education and linguistic policy affairs – and the Valencian Institute of Statistics, a number of schools include one or two of these programmes in their curricula, as shown in Table 3.1 below. We have subdivided existing centres on the basis of the three main geographical areas that make up the Valencian Community.

Table 3.1 Number of schools officially applying any or two of the PIP, PEV or PIL programmes

	Primary schools	*Total n. primary schools*	*Percentage on total*	*Second. schools*	*Total n. second. schools*	*Percent. on total*
Castelló	144	299	62.9	37	51	72.5
Valencia	355	844	42.0	112	357	31.65
Alacant	145	583	24.9	48	186	25.60

Source: IVE (*Institut Valencià d'Estadística* – Valencian Statistics Institute, 1999–2000)

As shown in Table 3.1, Castelló is the province where the most schools have adopted bilingual programmes, in both primary and secondary education. Concerning primary-education centres, almost 80% of schools seem to have applied bilingual programmes in Castelló, whereas approximately 60% of primary schools in Valencia and 75% in Alacant had not incorporated any of these programmes in the 1999–2000 academic year. A whole array of factors might have caused these differences. One of them might relate to the sociolinguistic situation of each province. Concerning the language that is mainly used in their capital cities, we can state that most people employ Catalan in both formal and informal encounters in Castelló city, whereas in Valencia and Alacant the number of Catalan speakers is considerably reduced. In fact, according to the Valencian Institute of Statistics (IVE), Castelló is the province where Catalan is mostly spoken, involving more than 50% of its inhabitants, followed by Valencia, where approximately 40% of its total population speak the language. Finally, we may say that Alacant is the region where Catalan is least used, as the number of Catalan speakers amounts to less than one-third of the total number of its inhabitants. Regarding the total number of Catalan speakers in the Valencian Community, we can say that almost 60% of its population do not use the language. This worrying fact affecting language maintenance has been tackled by the community educational authorities, as shown by the bilingual programmes described above, and by other relevant educational institutions, such as the university. Universities in the Valencian Community have implemented various linguistic policies in order to promote the use of the Catalan language. Considering that the subjects of the present study belong to University Jaume I (Castelló), we shall focus on its own linguistic policy plan.

This linguistic policy plan stems from the statutes of this institution, which regard Catalan as the only official language. The main objectives of this plan are based on results from a previous analysis on the use of the Catalan language in Jaume I University which was carried out by the Languages and Terminology Service during the 1997–1998 academic year. According to that survey, about 60% of students select Castilian as the language of their instruction, almost 75% of administrative personnel have great difficulty in writing reports in Catalan, and about 80% of lecturers reported providing instruction in Castilian. On the basis of these findings, the promotion of the Catalan language among all university members was considered to be of paramount importance. Global objectives involve a gradual development of University statutes and, thus, a generalised use of the Catalan language in all sections of the institution. For this purpose the following actions have been taken:[1]

- A training programme addressed to lecturers, administrative personnel and students on the basis of each sector's needs.
- A linguistic normalisation programme that fosters the use of Catalan in instruction, research and administration tasks.
- A culture-orientated programme that locates this university within the general framework of existing universities in the Valencian Community.

The above plan currently being developed at Jaume I University is assumed to affect our subjects to a certain extent, as they may receive input in both Catalan and Castilian. In fact, considering data provided by a survey[2] on the use of Catalan in different degree courses, we may say that approximately 20% of the total tuition was conducted in Catalan; thus Castilian instruction would account for 80%, without considering classes taught in English. The use of both languages is supposed to maintain and increase their bilingual competence. This fact is closely linked to one of our objectives, which is to find out whether bilingualism facilitates multilingual competence. As we are particularly interested in our subjects' use of English as a third language, we shall also consider past and present multilingual education in the Valencian Community in order to present a more illustrative picture of the sociolinguistic situation in which our subjects find themselves.

Multilingual Education in the Valencian Community

The creation of the European Union has contributed greatly to the importance attached to the learning of foreign languages. The learning of English, previously considered an imposition by the education system, is now regarded as a necessity in our society. This is certainly the case in the Valencian Community, where the inclusion of English as a compulsory school subject in the late stages of primary education did not seem to fully meet the society's demand. In fact, most parents' associations organised extra-curricular English courses for children under the age of eight, as English was not included as a compulsory or even an optional subject in their curriculum. Considering that demand and the increasing need to learn English, the Valencian autonomous government implemented a multilingual educational programme[3] in 1998, known as the Enriched Bilingualism (*Bilingüisme Enriquit* rule, published in DOGV n. 3285. 3-7-1998). In this section, we will firstly address those conditions in which the subjects of the present study started learning English at both primary and secondary school. It is also our aim to describe the goals of the above-quoted multilingual programme (Enriched Bilingualism), and its implementation in the PIP, PIL and PEV bilingual models. Finally, we shall comment on the number of schools that have already incorporated this multilingual model into their school curriculum. This may provide us with further relevant information on the linguistic characteristics of the community our subjects live in.

Interest in multilingualism has increased considerably during the last 20 years. In the mid- and late-1980s, foreign language learning in the Valencian Community schools started in the second cycle of primary education. In this period, several laws and rules[4] were passed concerning the adoption and inclusion of the Catalan language in school tuition. On the basis of that legislation, different educational institutions started teaching some of their curricular subjects in Catalan, while maintaining traditional Castilian tuition groups. Therefore, school learners in these years had the opportunity of receiving instruction in their mother tongue. In fact, this was the case for our bilingual subjects, whereas the monolingual learners in this study were never taught in Catalan, except for the Catalan language classes, which accounted for a very low percentage of their total formal instruction. Concerning the learning of a foreign language as a compulsory school subject, all our subjects chose English.

Therefore we may assume that the subjects of the present study were immersed in a multilingual educational model, as instruction was conducted in Catalan, Castilian and English, although this last language was employed to teach the language only in the late stages of secondary education. The existence of these three languages in the primary and secondary education curricula, together with society's plurilingual interest, promoted the birth of bilingual programmes on the one hand, and the subsequent introduction of a foreign language at the very early stages of compulsory education on the other. Therefore, those educational programmes (referred to above) that were the basis of instruction for our subjects during their school years have been modified since then.

In this respect, in 1998, educational authorities in the Valencian Autonomous Community implemented the Enriched Bilingualism programme which involved the introduction of a foreign language within existing bilingual programmes. In order to incorporate the foreign language in the early stages of the primary school curriculum, certain requirements had to be met. Centres interested in the teaching of a foreign language from the beginning of primary education were required to design a linguistic policy document. In addition, schools had to present written proof of (1) the consensus reached regarding such a document; and (2) the availability of trained teachers who could guarantee the successful modification of previously established bilingual programmes. The Enriched Bilingual programme also incorporated certain guidelines for the correct introduction of a foreign language in the three existing bilingual programmes.

The basic amount of foreign-language tuition required in all bilingual programmes (PIP, PIL and PEV) was set at an identical level, and in all cases it was to gradually increase. According to the planning provided by the educational authorities,[5] there would be at least one and a half hours' tuition during the first cycle of primary education. In the second cycle, foreign language instruction should amount to two and a half hours per week, while three and a half hours' minimum tuition would be provided in the third cycle of primary education. The hours of foreign-language instruction could be increased in each cycle, depending on the specific circumstances and requirements of each school. Following these guidelines, different primary schools in the Valencian Community decided to incorporate a foreign language into their curricula by adapting their bilingual programmes, as is shown in Table 3.2.

Table 3.2 Incorporation of a foreign language in bilingual programmes during the 1999–2000 academic year

	PEV/PIL	PIP	Total	Total n. primary schools	Percentage
Castelló	10	2	12	229	5.2
Valencia	56	20	76	844	9
Alacant	6	2	8	583	1.3

Source: Conselleria de Cultura i Ciència. Direcció Territorial València.

As shown in the above table, few centres have yet been able to incorporate the Enriched Bilingualism model into their curriculum. Although the percentages illustrated above may seem very low, we must bear in mind the fact that these models were implemented one year after the legislation was passed. The implementation of the multilingual model gives rise to many difficulties regarding economic and organisational factors. However, we can assume that an attempt is being made to incorporate a foreign language from the beginning of children's education, thus providing them with a multilingual setting that might reflect current linguistic trends in our society.

Other institutions offering non-compulsory education have also shown their concern for foreign language learning. We refer in particular to universities in the Valencian Community, which have taken into consideration the needs and demands of present-day society, which will have to be met by their students. Given the fact that our subjects are university students receiving English instruction as part of their degree courses, we shall examine the current framework in which the English language is learned and taught in Jaume I University. In so doing, special attention will be paid to the setting in which our study has been conducted.

Foreign Language Learning in the University Setting

Existing universities in the Valencian Community, namely Universitat de Valencia, Universitat d'Alacant, Universitat Politécnica de Valencia and Universitat Jaume I, provide students with the possibility of learning at least one foreign language. All these universities provide a modern-languages department and a language laboratory or self-access centre, where learners from different disciplines can learn and improve their skills in various foreign languages. In all cases, the language that is most frequently chosen by students is English. This language is offered as an optional component of several degree courses, and as a complementary course provided by the University Languages Service. There is only one exceptional case where English is part of all degree courses, and this is at Jaume I University in Castelló. For the purposes of our study, we will now focus on that particular setting, as all our subjects belong to this institution.

We will first present a general overview of English language teaching and learning in existing studies, taking into account the fact that it is a compulsory subject for all BA degrees and diplomas. Further services that are offered to students in facilitating English language learning will also be dealt with. We shall particularly focus on one specific goal of the Linguistic Policy Plan developed by the Languages and Terminology Service of Jaume I University, which involves the promotion of multilingualism. In addition, the most outstanding research carried out in the Valencian Community concerning foreign language acquisition will also be briefly discussed, as our study attempts to expand the scope of investigation developed in this multilingual setting.

Jaume I University is made up of three main centres, those of the Faculty of Human and Social Sciences, the Faculty of Law and Economics and the Higher School of Technology and Experimental Sciences. Within these faculties, various BA degrees and diploma courses can be studied, and common to all of them are Computing and English Language as compulsory subjects. Despite the fact that all Jaume I students study English, the syllabus has been adapted to the needs and specific characteristics of each discipline. Thus we might say that we deal with courses in English for Academic Purposes. The amount of tuition in English varies with each discipline. However, we can state that at least six credits (i.e. a total of 60 tuition hours) are offered on all degree and diploma courses. In the particular case of our subjects, English Language constituted seven and a half credits out of the total amount of credits included in their degree, which corresponds to 75 hours of formal English instruction.

Given the small amount of English tuition in degree courses, the Languages and Terminology Service offers further training in foreign languages as a complement to the official instruction. Bearing this in mind, certain actions have been implemented, namely analysing the particular needs of students regarding the use and knowledge of the English language, providing further training in the language, and offering various scholarships for studying or working in English-speaking countries. English instruction is provided in the Self-Access Centre of the University, where students can find material for developing autonomous language learning. In this Centre they can also attend conversation clubs in order to practise or improve their fluency in the English language.

Despite the quantity of foreign language instruction on offer in this institution, common problems associated with learning outcomes have been identified by certain researchers. Palmer and Posteguillo (1996) rightly point out that the existence of a self-access language centre does not necessarily guarantee language acquisition. On the same lines, Alcón (2000a) analyses the development of autonomy in instructional settings. This author (1994, 1997) also notes the way in which classroom negotiation and controlled input can influence learners' acquisition of the target language. Other authors, such as Alcón and Codina (1996), and Alcón and Guzmán (1995), have analysed the role of certain external factors in foreign language learning, paying special attention to classroom interaction and the setting in which instruction takes place. The influence of the learning situation has also been studied by scholars in other Valencian universities. Such is the case of Bou (1993), from Universitat de Valencia, who has examined the use of communication strategies in a specific learning environment. From this brief account of investigation conducted in this particular setting, we can state that relevant research projects have been conducted focusing on distinct aspects of foreign language learning. Nevertheless, none of the above studies has analysed the role of bilingualism in acquiring another language. In fact, most existing studies dealing with Catalan-Castilian speakers learning a further language have focused on the Catalonian region. We find instances of these studies in Hoffman (1991), Muñoz (2000) and Sanz (2000). Considering the sociolinguistic differences between Catalonia and the Valencian Community pointed out in this chapter, we believe that research on foreign language development in the Valencian Community should account for them. We have particularly dealt with Catalan-Castilian learners of English as a third language and the development of their pragmatic competence. For this purpose, we have focused on a specific pragmatic aspect, that of requesting, involving both learners' production and their awareness, as described next in the second part of this volume.

Notes

1. *Source: Servei de llengües i Terminologia UJI, Pla de Política Lingüística* – (UJI Languages and Terminology Service, Linguistic Policy Plan)
2. *Source:* UJI Languages and Terminology Service, Linguistic Policy Plan Course 1999–2000, Sociolinguistic Data: Tutition in Catalan. *(Servei de Llengües i terminologia UJI, pla de política lingüística. Dades Sociolingüístiques: docència en Català).*

3. The programme is assumed to be multilingual because it includes three languages: Catalan, Castilian and English.
4. We refer to the 1984 law on the implementation of Catalan in primary and secondary schools and to subsequent norms like those of 1986, 1990 and 1992, which regularised tuition of an amount of subjects in Catalan. These facts would then constitute the basis for existing bilingual programmes.
5. This chronogram was published in an official publication, namely *DOGV*, nº 3.285, 14 July 1998.

Part 2
The Study

Chapter 4
The Method

Participants

Participants in the present study were 160 female students from Jaume I University based in Castelló, who were engaged in an English for Academic Purposes (henceforth EAP) course which lasted one semester (February to June 2000). These students belonged to two different disciplines, as they were studying Industrial Design Technical Engineering (N=80), on the one hand, and Primary Teacher Education (N=80), on the other. The EAP course which all of them were attending was part of their degree syllabus and it was a compulsory subject. The reason that we decided to conduct this study in Jaume I University was partly the fact that it is the only university in the Valencian Community that offers EAP courses in all its degrees as compulsory subjects in an attempt to foster multilingualism (see Chapter 3 for further information). All of our subjects were in their first degree course and none of them had ever been to an English-speaking country before. They were all Spanish and born in the Castelló region. However, not all of them were living in Castelló city, as 60% of them came from several towns of the area, namely Vall d'Alba (10%), Borriol (10%), Benicàssim (5%), Vila-real (20%), Nules (10%) and Onda (5%).

Their ages ranged from 19 to 22 years old, the average age being 20.5 years. We chose this age group because it allowed us to focus on students who either had been engaged in a bilingual programme or who had been educated within the framework of a monolingual programme. In the first case, most of the school subjects were taught in Catalan, with the exception of Castilian language and literature in primary education, whereas in monolingual schools, which usually meant private centres, most subjects were taught in Castilian. Hence our subjects' distribution in terms of the primary-education programme they had been engaged in is as follows:

Table 4.1 Distribution of subjects

PEV or PIP programme	Monolingual programme
40%	60%

It should be mentioned that none of the above programmes is implemented in secondary education. Nevertheless, some centres attempt to provide learners coming from bilingual programmes with a high percentage of instruction in the Catalan language, while other secondary schools present monolingual curricula with a focus on Castilian. We can state that learners who have been immersed in a bilingual programme can continue receiving instruction in most subject matters (like maths, chemistry, history or physics) in Catalan in secondary education. By the same token, those learners who have been educated on the basis of a monolingual programme in primary schools may also follow this same condition in secondary education. For that reason, we selected those subjects who, having received instruction within bilingual programmes in primary schools, continued within that same framework in secondary education, on the one hand, and those who did not receive instruction in Catalan either in primary or in secondary schools, on the other.

In order to ascertain the actual degree of bilingualism of our subjects, we distributed a bilingualism test which was designed according to Li Wei's classification of bilingual competence (2000: 6–7) and Baker's (1995) definition of the phenomenon. The test consisted of 18 questions aimed at ascertaining the degree of bilingual competence of our subjects. Some of the items included in the test are as follows:

Example (1)
(1) What language do you usually employ when you write?
   Catalan ☐   Castilian ☐   Other: ....
(4) How would you evaluate your competence in Castilian and Catalan?
           Speaking   Listening   Writing   Reading
   Catalan
   Castilian
   A: Excellent command B: Good command C: With difficulties D: No idea
(7) What language do you use at home?
   Catalan ☐   Castilian ☐   Other: ....

In view of the results provided by the bilingualism test, we chose either those students who had received instruction in the Catalan language in high school after being involved in a bilingual programme at primary school, or those who were not exposed to instruction in Catalan in high school and had not been engaged in the framework of a bilingual programme at primary school. Hence, our subjects' distribution in terms of bilingualism was as follows: we regarded as bilingual those subjects who had been trained at both primary school and high school with a predominance of Catalan over Castilian language and who also made regular use of Catalan in their daily communication with friends, at home and at the university. These subjects also considered Catalan as their mother tongue and as the mother tongue of their parents. On the other hand, we considered as monolingual those subjects who had not received prior instruction in Catalan at primary and secondary schools and who had never used Catalan either in formal or in informal situations. Interestingly, most of these subjects were living in Castelló city and their parents came from towns and cities belonging to Castilian-speaking areas of Spain. Therefore, despite the fact that they were born in this bilingual community, they had never had the chance or the need to communicate in Catalan, or the need to read the press or watch TV in that language. Additionally, these subjects had never studied the language because they came from private schools, which some years ago (in the 1980s) did not necessarily include instruction in or about the Catalan language.

A second criterion in selecting our informants was their proficiency level in the target language, i.e. English. All our subjects had studied English as a foreign language both at primary school and at high school. However, they did not have the same proficiency level. Hence they were administered a proficiency-level test which consisted of four main parts: listening comprehension, reading comprehension, writing, speaking and grammar. The tests were corrected on the basis of the ACTFL Proficiency guidelines suggested by Byrnes et al. (1986). As we were mainly concerned with learners' production as part of their communicative competence, we also considered the ACTFL Proficiency Guidelines revision related to *speaking* that was provided by Breiner-Sanders et al. (1999). According to these authors, novice-level (or beginner) speakers can respond to simple questions, convey minimal meaning to interlocutors experienced in dealing with foreigners by using isolated words, lists of words and recombinations of words and phrases, and may satisfy a number of limited needs. Intermediate learners can participate in simple, direct conversations, to create the language and communicate personal meaning, and can obtain and give information, sustain uncomplicated communicative exchanges and satisfy simple personal needs. The teacher and researcher selected those learners who could be regarded as beginners and those who were considered intermediate learners. Subjects who showed higher or lower levels were not taken into account in this study.

On the basis of the proficiency level in the target language and the degree of bilingual competence, we distributed our subjects into four groups as follows:

Table 4.2 Distribution of subjects according to bilingual competence

	Bilingual n.	*Monolingual n.*	*Total*
Beginner	40	40	80
Intermediate	40	40	80
Total number of subjects	80	80	120

To avoid the effect of extraneous variables, all the participants were female students and there was an equal number of students belonging to the two disciplines mentioned above, namely those of Industrial Design Technical Engineering and Primary Teacher Education.

Data Collection Procedure

In order to examine our subjects' knowledge of request-act formulations, we first distributed a pre-test which contained several prompts or scenarios that aimed at eliciting requests strategies (i.e. linguistic formulations involved in making requests). Situations differed according to degrees of familiarity, dominance, social distance and obligation in conducting the action requested. Examples of two items in the pre-test are provided next.

Example (2)

(4) Your new English teacher does not speak Spanish and she cannot understand it either. However, she speaks very quickly and you cannot follow her. You know that she is not very friendly. What would you say?

(6) You need your mother's car to go to Madrid. She doesn't like lending you her car because last time you had an accident. However, you need it because there is no other possibility of going there and you have already told your friends. What would you say to your mother?

Results from this task were compared with those of a post-test that was administered after the study had taken place. This allowed us to ascertain the effects of instruction on the subjects' use of request formulations. The structure of the post-test was the same as that of the pre-test described above.

The tasks chosen to elicit requestive behaviour consisted of an open role-play, an open discourse-completion test and a discourse-evaluation test. These tasks were selected on the basis of previous research examining the advantages of one given elicitation method over another (Kasper and Dahl, 1991; Rose 1992). According to Houck and Gass (1996) the advantage of a production questionnaire like the discourse-completion test (henceforth DCT) lies in the fact that it enables us to collect a large amount of data in a relatively short time. Additionally, the researcher can easily control variables such as that of context. Nevertheless, the DCT, and particularly the closed version, have been criticised for being too artificial and for resembling a test situation rather than a real-life one. Unlike open DCTs, closed DCTs include rejoining or adjoining devices which guide the learner towards the required pragmatic item. These devices refer to the presence of replies and answers corresponding to a given request formulation in the test. When adjoining items are present in a DCT, learners are provided with the answer to the request linguistic realisation they are assumed to produce.

The role of rejoinders may be related to the participation of a potential interlocutor in the speech acts being performed. By inserting rejoining devices, learners may be further aware of the communicative function involved in their performance. In contrast, learners may be too directed towards a desired form and they may not have the chance to select or interact freely as it happens in everyday communication. For that reason, we decided to make use of an open version of that production questionnaire. The open discourse-completion test we resorted to included 20 prompts that required the use of request formulations. As in the pre-test and post-test tasks described above, situations included in the written production test varied in terms of familiarity, dominance or degree of imposition in making the request. Some examples are provided below.

Example (3)

Situation 3: You have just arrived at Heathrow Airport and you do not know where to get a bus to Victoria railway station. You decide to go to the information desk. What would you say?

Situation 9: Your best friend has moved to another town. You phone his/her mother's house because you want to know your friend's new phone number. What would you say?

Actually, we made use of two discourse-completion tests (Discourse-completion Test 1 and Discourse-completion Test 2), which included 10 situations each and which were administered in two instalments, before and after the training period, in order to take into account the effect of instruction and, thus, the teachability of requests. This task was written and it was carried out individually.

Taking into account the above-mentioned criticism and the disadvantages of written questionnaires in collecting pragmatic information (Rose, 1994), we also made use of a different task type which has been acknowledged as more ethnographic and similar to authentic language use, namely that of role-play. As in the case of discourse-completion tests, there exist at least two versions of the oral test. There are some researchers who have made use of closed role-plays in devising some pedagogical effects, as these include suggestions for responses. House (1996) states that closed role-plays promote learners' acquisition of specific formulae, although they do not allow for free interaction, as would be the case with open role-plays. Wolfson (1989) regards open role-plays and other sorts of ethnographic data collection as the most reliable means of learning about the sociolinguistic constraints implied in the use of a given speech act. For that reason, the second task type aimed at eliciting requestive behaviour in our study was that of the open role-play. Two role-plays (Role-play 1 and Role-play 2) were also administered on two different occasions, that is, before and after the instructional process, in order to determine the effects of training. The role-play task consisted of 10 prompts or brief descripts (five in each role-play test) of situations that identified the status of the speaker and the hearer in the exchange to be produced, but no further guidelines were offered. It was carried out in pairs because it required oral interaction. These are some examples of the prompts used:

Example (4)

Prompt E: You both work in a tile factory. One of you is a secretary who needs two days off because your (his/her) mother is ill.

Prompt D: You are two friends; one of you wants the other to ask the teacher a question about vocabulary, because there is a word s/he does not understand, but s/he is not very good at English.

In addition to the tasks that elicited request-act use, we considered our learners' pragmatic awareness. For this purpose, we decided to use a discourse-evaluation test, since the validity of this instrument in measuring pragmatic awareness had been demonstrated by previous research in the interlanguage pragmatics field addressing second language learners (Hudson et al., 1995), and in Fouser's (1997) study, which focused on learners of English as a third language. The discourse-evaluation test consisted of several exchanges including request acts which subjects had to evaluate on the basis of the appropriateness of the request formulation for the context in which it was used. Additionally, learners were required to justify their evaluation and to note down suggestions in those cases where they found the request formulation inappropriate for the context. Some items included in the discourse evaluation test are presented next.

Example (5)

Situation 1. You are in a hurry but you need to post an important letter. The post office is closed and you are taking a train in 10 minutes. You tell your father/mother:

Could you send this letter for me, please?

Appropriate ☐   Inappropriate ☐

Explain why:

If inappropriate, provide an alternative expression

SUGGESTION:

Like the discourse-completion test and the role-play tasks, the discourse-evaluation test was administered before and after the instructional process. Both discourse-evaluation tests (Discourse-evaluation Tests 1 and 2) contained nine situations. Discourse-evaluation Test 1 was distributed after students had fulfilled Role-play Task 1 and Discourse-completion Test 1 in previous sessions.

We should point out the fact that both beginner- and intermediate-level participants were provided with paraphrases and explanations of the situations included in all tasks when it was necessary, as we found that a full understanding of the situations was of paramount importance in order to complete the tasks. Learners at a beginner proficiency level asked for these explanations more often than their intermediate-level counterparts did.

After the administration of the tests and tasks mentioned before (i.e. pre-test, Role-play 1 and DCT1), we started the instructional period. This process was based on Kasper's (1996) suggested stages for teaching pragmatic items explicitly in the classroom. Thus it consisted of awareness-raising tasks and practice. Learners were first faced with a gradation of linguistic formulations for requests based on politeness criteria, which included indirect, conventionally indirect and direct forms, as shown in Trosborg's (1995) typology. This gradation is illustrated as follows:

Degree of politeness

Direct				Indirect
(less polite)		(more polite)		
Lend me your pencil!	Can you lend me your pencil?	Would you lend me your pencil?	Would you be so kind as to lend me your pencil?	I'm afraid I can't write this down. I don't have a pencil

Figure 4.1 Degrees of politeness

They compared the similarities and dissimilarities of those expressions with those in their mother tongue, and were asked to identify these strategies in transcripts that contained excerpts from authentic language use. Transcripts were based on Barraja-Rohan and Pritchard's (1997) book. We decided to make use of this research-based pedagogical material because it dealt with pragmatic aspects of English use, and thus served our purposes. After that, they were required to say aloud those linguistic formulations they would use in these specific situations:

Situation 1: You have forgotten your wallet and you need to buy some photocopies for the next class. Ask your classmate to lend you some money.

Situation 2: You have been waiting for the bus for almost half an hour. A person arrives at the bus stop. Ask him/her for information.

Situation 3: There is plenty of work at your office this weekend, but it is also your sister's wedding. Ask your boss for a morning off.

Their responses were discussed in class. The training was implemented within their established schedule for English classes, which consisted of four to six sessions depending on the amount of classes provided for each degree course (i.e. Industrial Design Technical Engineering and Primary Education). As we were dealing with two different degree courses, a second teacher took part in the data-collection procedure under our supervision. Thus, both instructional sessions and tasks were administered by ourselves and by a professor from the English Studies Department who conducts research in the field of second language acquisition.

Once the instructional process was finished, the participants were asked to act out the situations included in Role-play 2. This would allow us to compare their performance in Role-play 1 before receiving information on the use of request forms. After that, they completed Discourse-completion Test 2, which offered the same situations and added new ones to those they had faced in the role-play task. This was done in order to compare task effects in their performance. As we had done before the instructional process, we also required learners to evaluate request-act use in different situations included in Discourse-evaluation Test 2.

Data from the role-play tasks was tape-recorded and transcribed for later coding. Subjects' responses to the discourse-completion-test and discourse-evaluation-test tasks were also analysed and codified afterwards. In order to codify our data related to pragmatic production, that is, the use of request formulas, we first of all considered the amount and type of strategies employed by our subjects in situations provided on the basis of Trosborg's (1995) suggested taxonomy of request-realisation strategies presented in Chapter 2, also illustrated below:

Table 4.3 Type of request strategy

TYPE	STRATEGY	EXAMPLE
Indirect request	1. Hints (mild or strong)	I have to be at the airport in half an hour My car has broken down
Conventionally indirect	2. Ability/Willingness/ Permission	Could you lend me your car? Would you lend me your car?
Hearer-oriented		May I borrow your car?
	3. Suggestory formulae	How about lending me your car?
Speaker-oriented	4. Wishes 5. Desires	I would like to borrow your car I need to borrow your car
Direct request	6. Obligation	You must lend me your car
	7. Performatives	I would like to ask you to lend me your car I ask you to lend me your car
	8. Imperatives/ Elliptical phrases	Lend me your car Your car (please)

Source: Trosborg (1995: 205)

Additionally, we took into account their use of peripheral elements accompanying the head act, which were counted and coded following Sifianou's (1999) classification also described in Chapter 2 and presented below.

Table 4.4 Sifianou's classification of peripheral elements in request realisation

Internal modification	Openers		diminutives
		Softeners	
	Hedges		miscellaneous
			tag questions
	Fillers	Intensifiers	
		Hesitators	
		Cajolers	
		Appealers	
		Attention-getters	
External modification	Commitment-seeking devices		
	Reinforcing devices	Grounders	
		Disarmers	
		Expanders	
		Please	

Source: Sifianou (1999: 159)

Regarding our subjects' level of pragmatic awareness, we considered the amount of reasons provided for their evaluation regarding requestive behaviour and the amount of reasons connected to politeness issues, such as the role of the speaker, the social distance between speaker and hearer, the situation in which the request move was produced or the degree of imposition involved in the request formulation.

Data-collection procedures and instructional sessions took place during the second semester of the 1999–2000 course, starting in February 2000 and finishing in June 2000. The following table illustrates stages in the data-collection process and it also relates tasks to the aim of the tests, which relates to the hypotheses guiding the study. Although the training period consisted of four to six sessions, as specified above, we believe that prior practice involved in the pre-test, Role-play 1 and Discourse-completion 1 provided participants with further insights into pragmatic production. On that account, we have also highlighted these stages as part of the global instructional process.

Table 4.5 Goals of each task/test

	Task/Test	Goal
1st	Level placement test	Proficiency level of participants
2nd	Bilingualism test	Participants' degree of bilingual competence
3rd	Pre-test	Participants' knowledge of request forms Hypothesis – Chapter 5
4th	Role-play 1	Hypothesis – Chapters 5, 6 and 7
5th	Discourse-completion Test 1	Hypothesis – Chapters 5, 6 and 7
6th	Discourse-evaluation Test 1	Hypothesis – Chapter 8
7th	Training period	Hypothesis – Chapter 5
8th	Role-play 2	Hypothesis – Chapters 5, 6 and 7
9th	Discourse-completion Test 2	Hypothesis – Chapters 5, 6 and 7
10th	Discourse-evaluation Test 2	Hypothesis – Chapters 8
11th	Post-test	Hypothesis – Chapter 5

Methodological Decisions Taken in the Analysis of the Data

As has been previously stated, our main aim was to ascertain the role of instruction, the effects of proficiency level and tasks, and the role of bilingualism in producing and identifying request-act forms. Decisions concerning research design and the application of statistical procedures were taken on the basis of Hatch and Lazaraton's (1991) research manual for applied linguists. Additionally, an expert in the field of statistics belonging to a public research institute (i.e. *Organisme Públic Valencià d'Investigació*) advised us on the selection of those tests that best suited our goals. Regular interviews were also held during our data analysis to discuss specific doubts.

In order to identify reliability criteria, a pilot study including all tasks had been conducted in November 1999 with a reduced population under the supervision of a senior researcher. Results from that pilot study helped us eliminate or modify those situations in pragmatic production tasks that did not elicit requestive behaviour. Interpretation of our data was also based on Trosborg's (1995) typology and criteria to identify appropriate request formulations and evaluation were discussed with that senior researcher from the second/foreign language acquisition field.

On the basis of statistics experts' advice and decisions derived from the pilot study under the supervision of a senior researcher from the field of second/foreign language acquisition, we interpreted and analysed the data collected in the present study. The fact that our data was normally distributed (Kolmogorov-Smirnov = 0.701) and consisted of a wide sample (cases n = 160) enabled us to make use of statistical parametric tests. These tests provide stronger assumptions and perceived differences are considered more significant than results deriving from non-parametric measures. Parametric tests were employed during the whole research process involved in the present study.

In testing the hypothesis posited in Chapter 5, that is, the role of instruction in fostering our subjects' pragmatic competence, we compared their performance in the pre-test and the post-test, on the one hand, and in Role-play 1, Discourse-completion 1, Role-play 2 and Discourse-completion 2 on the other. We then compared the amount and type of request realisations elicited by these tasks at four stages: before being engaged in this study (pre-test), at the beginning of the instructional period (DCT1 and Role-play 1), at the end of this same period (DCT2 and Role-play 2), and after taking part in the study (post-test). Results obtained by contrasting the learners' performance in the pre-test and the post-test (i.e. stages 1 and 4) would highlight any similarities or dissimilarities in their use of request acts before and after the instructional process. Comparing results from tasks conducted immediately before and after the training period, those of role-play (1 and 2) and written completion test (1 and 2), (stages 2 and 3), would enable us to discover further instructional effects related to the beginning and end of the instructional process. In order to account for statistically significant differences in these tests completion, we chose a paired t-test, as we were interested in the performance of one group on two different measures, that is, before and after the instructional process or study. This parametric statistical procedure would allow us to see whether differences in strategy use were statistically significant.

In order to investigate the effects of proficiency on request-strategy use (see Chapter 6), we focused on the number and type of linguistic realisations produced by beginner and intermediate learners in those tasks that aimed at eliciting the use of request formulations, namely the role-play and the discourse-completion test. Dissimilarities between the two groups of subjects were identified by applying a *t*-test for independent measures. The reason we chose this statistical procedure related to the fact that the data was continuous; we dealt with two level groups (i.e. beginner and intermediate) and contrasted their performance in the same tasks.

We also made use of the parametric test described above in analysing the third hypothesis of the present study. We were particularly interested in contrasting learners' behaviour in oral and written task types, that is, role-plays and written discourse-completion tests. To that end, we attempted to discern significant differences among means related to request formulations employed in these two task types. Hence we focused on one group in two different moments that coincided with subjects' performance in different tasks types (oral and written). The paired t-test would provide us with significant (or not) mean differences in strategy use.

Finally, Chapter 8 deals with differences in our subjects' degree of pragmatic awareness. The t-Test for independent measures was employed in addressing significant differences between monolingual and bilingual subjects' responses in Discourse-evaluation Tests 1 and 2. As in the previous case, we dealt with two subgroups (bilingual and monolingual) and independent variables related to pragmatic awareness issues. We considered the number of accurate identifications of appropriate or inappropriate requestive behaviour presented during the test, and the number of suggestions provided in cases where request formulations were not considered appropriate. A major focus was on the number of reasons provided by subjects in relation to their evaluation, and on identifying whether these reasons related to politeness issues. Although it was not the main aim of Chapter 8, we also examined the extent to which bilingualism would affect not only pragmatic awareness but also pragmatic production. In so doing we made use of the t-test for independent variables.

The application of those statistical procedures quoted above, namely the t-test for independent measures and the paired t-test, enabled us to determine the significance of our results, which are described more fully in the following chapters.

Chapter 5
The Role of Pragmatic Instruction in Developing Foreign Language Learners' Pragmatic Competence

Hypothesis and Research Questions

As mentioned in Chapter 2, we have argued for a particular proposal for fostering pragmatic competence in the foreign language classroom. This suggestion focuses on the comprehension of pragmatic information in the language classroom. Pragmatic production should be based on criteria of appropriateness, thus pointing to the need for accessing those systematised pragmatic patterns that are provided by previous studies in the fields of second language acquisition and interlanguage pragmatics. Results from these studies on the role of pragmatic instruction in the language classroom have shown a positive improvement being made by those learners who have benefited from an instructional period. Furthermore, Norris and Ortega's (2000) study quoted in Chapter 2 suggests the advantage of explicit over implicit instruction. Teaching pragmatics explicitly involves awareness-raising as well as production tasks. The former task type includes description, explanation and discussion of pragmatic features, whereas the latter type engages learners in role-play and simulation activities.

In the light of the results obtained by previous studies on the effect of explicit instruction in speech acts' use, we have formulated the first hypothesis of our study as follows:

Hypothesis 1: Pragmatic instruction will affect the learners' degree of pragmatic competence. (Kasper, 1997; Kasper and Rose, 1999)

Despite the positive findings described in several studies (Fuyuka *et al.*, 1998; House, 1996; Tateyama *et al.*, 1997), the extent to which explicit formal instruction affects pragmatic development deserves further research, as claimed by Kasper (1997). With regard to that, we wonder whether explicit request instruction might result in a wider variety of linguistic formulations, whether learners will resort to mitigation devices to a greater extent after the instructional process, and whether the predicted positive effect of instruction will affect oral and written practice in the same way. Another aim of our study derives from Ellis' (1992, 1997) developmental study on the acquisition of request acts by two children (see Chapter 2 for further details). As has been mentioned, learners' production revealed certain development which was related to an increase in the use of mitigation devices when performing request moves. Taking Ellis' (1992, 1997) findings into account, the following research questions were formulated:

RQ1: Will learners make use of further mitigation devices after the instructional process?

RQ2: Will the use of these devices increase as instruction progresses?

In addition to that, we also examined the effects of instruction on the bilingual and the monolingual group. In doing so, we considered the pragmatic production of third language learners and contrasted their performance with that of monolingual learners. On the basis of previous research in third language acquisition, which highlighted the advantage of multilingual over monolingual learners (Cenoz and Jessner, 2000), the following research question was formulated:

RQ3: Will bilingual and monolingual learners' performance before and after instruction differ?

Results and Discussion

The first hypothesis of the present study concerned the effect of pragmatic instruction on the learners' performance. As mentioned in the previous section, this hypothesis assumed that pragmatic instruction would affect the learners' pragmatic competence. For the purposes of the present study, we have focused on one aspect of our participants' pragmatic competence, that of the production of request strategies. In order to test the effects of instruction, we first of all compared the learners' use of request formulations in the pre-test that was distributed before the study with that in the post-test, which was completed after the participants had completed all the tasks. We understand that the study consisted not only of instructional sessions but also of the participants' performance of various task types (two role-play tasks, two discourse-completion tests and two discourse-evaluation tests), which were administered at the beginning and end of the instructional period. Our analysis at this stage was quantitative on the one hand, (that is, accounting for the amount of strategies employed), and qualitative on the other (as we also considered whether there were any differences regarding the strategy types used at/on these two stages/occasions). Additionally, we also examined our subjects' use of peripheral modification devices in performing request acts.

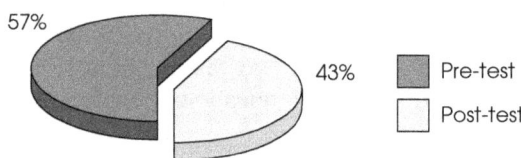

Figure 5.1 Global strategy use before and after the study took place

Figure 5.1 (above) shows differences in strategy use relating to pre-test and post-test data, which reveal an increase in the amount of strategies employed after the study was conducted. Some examples illustrating the use of request realisations in pre-test and post-test are presented below:

Example (1)

Pre-test

Situation 5: You cannot stand smoke or people smoking next to you. After an experiment in the company you work for, your boss lights up a cigarette while standing in a non-smoking area. He is talking to you about the experiment because you are the lab. assistant. What would you say to your boss about that cigarette?

S10: Can you put out that cigarette?
S11: Can you not smoke?
S5: Could you not smoke?

Post-test

Situation 4: You are having dinner at a restaurant and you want the waiter to bring you the bill. You say:

S10: Excuse me, could you bring me the bill, please?
S11: Excuse me, would you bring me the bill?
S5: Can you bring the bill, please?
[S10: bilingual intermediate]
[S11: monolingual intermediate]
[S5: bilingual beginner]

In order to find out whether the above difference in strategy use was statistically significant, we applied a paired t-test because it allowed us to calculate differences in strategy use relating to two moments in time, before and after the study had taken place. Another reason that we chose the paired t-Test was the fact that our sample (n=160) enabled us to make use of a parametric statistical procedure.

Table 5.1 shows the difference in the use of request realisations in the pre-test and the post-test. These differences are displayed in terms of means, t-value and statistical significance.

Table 5.1 Differences in pre-test and post-test amount of strategy use

	Mean	t	Sig.
Pre-test strategy use	3.23	–6.223	0.000*
Post-test strategy use	4.31		

*$p < 0.001$

According to the results obtained from the paired t-test statistics, our subjects produced more linguistic request realisations in the post-test than in the pre-test, that is, before carrying out the present study. This fact is also displayed by the t-value (t = –6.223) and the difference in strategy use in these two moments seems to be statistically significant ($p < 0.001$). In fact, our results point to a 99% probability level. This means that the number of request strategies increased considerably after the study took place, thus pointing to the effects of instruction. Regarding the strategy type employed in these two tests, we focused on our subjects' use of conventionally indirect, direct and indirect request formulations to see whether differences not only applied to quantity but also quality, as shown by Table 5.2.

As shown in Table 5.2, the paired t-test did not report statistical differences in our subjects' use of indirect request strategies before and after taking part in the study. However, there were differences in their use of conventionally indirect and direct request forms. We found that subjects resorted more often to conventionally indirect strategies in the post-test than in the pre-test. The t-value (t = –5.028) for such distinction denotes statistically significant differences that point to a 95% probability level. Subjects also employed more direct request strategies after taking part in the study; the difference regarding direct-strategy use before and after conducting the study is as significant as the use of conventionally indirect

Table 5.2 Differences in pre-test and post-test strategy type use

	Mean	t	Sig.
Pre-test Conventionally indirect	2.86	−5.028	0.039**
Post-test Conventionally indirect	3.78		
Pre-test direct strategy use	0.34	−2.086	0.000*
Post-test direct strategy use	0.52		
Pre-test indirect strategy use	0.02	1.642	0.203
Post-test indirect strategy use	0.03		

*$p < 0.001$ **$p < 0.05$

strategies. In fact, as illustrated in Table 5.2 above, the t-value ($t = -2.086$) points to a 99% probability level ($p = 0.000$), whereas significance in contrasting conventionally indirect use implied a 95% probability level. Hence, differences in the use of direct and conventionally indirect forms after taking part in the study may be considered as statistically significant on account of those results provided by the paired t-test above.

As stated in the previous subsection, our first hypothesis also evoked an interest in devising differences in the production of peripheral modification devices before and after engagement in the study. In that respect, we examined participants' global use of modification items, following Sifianou's (1999) classification of peripheral modification devices.

Although Figure 5.2 denotes a strong contrast between our subjects' use of peripheral modification in the pre-test (8%) and in the post-test (92%), we applied a statistical test to find out the level of significance involved in that distinction. The statistical analysis selected for that purpose was also the paired t-test, as we were comparing results obtained at two different times, and these results referred to the same variables, particularly those of modification items.

Pragmatic Instruction

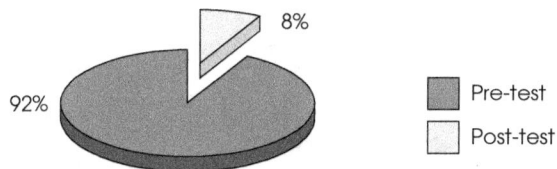

Figure 5.2 Peripheral modification devices in pre-test and post-test

Table 5.3 Differences in modification devices used in the pre-test and post-test

	Mean	*t*	*Sig.*
Pre-test modification devices	0.37	−32.680	0.000*
Post-test modification devices	4.31		

*$p < 0.001$

As shown in Table 5.3, there seems to be an important difference in the number of modification devices employed before and after the study. In fact, few modification devices were used before the study (i.e. in the pre-test), while participants largely modified the request head acts after taking part in this investigation. The high contrast level obtained ($t = -32.680$) and the level of significance of such contrast ($p = 0.000$) leads to statistically significant differences in the use of modification elements, thus pointing to a 99% probability level.

At this stage, we can state that the results relating to our subjects' performance before and after taking part in the study support our first hypothesis and thus point to instructional effects. Nevertheless, in order to further examine the effect of instruction on the requestive behaviour of foreign language learners, we also compared linguistic realisations employed in the first tasks (that is Role-play 1 and DCT1), with those performed at the end of the training period (Role-play 2 and DCT2), as shown in Figure 5.3 (below).

Although little contrast might be observed in Figure 5.3 (above) regarding global strategy use at the beginning and end of the training period, we still attempted to confirm this apparent lack of divergence. In accounting for significance levels, we also resorted to the paired *t*-test, for we were considering the same variables at two different moments as in the

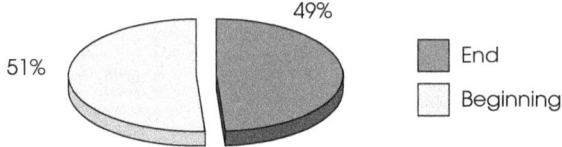

Figure 5.3 Strategy use at the beginning and end of the instructional process

previous analyses. Means, *t*-value and levels of significance are best displayed in Table 5.4 (below).

Table 5.4 Differences in global strategy use at the beginning and end of the instructional process

	Mean	t	Sig.
Beginning of instruction	7.26	0.675	0.501
End of instruction	7.04		

According to the results displayed in the paired *t*-test statistical analysis, the difference in the total amount of strategies employed at the beginning and end of the instructional process is not statistically significant. Hence we would say that no increase in terms of quantity in using request realisations can be reported. The number of strategies employed did not seem to vary a great deal during the instructional period. However, we were also interested in discovering whether the types of strategy employed were also similar at the beginning and end of the training period. Bearing this aim in mind, we focused on our subjects' use of conventionally indirect, direct and indirect request forms, as illustrated in Figure 5.4 (below).

After examining the types of linguistic formulation employed by our subjects before and after receiving formal instruction in the use of request acts, a paired *t*-test was also applied to our data in order to account for statistically significant differences.

Contrary to our findings relating to the lack of difference in the total number of strategies employed at the beginning and end of the instructional period, we found that there were significant differences in our subjects' use of request forms. Therefore, our findings point to differences in terms of quality, though not quantity. As presented in Figure 5.4 and Table 5.5, conventionally indirect strategies were more often employed

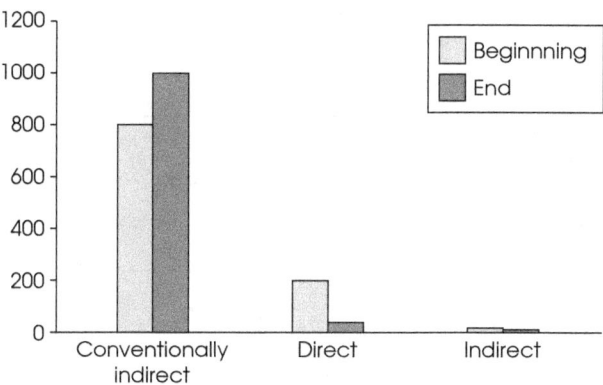

Figure 5.4 Strategy type used at the beginning and end of the instructional process

after the instructional process. In fact, differences relating to the use of these strategies at these two points revealed statistical significance according to results provided by the *t*-test (t = –3.588) with a 99% probability level (p = 0.000). On the contrary, direct strategies were more often employed at the beginning than at the end of the instructional process. Differences in direct-strategy use may also be interpreted as statistically significant on account of the results and probability level provided by the *t*-test, which also amounts to 99% (p = 0.000). The third subgroup of strategies analysed was that of the indirect type, which seemed to be more often employed at the beginning than at the end of the instructional process. As shown in Table 5.5 (below), mean scores point to a lack of indirect strategies at the end of the instructional process whereas some linguistic realisations belonging to the indirect type were used at the beginning. The probability level (p = 0.000) and *t*-value (t = 4.015) denote statistical significant differences in indirect strategy use at the beginning and end of the instructional period.

As has been previously mentioned, we were interested in ascertaining whether instruction had also affected both our subjects' use of request forms and peripheral modification devices. This last aspect was examined by contrasting their performance in pragmatic production tasks distributed at the beginning and end of the instructional period. Table 5.6 shows differences in use of modification at the beginning and end of the instructional process. These differences were obtained by applying a paired *t*-test to our data.

Table 5.5 Differences in strategy type use at the beginning and end of instruction

	Mean	t	Sig.
Before instruction Conventionally indirect	5.53	−3.588	0.000*
After instruction Conventionally indirect	6.67		
Before instruction direct strategy use	1.60	9.212	0.000*
After instruction direct strategy use	0.38		
Before instruction indirect strategy use	0.11	4.015	0.000*
After instruction indirect strategy use	0.00		

*$p < 0.001$

Table 5.6 Total modification devices used at the beginning and end of instruction

	Mean	t	Sig.
Modification devices before instruction	2.77	−24.792	0.000*
Modification devices after instruction	8.98		

*$p < 0.001$

Results from the *t*-test showed significant differences in our subjects' use of modification devices and they provide an answer to the first research question that was formulated in the first subsection of this chapter. In line with our results contrasting pre-test and post-test phases (see Table 5.3 above), a wider range of modification devices were used at the end than at the beginning of the instructional process. The probability level denoting statistical significance amounted to 99% ($p = 0.000$).

Considering the results presented above, we can state that our first hypothesis is supported, as the influence of instruction has been reported by contrasting both pre-test and post-test results on the one hand, and tasks performed at the beginning and end of the instructional period on the other. We should also point out the fact that the subjects' use of request formulations varied in terms of both quantity and quality. Besides, only differences in terms of quality or strategy variation were found in contrasting tasks carried out at the beginning and end of the training period. Nevertheless, the number of strategy subgroups, namely direct, indirect and conventionally indirect types, also varied as instruction progressed. In fact, we can point to a tendency to use more conventionally indirect strategy types and to decrease the use of direct-request realisations as subjects' knowledge of the use of request acts increased (see Tables 5.2 and 5.5). This finding is in line with Ellis' (1992) study, where subjects showed more variation in the use of realisation formulas as instruction progressed. Our results also seem to confirm Cohen and Olshtain's (1993) results, which point to a wider use of request-act realisations on the part of foreign language learners of English after a tutoring process. Findings also provide an answer to the second research question presented in the previous subsection of this chapter.

The third research question formulated in the first subsection dealt with the effect of instruction on our bilingual and monolingual subgroups. In order to provide an answer to this third question, we contrasted bilingual and monolingual learners' use of request formulations before and after being engaged in explicit instruction sessions. Results are displayed in Tables 5.7 and 5.8 (below).

Table 5.7 Request formulas employed by each subgroup before instruction

Strategy Type	Subgroup	Mean	t	Sig.
Conventionally indirect	Bilingual	6.28		
	Monolingual	4.79	−3.654	0.000*
Direct	Bilingual	1.69		
	Monolingual	1.51	−7.05	0.482**
Indirect	Bilingual	0.19		0.007*
	Monolingual	0.02	−2.730	

*$p<0.001$, $p<0.05$
**$p>0.1$

Table 5.8 Request formulas employed by each subgroup after instruction

Strategy Type	Subgroup	Mean	t	Sig.
Conventionally indirect	Bilingual	7.73	−3.446	0.001*
	Monolingual	5.61		
Direct	Bilingual	0.38	0.000	1**
	Monolingual	0.38		
Indirect	Bilingual	0.00	***	***
	Monolingual	0.00		

*$p<0.001, p<0.05$
**$p>0.1$
***no data

As displayed in Tables 5.7 and 5.8 (below), bilingual learners produced more conventionally indirect requests before and after instruction, whereas differences in indirect-strategy use relate only to performance before instruction. According to Table 5.8, no differences were found between bilingual and monolingual learners in their use of indirect-request strategies after instruction. Both bilingual and monolingual learners made use of a similar number of direct-request strategies. Considering these findings, we can say that bilingual learners outperformed monolinguals in their use of conventionally indirect strategies both before and after being engaged in instructional sessions, and also in their use of indirect strategies before instruction. Nevertheless, no statistical differences were found in these learners' production of direct requests and indirect strategies after instruction. Therefore, we can state that bilingualism was more significant than the effects of instruction where the use of conventionally indirect requests was concerned.

Bilinguals' performance reported above is in line with previous studies that point to bilingual and multilingual learners having an advantage in terms of their interactional competence (Hoffmann, 2001; Oskaar, 1990). In fact, we understand pragmatic competence as part of interactional competence, and conventionally indirect requests may be regarded as an instance of appropriate pragmatic behaviour (Brown and Levinson, 1987; Trosborg, 1995).

In drawing a contrast between the two learner subgroups, we have considered their performance in a written and an oral task before and after they were exposed to explicit instruction. As stated in the previous subsection of this chapter, one of our research aims was to analyse whether instructional effects would affect oral and written tasks in the same way or to the same extent. In order to answer this question, we analysed our data on the basis of a paired t-test including role-play and discourse-completion test results at the beginning (Role-play 1 and Discourse-completion 1) and end (Role-play 2 and Discourse-completion Test 2) of the instructional process. Results are displayed in the following two tables, where Table 5.9 represents request-strategy use in the oral task on two occasions, and Table 5.10 illustrates strategy use in the written task before and after the instructional process.

According to the results displayed in Tables 5.9 and 5.10, we can state that differences in strategy use also correspond to our previous findings as specified in Table 5.5. We may also say that instruction affected both our subjects' oral and written practice. There is only one exception that refers to the use of indirect strategies in the role-play task on these two occasions. As illustrated in Table 5.9, the difference cannot be considered as statistically significant. The less frequent use of indirect strategy types seems to confirm Trosborg's (1995) results, which showed that learners of English as a foreign language did not frequently resort to hints in the role-play task. Following Trosborg (1995), we also believe that this finding might be attributed to the nature of the task and the difficulty implied in making indirect requests, since we were dealing with beginner and inter-mediate learners and no specific formulae had been previously taught in

Table 5.9 Differences in Role-play 1 and 2 strategy type and modification devices used

	Mean	t	Sig.
Role-play 1 Conventionally indirect	2.22	−1.677	0.096#
Role-play 2 Conventionally indirect	2.49		
Role-play 1 Direct strategy use	0.48	4.613	0.000*
Role-play 2 Direct strategy use	0.18		
Role-play 1 Indirect strategy use	6.25E–03	1.000	0.319
Role-play 2 Indirect strategy use	0.00		
Role-play 1 Modification devices	0.78	−9.850	0.000*
Role-play 2 Modification devices	2.15		

*$p < 0.001$ #$p < 0.1$

Table 5.10 Differences in DCT 1 and DCT2 strategy type and modification devices used

	Mean	t	Sig.
DCT 1 Conventionally indirect	3.31	−3.065	0.003**
DCT 2 Conventionally indirect	4.18		
DCT 1 Direct strategy use	1.13	8.419	0.000*
DCT 2 Direct strategy use	0.20		
DCT 1 Indirect strategy use	0.11	4.087	0.000*
DCT 2 Indirect strategy use	0.00		
DCT 1 Modification devices	1.99	−24.257	0.000*
DCT 2 modification devices	6.83		

*$p < 0.001$ **$p < 0.05$

illustrating the use of hints. Furthermore, the culture-bound nature of this type of request strategy might have also affected learners' performance. In view of the results relating to our first hypothesis, we are able to state that our learners' pragmatic competence was influenced by the instructional period they were engaged in. The effects of instruction pointed to positive outcomes, as a trend towards polite behaviour in the use of request strategies was illustrated by means of an increase in the use of conventionally indirect strategies and a decrease in the use of direct formulations. Furthermore, after the instructional process, and also after the study took place, learners produced more request-act modification devices, thus corresponding to previous research on pragmatic development (Ellis, 1992, 1997). These results also seem to confirm Olshtain and Cohen's (1990) claim for the teaching of mitigating devices and situational features in the foreign language context. Like ours, their study also showed positive outcomes in the use of modification devices after a training period. Therefore, our results seem to support both our hypothesis and previous studies on the positive effect of explicit instruction in developing foreign language learners' pragmatic competence (Kasper, 1997; Rose and Kasper, 2001). In line with House (1996),

Tateyama *et al.* (1997), Fuyuka *et al.* (1998), Norris and Ortega (2000) and Takahashi (2001), we can argue for the improvement of learners' pragmatic competence after being engaged in a training period. Despite the fact that learners in the above-quoted studies did not share a linguistic background with our subjects, we found a correspondence regarding the beneficial effect of explicitly teaching the use of particular speech acts.

Although our hypothesis addressed the role of instruction in pragmatic production, we also wondered whether training in request-act use would influence our subjects' pragmatic awareness. In order to account for this fact, we examined data collected by means of the discourse-evaluation test, which was also distributed on two occasions, that is, at the beginning and end of the instructional process. Data provided by the discourse-evaluation test consisted of subjects' identification of appropriate or inappropriate request forms, suggestions for those formulations found inappropriate and reasons that justified our subjects' evaluation. Findings may be best illustrated in the following figure and in Table 5.11, which displays results after applying a paired *t*-test to our data.

As shown by Figure 5.5, subjects seemed to provide more reasons for their evaluation and suggestions relating to inappropriate formulations at the beginning than at the end of the instructional process. In fact, differences in the reasons provided may not be considered significant according to the paired *t*-test results. In this sense, no instructional effects would then be reported. However, considering the identification of appropriate and inappropriate request forms, we can say that the training

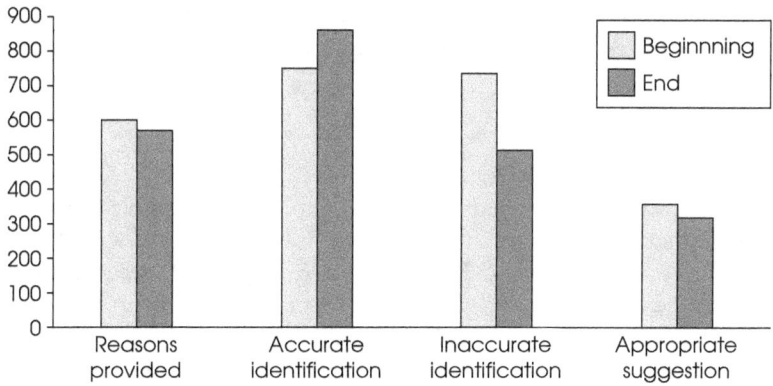

Figure 5.5 Effects of instruction on pragmatic awareness

period had a positive influence on our subjects' performance. According to Table 5.11, differences in this respect indicated a probability level of 0.000 ($p < 0.001$).

Table 5.11 Pragmatic awareness at the beginning and end of instruction

	Mean	t	Sig.
Reasons Provided – Beginning	3.85	0.997	0.320
Reasons Provided – End	3.68		
Accurate Identification – Beginning	4.95	–3.927	0.000*
Accurate Identification – End Direct strategy use	5.58		
Inaccurate Identification – Beginning	4.97	10.113	0.000*
Inaccurate Identification – End	3.35		
Suggestions Provided – Beginning	4.67	2.374	0.019**
Suggestions Provided – End	4.31		

*$p < 0.001$ **$p < 0.05$

On the basis of our results presented in this subsection, we can state that instruction not only affects pragmatic production, but it also seems to play a role in pragmatic awareness. Since the main focus of instruction was on pragmatic production, we believe that instruction addressing awareness issues in a more detailed way might have promoted different results, which would presumably reflect a greater influence on the learners' pragmatic awareness.

Conclusions

Our hypothesis concerned the role of explicit instruction in fostering learners' pragmatic competence. Tutoring sessions were held during a semester and they followed Kasper's (1996) suggested stages, those of description, explanation and discussion of pragmatic features. In testing our first hypothesis, we contrasted the subjects' use of linguistic request formulations and peripheral modification devices in the pre-test with routines employed in the post-test. Thus, analysis was both quantitative and qualitative. We counted the total number of strategies employed on the one hand, and noted differences in strategy types used in these two tests on the other.

Results from the paired *t*-test pointed to a significant increase in terms of both the number and type of strategies employed in the post-test, compared with their use in the pre-test. Subjects resorted more often to conventionally indirect and direct request forms in the post-test. Additionally, we also reported subjects' tendency to use a wider range of peripheral modification devices after the study had taken place (i.e. post-test). In this sense, Hypothesis 1 of the study was supported by our findings, and it also confirmed previous studies which attributed a positive role to the explicit teaching of pragmatic items from the target language (Norris and Ortega, 2000; Olshtain and Cohen, 1990).

Furthermore, we contrasted bilingual and monolingual learners' performance before and after being exposed to explicit instruction, and we found that bilingualism influenced learners' performance even after instruction had taken place. Yet the effects of bilingualism related mainly to the use of conventionally indirect strategies, since there were no statistical differences between the two learner groups as far as direct realisation strategies were concerned.

In the light of the positive results obtained, we decided to further examine the role of instruction in our subjects' performance. In so doing, we contrasted the use-request formula in the first tasks (Role-play 1 and Discourse-completion Test 1), distributed at the beginning of the instructional process, and in the tasks administered immediately after tutoring sessions had finished (Role-play 2 and Discourse-completion Test 2). Results from the paired *t*-test did not show important dissimilarities in the global number of strategies employed. However, the use of particular strategy types and peripheral modification items differed significantly in both sets of tasks. Thus there were qualitative (though not quantitative) differences during the training period, as participants resorted to certain strategy types in completing Role-play 1 and Discourse-completion Test 1, and showed a preference for other linguistic request realisations in Role-play 2 and Discourse-completion Test 2. In addition to that, they also denoted a clear preference for resorting to a particular strategy type, that of the conventionally indirect subgroup. Coinciding with Ellis' (1992) study, our subjects' performance varied as instruction progressed, thus indicating the positive role of tutoring sessions in foreign language learners' use of particular formulae in request acts.

Related to instructional effects is the proficiency level of learners of English as a foreign language and its influence on the development of pragmatic competence, which is discussed in the following chapter.

Chapter 6
Effects of Proficiency Level on Pragmatic Production

Hypothesis and Research Questions

Previous studies have concluded that there exists a mismatch between foreign language learners' grammatical and pragmatic competence (Kasper, 1997). In foreign communities we find advanced learners who may produce accurate linguistic structures but who are unable to use them appropriately in different situations or contexts. Appropriateness seems to be largely ignored in second and foreign language learning settings, thus probably resulting in the above-quoted mismatch (i.e. knowledge about the language but not about how to use it). Studies in the interlanguage pragmatics field have accounted for this imbalance when showing pragmatic production of intermediate and advanced learners of the target language (see Chapter 2 for a revision), since no differences were reported between learners of these two proficiency levels in terms of their pragmatic competence.

As discussed in Chapter 2, the target language proficiency level has been regarded as a major factor in language learners' pragmatic competence. In fact, proficiency effects have been reported by various studies in the field of interlanguage pragmatics (Hill, 1997; Takahashi and DuFon, 1989). Regarding request-act production, several scholars have pointed to significant changes in the type of linguistic formulations used which were related to an increase in the proficiency level of their subjects (Ellis, 1997; Takahashi and DuFon, 1989). Nevertheless, as has been previously mentioned, other studies report little influence of the learners' proficiency on their performance (Takahashi, 1996). We should point out the fact that most of these studies have considered learners at an intermediate and advanced proficiency level. However, as raised by Kasper and Rose (1999), few studies have dealt with learners at a beginner level. Therefore, it seems appropriate to study learners at lower levels in order to ascertain to what extent the learners' proficiency level in the target language affects both their performance and their pragmatic development. Thus, our population consisted of learners at an intermediate and beginner proficiency level in the target language, and our research aim was to ascertain to what extent the learners' level would affect request-act use. On the basis of previous findings reported in Chapter 2, we formulated the following hypothesis:

> *Hypothesis 2: There will be a mismatch between beginner and intermediate learners on those developmental stages concerning grammatical and pragmatic competence. (Kasper, 1997; Kasper and Rose, 1999)*

Considering the above hypothesis, and previous findings that revealed an imbalance between foreign language learners' grammatical and pragmatic competence, we formulated the following research questions:

> RQ1: Will there be a great difference between intermediate and beginner learners in their overall performance?

> RQ2: Will their level be connected to a particular type of linguistic request realisation?

> RQ3: Will there be any difference in their global use of peripheral elements accompanying the request head act?

Considering the characteristics of our learners and our interest in establishing a link between the areas of interlanguage pragmatics and third language acquisition (see Chapters 2 and 3), we further wondered whether bilingual learners would employ a wider range of request strategies than monolinguals both in the beginner and intermediate subgroup:

> RQ4: Will beginner bilinguals outperform beginner monolinguals? Will this also be case with intermediate bilingual and monolingual participants?

Results and Discussion

As stated in the previous section, the second hypothesis of our study referred to the use of request realisations by subjects at different proficiency levels. The hypothesis stated that there would be a mismatch between our subjects' linguistic and pragmatic competence, as predicted by previous studies. For this purpose, we examined the use of conventionally indirect, direct and indirect request realisations by beginner and intermediate learners of English. First of all a comparison was made of beginner and intermediate subjects' overall use of request formulations, as shown in Figure 6.1.

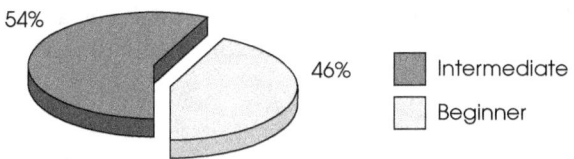

Figure 6.1 Effects of proficiency on global strategy use

Intermediate learners seemed to resort to request strategies more frequently (54%) than subjects at a beginner proficiency level (46%). Despite this apparent distinction in strategy use, we aimed at confirming the difference by applying a statistical analysis to our data. As we were dealing with the effect of two proficiency levels on one independent variable (i.e. strategy type, whether it be conventionally indirect, direct or indirect), and considering our data was continuous, we applied the t-test for independent sample data as a statistical procedure. Our interest lay in discovering whether or not the null hypothesis (no differences between groups) was rejected. Results are displayed in terms of means in strategy use, t-value and significance.

Table 6.1 Effects of proficiency in overall strategy use

	Mean	*t*	*Sig.*
Beginner Group	13.03	−2.658	0.0099**
Intermediate Group	15.55		

**$p < 0.05$

As may be observed in Table 6.1, results point to a significant difference between beginner and intermediate learners' use of request realisations in terms of quantity. The difference in mean scores reveals that subjects at an intermediate proficiency level produced more request formulations than those at a beginner level. These findings would reject the null hypothesis, and thus account for differences between the two groups of learners. We may assume, then, that a better command of the target language enables a more frequent use of request formulations when these are elicited. Apart from discovering the frequency of global strategy use, we were also interested in finding out whether there was any sort of connection between our learners' proficiency level and the strategy type employed. For this purpose, we compared beginner and intermediate subjects' use of conventionally indirect, direct and indirect request forms as follows.

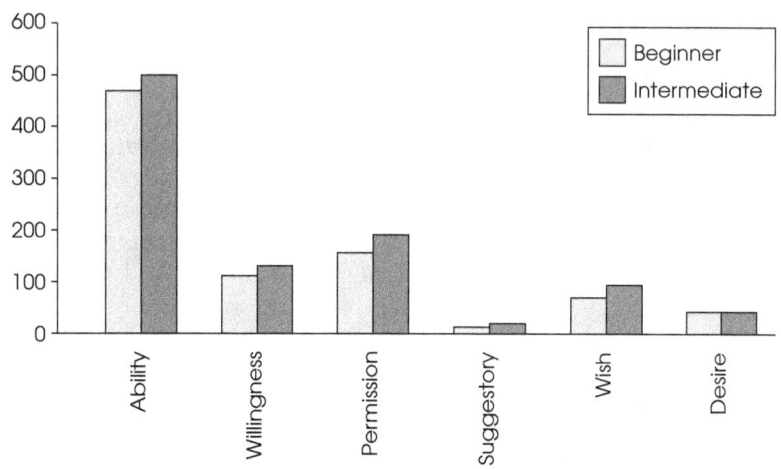

Figure 6.2 Effects of proficiency on the use of conventionally indirect request forms

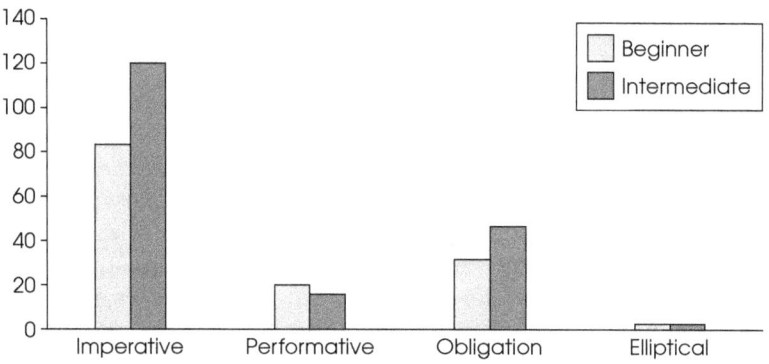

Figure 6.3 Effects of proficiency on the use of direct request forms

Effects of Proficiency Level

Our findings revealed significant differences in beginner and intermediate learners' use of specific realisations with a probability level of < 0.05, where intermediate learners always outperformed beginner ones. Nevertheless, there were two particular realisations which seemed to slightly contradict the findings reported in Figure 6.1 and Table 6.1. These refer to the use of desire (e.g. *I would like to borrow your bag*) and performative (e.g. *I ask you to lend me your bag*) request formulations, which are presented in Figures 6.2 and 6.3, and the statistical significance is displayed in Table 6.2.

Table 6.2 Effects of proficiency on the use of desire and performative request realisations

	Mean	*t*	*Sig.*
Beginner group Conventionally indirect DESIRE	0.50	0.000	1
Intermediate group Conventionally indirect DESIRE	0.50		
Beginner group direct PERFORMATIVE	0.29	0.714	0.476
Intermediate group direct PERFORMATIVE	0.21		

According to the probability levels shown in the above table, we can state that our learners' use of desire and performative realisations was not related to their proficiency level, as no significant differences were found between these two groups. Therefore, though the global use of conventionally indirect and direct forms points to a wider use of request forms on the part of intermediate than on the part of beginner subjects, we may also state that it was not so for all particular realisations.

Findings presented in Table 6.2 suggest that there is a certain connection between proficiency-level variable and global strategy use with a level of probability of 0.013. This means that the higher the proficiency level of our subjects, the more request strategies they will employ. After observing proficiency effects in conventionally indirect and direct strategy use, we wondered whether our subjects' level of target language would also have affected their use of peripheral modification devices, and whether the use of such items also bore a correlation with the proficiency level variable. In testing this we made use of the t-test for independent samples to ascertain differences between groups. These results are best illustrated in Table 6.3 below.

Table 6.3 Effects of proficiency in peripheral modification devices use

	Mean	t	Sig.
Beginner group	9.09	−9.716	0.000**
Intermediate group	14.40		

*$p < 0.001$

In line with results obtained concerning global and particular strategy use, we may say that the subjects' proficiency level also affected their use of peripheral modification devices in performing request acts. Table 6.3 shows that intermediate subjects produced more peripheral modification devices than those belonging to the beginner group. Differences in modification-device use point to a t-value of 09.716 and a probability level of $p < 0.001$ (i.e. 99%). Therefore, the t-test seems to reveal statistically significant differences between intermediate and beginner groups. The proficiency level seems to be related to the subjects' use of peripheral modification devices. In fact, results suggest that the higher the proficiency level of our subjects, the more peripheral modification devices they employed. This finding is not surprising if we take into account results on our subjects' global request-strategy use. Intermediate learners displayed a higher use of conventionally indirect and direct formulations, and peripheral modification devices only appear in this type of linguistic formulation in order to mitigate the impositive nature of the request move.

Besides this, we also wondered whether particular learner characteristics, namely bilingualism or monolingualism, would affect subjects of different proficiency levels in the same way, as formulated in the fourth research question presented in the first subsection of this chapter. In providing an answer to that question we made use of the t-test for independent samples and contrasted, on the one hand, beginner bilingual and beginner monolingual learners' production of request realisations. Results are displayed in Table 6.4.

Table 6.4 Beginner bilingual and monolingual subjects' use of request strategies

		Mean	t	Sig.
Conventionally Indirect	Bilingual	13.05	−3.064	0.003*
	Monolingual	9.45		
Direct	Bilingual	1.85	−1.083	0.2
	Monolingual	1.48		
Indirect	Bilingual	0.20	−2.049	0.04*
	Monolingual	0.00		

*$p<0.05$

On the other hand, we contrasted the use of request strategies by intermediate bilingual and intermediate monolingual learners. Results from applying the *t*-test to our data are shown in Table 6.5.

Table 6.5 Intermediate bilingual and monolingual subjects' use of request strategies

		Mean	t	Sig.
Conventionally Indirect	Bilingual	14.95	−3.175	0.002*
	Monolingual	11.35		
Direct	Bilingual	2.28	−0.055	0.956
	Monolingual	2.30		
Indirect	Bilingual	0.02	−1.782	0.079
	Monolingual	0.18		

*$p<0.05$

As shown in Tables 6.4 and 6.5, we can state that bilingual learners employed a wider range of conventionally indirect strategies within both the beginner and the intermediate subgroup. Hence, differences related to bilingualism apply to learners of different proficiency levels. However, no significant differences were found in the use of direct strategies, whereas the use of indirect requests by beginner bilinguals slightly exceeded that by beginner monolinguals (see Table 6.4). We may state that there seems to be a tendency to show appropriate pragmatic behaviour on the part of bilingual learners, which might be illustrated by the use of conventionally indirect request realisations. The learners' proficiency level seemed to influence their performance, although this was not the case for all strategy subtypes, and bilingualism might have affected such results, although further research in that respect would be necessary.

To sum up, we can state that our second hypothesis has been partly disproved, as no mismatch was found between our intermediate and beginner learners' linguistic and pragmatic competence. Furthermore, some degree of relationship was found between the proficiency-level variable and the use of conventionally indirect and direct strategy types and peripheral modification devices. For that reason, we believe that our findings may hint at/imply the importance of linguistic competence in promoting pragmatic development, as both constitute the global notion of communicative competence (Alcón, 2000; Bachman, 1990; Celce-Murcia et al., 1995).

Despite the fact that our hypothesis was not fully supported by our findings, results are in line with previous studies dealing with the use of requests by learners at different proficiency levels (Takahashi and Dufon, 1989) and with longitudinal studies addressing learners at a beginner level. As described in Chapter 2, Ellis (1992) examined the use of request acts by two beginner subjects and reported a significant change in their performance. According to this author, developmental stages were identified which referred to an increase in the use of mitigation devices and more variation in the linguistic request formulations used. Taking these facts into account, we may say that our results shared some characteristics with Ellis' (1992) study. As has been previously discussed, a wider use of peripheral modification devices was reported by intermediate than by beginner learners. Similarly, intermediate learners employed a wider range of request linguistic realisations, which also denoted wider variation.

On the basis of previous studies, such as those of Kasper (1997) and Kasper and Rose (1999), we predicted a mismatch between our learners' linguistic and pragmatic competence. Conversely, we found that learners' use of linguistic request-act realisations and peripheral modification devices was related to their proficiency level. Intermediate learners outperformed beginners in terms of quantity and quality in using request forms. Nevertheless, we should take into account the fact that previous studies reporting a lack of difference in pragmatic production dealt with intermediate and advanced learners, which was not our situation. In fact, according to Kasper and Rose (2002), none of these studies had considered learners at a beginner proficiency level in the target language. This was the reason why we included beginner subjects in our study. Besides, we should also point out the fact that no differences were reported in particular strategy types, namely those belonging to the desire (conventionally indirect) and performative (direct) subgroup (see Table 6.2 for a detailed description). In view of these findings, we believe that just as proficiency effects have been widely examined within the field of second language acquisition, these should also be further analysed in the interlanguage pragmatics subfield in order to understand and allow for an identification of those developmental stages involved in language learners' pragmatic production.

Conclusions

The hypothesis in this chapter predicted a mismatch between our learners' linguistic and pragmatic competence in the target language. In testing this hypothesis we contrasted the use of request formulations by subjects at beginner and intermediate proficiency levels in the oral production (Role-plays 1 and 2) and written production (Discourse-completion Tests 1 and 2) tasks. Findings showed that intermediate learners outperformed beginner ones in terms of quantity and quality in using request forms. In fact, learners' use of request formulations and modification devices appeared to be related to their proficiency level. We should also point out that no differences between these two learner groups were found regarding the use of specific request formulations, namely those of the desire (conventionally indirect) and performative (direct) subgroup. This means that our second hypothesis was partially disproved.

Furthermore, findings also pointed to bilingualism having an effect on the use of request strategies by beginner and intermediate learners, particularly as far as conventionally indirect strategies were concerned. Results confirmed the findings reported in Chapter 5, which highlighted the role of bilingualism in learners' use of conventionally indirect requests. Yet the effects of bilingualism were not reported in connection with beginner and intermediate learners' use of direct strategies. These facts seem to call for further research into the role of bilingualism and the proficiency level of language learners in their pragmatic production.

In interpreting these findings, two points should be taken into account. On the one hand, previous studies reporting no differences in their subjects' pragmatic production dealt with intermediate and advanced learners, which was not the case with us. In fact, according to Kasper and Rose (1999), none of those studies had considered learners at a beginner proficiency level, and that was the reason why we included a beginner group in our study. On the other hand, although no clear mismatch between our subjects' grammatical and pragmatic competence was reported by our findings, they bore certain similarities with longitudinal studies addressing beginner learners (Ellis, 1992, 1997). Like Ellis' (1992) subjects, ours showed a tendency to use more mitigation devices and request formulations in line with their proficiency level.

Chapter 7
The Effects of the Task on Pragmatic Production

Hypothesis and Research Questions

In Chapter 2 we described the need to employ a wider range of elicitation techniques in studies focusing on speech acts. Existing studies have made use of oral role-plays, discourse-completion tests, rating scales and cartoon oral-production tests. However, most of these studies have resorted to one of these instruments in fostering learners' use of a particular speech act. As reported by Kasper and Rose (1999, 2002), one of the main themes that should be incorporated in further research is that of implementing several elicitation techniques. In fact, authors such as Rose (1992, 1994), Rose and Ono (1995) and Johnston et al. (1998) have observed differences in their subjects' performance that related to the task type they were required to perform. These studies have ascertained the main differences between written and oral methods, and within the latter, related to open and closed options. Results point to the advantage of written instruments over oral ones in terms of the large number of participants to whom this test may be administered, and also in terms of the possibility of controlling variables, such as the context, on the part of the researcher. Nevertheless, oral methods like open role-plays provide more authentic data, as participants have more chances to interact freely than in written discourse-completion tests.

Bearing these issues in mind, we decided to make use of both open role-plays and discourse-completion tests in an attempt to determine the extent to which the task type, that is oral or written, would affect learners' performance. Taking into account previous findings from research contrasting different elicitation methods in speech-act production (see Chapter 2), we formulated the following hypothesis:

Hypothesis 3: The task performed, whether it be an oral or a written task (i.e. role-play vs discourse-completion test) will affect the choice and use of request realisations. (Kasper, 2000; Rose and Ono, 1998; Sasaki, 1998)

The following research questions were also formulated in order to further examine task effects:

RQ1: Will learners use a wider range of request-head peripheral elements in the oral production task?

RQ2: Will the discourse-completion task elicit more request realisation strategies than the open role-play task?

RQ3: Will bilingual learners outperform monolingual ones in the oral and written task?

Results and Discussion

As reported in Chapter 2 and the first subsection of the present chapter, task effects on the use of particular speech acts have been identified by several scholars in the field of interlanguage pragmatics (Johnston et al., 1998; Kasper and Rose, 1999). On account of the results provided by these studies, we considered it necessary to examine the effect of different task types on our subjects' pragmatic production. For that reason, we analysed the effect of oral (i.e. role-play) and written (i.e. discourse-completion test) tasks on the use of linguistic request formulations. We first focused on the number of request strategies employed in these two tasks.

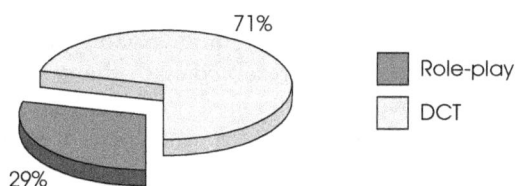

Figure 7.1 Task effects on global strategy use

In order to account for potential significant differences, we applied a paired *t*-test to our data, the focus being on the performance of a group (our subjects) in two different measures (role-play vs. discourse-completion test) during the semester when the present study was conducted. Results obtained from this paired *t*-test are then presented in terms of mean scores, *t*-value and level of significance.

Table 7.1 Task effects on global strategy use

	Mean	t	Sig.
Role-play	5.36	6.792	0.000*
Discourse-completion test	8.91		

*$p < 0.001$

As shown in Figure 7.1 and Table 7.1 (above), learners seemed to employ a wider range of linguistic request formulae in the discourse-completion test than in the Role-play task, and these differences are statistically significant. The differences between the oral and the written task might derive from (1) the presence of an interlocutor in the role-play task and the fact that the subjects' performance was tape-recorded; and (2) the nature of written and oral tasks, since both were open versions and in no case were adjoining devices present. Open role-plays are regarded as enabling free interaction among participants, as opposed to closed role-plays, where a response to the request act is provided (see Chapter 2 for further information). By the same token, we may assume that such freedom in interaction reduces the elicitation possibilities of a specific speech-act formulation, thus resulting in fewer examples of linguistic formulations than those provided by a written method, like that of the discourse-completion test.

We should also point out that, although situations in the discourse-completion tests ($s = 10$) doubled those present in the oral role-play task ($s = 5$), we considered only those situations that were identical in both tasks ($n = 5$). This was done in order to ascertain task effects and factors, as well as to control other possible intervening variables. By the same token, we could also argue that being presented with the same situation for a second time might have led to an increase in the use of request formulations in this second task, as would be the case of learners' performance in the discourse-completion test.

In addition to the quantitative analysis, we also carried out a qualitative analysis of the strategy type employed in each task. Thus we analysed the production of specific request strategies, namely those of the conventionally indirect, direct and indirect subgroups, in the oral and written tasks. The results of a paired t-test are shown in Table 7.2.

Table 7.2 Task effects on specific request strategy types

	Mean	t	Sig.
Role-play Conventionally indirect	4.71	5.722	0.000*
Discourse-completion test Conventionally indirect	7.49		
Role-play direct	0.65	6.046	0.000*
Discourse-completion test direct	1.33		
Role-play indirect	6.25E–03	3.939	0.000*
Discourse-completion test indirect	0.11		

*$p < 0.001$

In line with the quantitative results specified above, we may state that a wider range of request formulations belonging to the three examined subgroups (i.e. conventionally indirect, direct and indirect) were employed in the discourse-completion test than in the role-play tasks. The difference in the use of these three strategies in the two tasks is statistically significant. Findings also reveal that indirect requests were not present in the role-play task. As has been previously mentioned, we believe that the presence of an interlocutor and a tape-recorder might have overruled any other expected task effect. On the one hand, the need to communicate and make one's intention explicit in performing a request might have promoted the lack of indirect strategies in this task. On the other, although there were no time constraints in either the oral or the written task, being tape-recorded might have been understood as a timing measure. Therefore, participants might have felt some kind of pressure to produce request realisations in the oral task, which did not enable them to use highly elaborated linguistic formulae.

In formulating the hypothesis of this chapter, we were also interested in ascertaining possible task effects on the learners' use of peripheral modification items. This interest derived from the observation that the use of peripheral modification devices had been frequently related to native speakers' use of the target language (Trosborg, 1995). In this sense a more authentic task, e.g. the open role-play, would probably foster a wider use of peripheral modification items than a more artificial task (i.e. a discourse-completion test). On that account we examined our subjects' use of peripheral modification devices in the oral and the written task. In order to note down significant differences we resorted to the paired *t*-test, as in the previous analysis conducted in testing this hypothesis.

Table 7.3 Task effects on peripheral modification devices use

	Mean	*t*	*Sig.*
Role-play	2.93	24.166	0.000*
Discourse-completion test	8.81		

$p < 0.001$

Contrary to our prediction stated above, a wider use of modification devices was found in the written than in the oral task, the difference being statistically significant. These findings might be connected to the fact that a wider range of strategies were also elicited by the discourse-completion-test task. We should bear in mind the fact that this higher number of linguistic request realisations (i.e. compared to the number of request realisations elicited in the oral task) were accompanied by a modification device. Thus our data shows that the more request strategies were employed, the more chances there were to use peripheral modification devices.

On the basis of results related to this hypothesis, we may state that task effects were powerful enough to display statistically significant differences in our subjects' use of particular linguistic request realisations and modification devices in two different task types. Furthermore, we have pointed to the role of the interlocutor in request-act performance, as well as to the practical effects of the use of request formulations. This refers to the fact that learners were faced with the same situations in the role-play as in the written discourse-completion test, which was performed later on in a different session. For this reason, a change in the setting for the written task completion (which involved individual participation and no perceived time constraints) might have fostered the above-quoted increase in the use of request formulations, on the one hand, and of peripheral modification devices accompanying them, on the other.

We have also noted the lack of hints or indirect request formulations in the role-play task. This finding seems to confirm Trosborg's (1995) results from her analysis of the use of request formulations on the part of intermediate and beginner learners of English by means of a role-play task. Findings from this study also led to the lack of indirect request formulations in the subjects' performance, as has been the case in our own study. We agree with Trosborg (1995) that the linguistic complexity involved in producing hints might have prompted our results, bearing in mind the proficiency level of our subjects. However, we have also mentioned other possible reasons that may explain our results, which involve the presence of an interlocutor and perceived time constraints.

In addition to the above-mentioned task effects on the use of particular request strategies, our learners also resorted to different peripheral modification devices. On that account, we wondered whether the type of modification item employed in the two tasks would somehow correspond to our findings referring to the global use of modification items. Hence we attempted to discern whether most of the modification items belonging to the examined subcategories had been used in the written task. Results are illustrated in Figure 7.2, where frequency rates and type of modification devices used in the two tasks are shown.

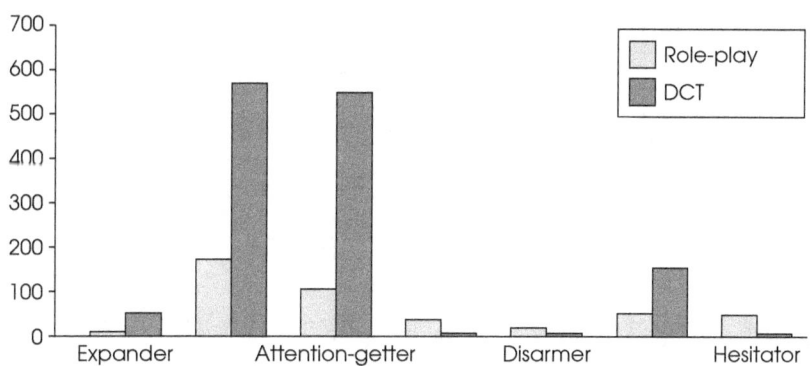

Figure 7.2 Task effects on subcategories of modification devices employed

As illustrated in this figure, more modification devices were employed in the discourse-completion test. However, we found particular cases where the use of modification devices seemed to be higher in the oral than in the written task. Softeners, disarmers and hesitators were more frequently employed in the role-play than in the discourse-completion test, whereas expanders, grounders, attention-getters and the word *please* were more often used in the written than in the oral task.

In examining statistically significant differences in the use of specific modification devices, we applied a paired *t*-test to our data. Results are displayed in Table 7.4:

Table 7.4 Task effects on types of modification devices used

	Mean	t	Sig.
Role-play expander	4.38E–02	4.772	0.000*
Discourse-completion test expander	0.31		
Role-play please	1.25	13.035	0.000*
Discourse-completion test please	3.77		
Role-play attention getter	0.74	13.681	0.000*
Discourse-completion test attention-getter	3.61		
Role-play softener	0.26	13.681	0.000*
Discourse-completion test softener	1.88E–02		
Role-play disarmer	8.75E–02	–2.567	0.011**
Discourse-completion test disarmer	1.88E–02		
Role-play grounder	0.29	7.605	0.000*
Discourse-completion test grounder	1.08		
Role-play hesitator	0.26	–5.236	0.000*
Discourse-completion test hesitator	6.25E–03		

*$p < 0.001$ **$p < 0.05$

On the basis of the results provided by the paired t-test above, differences in terms of modification devices employed are statistically significant. On the one hand, t-values corresponding to the more frequent use of expanders ($t = 4.772$), the word *please* ($t = 13.035$), attention-getters (13.681) and grounders ($t = 7.605$) in the discourse-completion test than in the oral task indicate a probability level of 0.000 ($p < 0.001$). On the other hand, the wider use of softeners ($t = -5.040$), disarmers ($t = -2.567$) and hesitators ($t = -5.236$) in the role-play task than in the written one accounted for a probability level of 0.011 ($p < 0.05$) in the case of disarmers and 0.000 ($p < 0.001$) regarding softeners and hesitation devices.

As has been previously mentioned, the fact that learners resorted to more elaborate modification devices in the discourse-completion test than in the oral task might be task-dependent. In this sense, lack of perceived time pressure in the written task might have allowed learners to note down reasons in performing the request (i.e grounder use). It might also have enabled them to use two or more different modification devices in accompanying one request formula (i.e. expander, *please*) in those cases where they felt the linguistic formula employed was not polite enough for the situation presented. This written task carried out individually also provided them with the chance to review their request formulations and see if these took into account a potential hearer (i.e. attention-getter). By the same token, we could state that the interaction involved in the oral task promoted the use of hesitation devices as well as the use of softeners and disarmers in softening the degree of imposition implied in the produced request formulae.

In order to further analyse task effects, we examined bilingual and monolingual learners' performance in the two tasks. Results from such analysis would provide us with an answer to the research question stated in the first subsection, which also relates to the hypothesis in this chapter. For this purpose, we applied a *t*-test for independent samples in our analysis of bilingual and monolingual learners' use of request strategies, as displayed in the following tables.

Mean scores displayed in Tables 7.5 and 7.6 show that bilingual learners made appropriate use of request strategies more often than their monolingual counterparts did in both the oral and the written task, with the exception of the use of indirect strategies in the oral task. However, findings from applying statistical test to our data only point to significant differences in learners' use of conventionally indirect strategies, while differences in the use of other strategy types were not statistically significant. These results further confirm bilingualism effects pointed out in Chapters 5 and 6, where bilingual learners always produced more conventionally indirect requests than monolingual participants, with a statistically significant difference in all such cases.

In this chapter, we have examined bilinguals' performance in an oral and a written task in an attempt to broaden the scope of findings deriving from testing our hypothesis. Bilingualism effects have not contradicted findings relating to the influence of the task type displayed in the present chapter (see Tables 7.1 and 7.2) and they have further confirmed results obtained in Chapters 5 and 6 of the present volume.

Table 7.5 Bilingual and monolingual subjects' use of request strategies in the oral task

		Mean	t	*Sig.*
Conventionally Indirect	Bilingual	5.54	−3.995	0.000*
	Monolingual	3.88		
Direct	Bilingual	0.68	0.372	0.2
	Monolingual	0.63		
Indirect	Bilingual	0.00	1	0.3
	Monolingual	0.00		

*$p<0.001$

Table 7.6 Bilingual and monolingual subjects' use of request strategies in the written task

		Mean	t	*Sig.*
Conventionally Indirect	Bilingual	8.46	−2.413	0.01*
	Monolingual	6.53		
Direct	Bilingual	1.44	−1.024	0.307
	Monolingual	1.21		
Indirect	Bilingual	0.18	−2.696	0.008
	Monolingual	0.00		

*$p<0.05$

Considering findings that refer to task effects on the use of linguistic request realisations and peripheral modification devices, we may assume that the nature of the task learners were required to carry out influenced their pragmatic production. Therefore, our results are in line with previous studies that report significant task effects on speech-act production, such as those of Hartford and Bardovi-Harlig (1992), Houck and Gass (1996) and Beebe and Cummings (1996). Regarding the wider range of strategies employed in the written than in the oral task, our study seems to confirm Beebe and Cummings' (1996) claim, which pointed out that contextual variables cannot be controlled in open role-plays, nor can the occurrence of a particular speech act be predicted. In this sense, it is not surprising that role-play moves did not always elicit requestive behaviour, since only prompts were provided and no further guidelines were provided.

The above-quoted authors compared oral with written data in the production of request forms and refusals by second language learners. Oral data revealed longer responses involving more turns. However, semantic formulas involved in the two tasks were similar. Also corresponding to their findings, we may say that our subjects' performance in the role-play task implied more than one turn, since it enabled learners to negotiate while producing the request act, as illustrated in the following example:

Example (1)

PROMPT A: *You are the human resources manager of a company. Your secretary has been arriving late for the last week and you wouldn't like him/her to come late again.*

S60: <Hola> Susan..eh,,, Good morning Susan!

S75: Good Morning!

S60: eh.. eh... **can you.. can you come to my office..?**...you arrived this moment? Eh... I want to talk with you.

S75: eh... yes?..what's the matter?

S60: eh.. during this last week eh... you... have been eh... arriving late and ...I don't know why.

S75: Oh! Eh... I'm sorry.. this this..haven't been again..

[S60 and S75: Monolingual Intermediate Subjects]

The above extract, taken from learners' recorded performances in the role-play task, shows that more than one turn was employed in that oral task as opposed to request acts used in the discourse-completion test. As shown in the following extract, learners merely wrote down one turn in request-formulae production. This fact may have been caused by the absence of an interlocutor in the written task.

Example (2)

SITUATION 1: *You have an appointment to see the doctor and you are sitting in the waiting room. It is getting late and you wonder whether your turn has passed. Suddenly, a nurse enters the room. What would you say?*

S50: Excuse me, nurse, what is the next number to see the doctor?

S32: Nurse, nurse, please. Why the doctor arrive late?

[S50: Intermediate bilingual subject]

[S32: Beginner bilingual subject]

Although our findings bear a certain degree of similarity to those of Beebe and Cummings (1996), we did not find a wider use of request formulations in the oral than in the written task. We should also note that our subjects were learning English as a foreign language, while most studies conducted within the field of interlanguage pragmatics focus on second language learners. We believe that the context in which a language is learned and the number of chances to use it affect not only acquisition processes, but also communicative competence and performance.

Task effects have been analysed in relation to the amount and type of linguistic request formulations and also to the learners' use of peripheral modification devices. These should also be understood as part of the entire request act, since they are one of the outstanding characteristics of real language use. The type of modification item employed varied according to the nature of the task in which it was employed. In this sense, the use of hesitators, softeners and disarmers seemed to be connected to the roleplay task, whereas grounders, expanders, attention-getters and the word *please* appeared to be related to the written task.

The type of task learners are engaged in has also received a great deal of attention in second language acquisition. We focused in particular on the influence of an open role-play and an open discourse-completion test on the learners' use of particular request formulas. Our third hypothesis predicted significant differences in the use of particular request realisations in the two task types. This hypothesis derived from research contrasting different elicitation methods (Kasper and Dahl, 1991; Sasaki, 1998), which pointed to the advantage of one method over another one. After analysing the data provided by the administration of the role-play and discourse-completion-test tasks, we observed significant dissimilarities in requestive behaviour. The written task elicited a larger number of request formulations than the oral task, whether these belonged to the conventionally indirect, direct or indirect subgroups. We have attributed this divergence to the fact that the written task was carried out individually, and thus no perceived time constraints were involved. Additionally, the written task was distributed after learners had been engaged in the oral task. In order to contrast task effects we included five situations in both tasks that were identical in terms of social parameters, degree of imposition involved and relationship between interlocutors. Owing to this fact, practice effects might have influenced learners' performance. However, our results also illustrated further influences that related to previous research (Beebe and Cummings, 1996).

In line with Beebe and Cummings' (1996) results, our subjects produced longer responses involving more than one turn in the open role-play task, whereas the discourse-completion test elicited one-turn request moves. The use of peripheral modification devices accompanying the request head seemed to be task-dependent. As shown in Figure 7.3 and in Table 7.2, the word *please*, attention-getters and grounders were most frequently employed in the discourse-completion test, while softeners, disarmers and hesitators were more often produced in the role-play task. In this sense, and taking account of previously described findings, we may assume that the hypothesis described in this chapter, which related to task effects on pragmatic production, was supported by our findings.

Conclusions

This chapter dealt with the influence of the task type on the subjects' use of request formulations and modification devices, as predicted by previous studies (Kasper and Dahl, 1991; Sasaki, 1998). In testing the hypothesis presented in the first section, we compared learners' performance in the open role-play with their use of requests in the open discourse-completion test. The oral task was carried out in pairs and the subjects' performance was tape-recorded, while the written task was done individually. In contrasting task effects on the subjects' use of request formulations, we included situations that were identical in terms of social parameters and degree of imposition involved, and we focused our analysis on the strategies elicited by these situations.

Results from applying a paired *t*-test showed significant differences in our subjects' use of request strategies, and such behaviour was considered task-dependent. We attributed this divergence to the fact that the written task was carried out individually and no perceived time constraints were involved. In our opinion, the presence of an interlocutor and the fact that our subjects' oral production was tape-recorded might have led to a decrease in the use of request formulations compared to the number amount employed in the discourse-completion test.

In line with Beebe and Cumming's (1996) study, our subjects presented longer responses involving more than one turn in the open role-play task, whereas the written task involved the use of one-turn request moves. The use of peripheral modification devices also appeared to be task-dependent. The particle *please*, attention-getters and grounders were frequently employed in the written task, while softeners, disarmers and hesitators were more often used in the role-play task. In this sense, and considering the above quoted findings. The hypothesis presented in this chapter was supported by our findings, which further confirm previous studies in the field of interlanguage pragmatics (those of Beebe and Cummings, 1996; Kasper and Dahl, 1991; Sasaki, 1998).

Request use might also be affected by other factors, as argued by Kasper (2000). According to this author, further research ought to examine the effect of individual factors on language learners' pragmatic competence. For this reason, we have also considered the learners' linguistic background and examined the effects of bilingualism on the beginner and intermediate subgroups.

Chapter 8
The Role of Bilingualism in Pragmatic Awareness

Hypothesis and Research Questions

In order to examine the effect of individual factors on the learners' pragmatic competence, we focused on our participants' linguistic background. We analysed the use and identification of request strategies on the part of Catalan/Castilian speakers learning English as a foreign language. In so doing, we attempted to meet some of the current needs for further research in two applied linguistics subfields, namely interlanguage pragmatics and third language acquisition. As quoted in Chapter 1, third language acquisition research has demonstrated the advantage of bilinguals over monolinguals with respect to metalinguistic skills (Jessner, 1997; Lasagabaster, 1997), and interactional competence (Jessner, 1999). However, few studies have been conducted in order to analyse the pragmatic competence of bilingual learners of a third language (Cenoz and Valencia, 1994; Fouser, 1997).

In order to shed more light on this relatively young field and on account of the increasing attention devoted to multilingualism and multilingual acquisition, we have studied bilingual and monolingual speakers learning a third language and have focused on their pragmatic awareness in evaluating the use of request strategies. Considering findings from previous research in the field of third language acquisition (see Chapter 1 for a detailed review), we formulated the following hypothesis:

> *Hypothesis 4: Bilingual learners studying English as a third language will show a higher degree of pragmatic awareness than monolingual learners. (Fouser, 1997; Jessner, 1999)*

Additionally, the following research questions were formulated order to further analyse the effects of bilingualism:

RQ1: To what extent will bilingual learners' awareness differ from that of monolingual subjects?

RQ2: Will bilingual subjects provide a wider range of reasons to justify their judgements than monolingual learners?

RQ3: Will bilingual subjects provide more suggestions for the inappropriate expressions they are required to evaluate than monolingual subjects?

RQ4: Will bilingual subjects offer more reasons related to politeness phenomena in justifying their evaluation than monolingual learners?

RQ5: Will bilingual learners identify inappropriate and appropriate request linguistic realisations more successfully than monolingual subjects?

RQ6: Will bilingualism affect pragmatic production?

Results and Discussion

In Chapters 5, 6 and 7, we have dealt with hypotheses that were related to pragmatic production issues, since we examined the influence of instruction, proficiency-effects and the influence of the task type on our subjects' use of request-act formulations and the peripheral modification devices accompanying them. The hypothesis presented in this chapter has a different perspective from the previous ones, in that it examines two themes previously mentioned in Chapter 1, pragmatic awareness and the effects of bilingualism on third language acquisition and use. According to this fourth hypothesis, those subjects learning English as a third language will show a higher degree of pragmatic awareness than monolingual learners (Fouser, 1997; Jessner, 1999).

In order to test the above assumption, we examined data obtained from the subjects' performance in the discourse-evaluation test, in which learners were required to evaluate the appropriateness of particular request formulations for specific situations. As has already been mentioned in Chapter 4, subjects could write down their suggestions in cases where they found an inappropriate formulation and they were also asked to note down the reasons for their evaluation both when it was positive (i.e. appropriate) and when it was negative (inappropriate). These reasons could be written in their own mother tongue, as half of our subjects were beginner students and we were not interested in pragmatic production but rather in awareness; proficiency effects were not taken into account. Regarding the learners' performance in the discourse-evaluation test, we carried out a quantitative and a qualitative analysis on the basis of the appropriate and inappropriate evaluations conducted, the appropriateness of the suggestions provided, the number of reasons presented for their evaluative comments, and the reasons that led to their assessment of politeness issues. Differences between monolingual and bilingual subjects are illustrated in Figure 8.1.

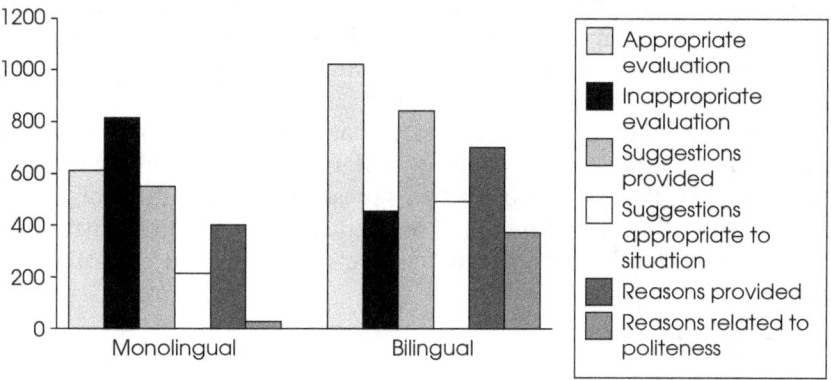

Figure 8.1 The influence of bilingualism on evaluating request-act use

Considering the results presented above, it seems that bilingual subjects outperformed their monolingual counterparts in recognising pragmatic failure, in providing suggestions for improvement and in justifying their evaluative comments. As shown by the first two items in Figure 8.1 (which refer to the acknowledgement of the degree of appropriateness of a given request routine to a particular situation), bilingual subjects gave a better performance in selecting those expressions that seemed more convenient for the description provided. When noting down their suggestions in cases where request routines were considered inappropriate, bilingual subjects also displayed a higher degree of pragmatic awareness compared with monolingual learners, as the former provided a wider range of suggestions and these suggestions seemed to be made on the basis of the context provided (i.e. situation).

The last items examined and illustrated in Figure 8.1 refer to the learners' comments on their performance, that is, the reasons provided by learners when justifying their evaluation. In our view, these features might be considered to be of the utmost importance in examining pragmatic behaviour, since they indicate the learners' understanding of the task they are performing, and they also enable us to acknowledge to what extent their pragmatic awareness truly deals with pragmatic (and not grammatical) issues. If subjects had merely focused on the grammatical nature of formulations employed in previous tests and presented during the training period, they could present suggestions that involved other formulations but could not possibly justify either their choice or their evaluation on pragmatic grounds. Instead, they would have merely concentrated on formal matters, leaving aside other contextual issues (e.g. participants, status distance, degree of obligation, degree of imposition). Bearing this idea in mind, we introduced these two items in the discourse-evaluation test so that we could present an in-depth analysis of the learners' degree of pragmatic awareness.

According to Figure 8.1, we may state that monolingual learners did not seem to present as many reasons as bilingual subjects in justifying their evaluation. Furthermore, those reasons presented were highly politeness-dependent in the case of bilingual learners, as opposed to the nature of reasons provided by monolingual subjects, as shown in the following extract:

Example (1)

Situation 2: You are sharing a flat with other students and today it is your turn to do the washing up. However, you have an important exam tomorrow, so you tell one of your flatmates: Do the washing up for me. I have to study for an important exam.

S11: Appropriate Reason: 'És apropiada per qué hi ha una relació de confiança entre els estudiants' (It is appropriate given the closed relationship between these students).

S90: Inappropriate Reason: 'Creo que sería más apropiado hacer la pregunta, no puedes dar por supuesto que el otro lo puede hacer'. (I think formulating the question may be more appropriate, you cannot take for granted the fact that your interlocutor will do it for you)

[S11: Beginner Bilingual Subject]

[S90: Beginner Monolingual Subjects]

Although Figure 8.1 above seems to signal out important differences between bilingual and monolingual learners in terms of pragmatic awareness, a *t*-test was also applied to our data in order to discern if these differences were statistically significant.

Table 8.1 Effects of bilingualism on pragmatic awareness

	Mean	t	F
Monolingual – appropriate evaluation	8.04	–7.253	19.344**
Bilingual – appropriate evaluation	13.03		
Monolingual – inappropriate evaluation	10.69	6.807	16.934*
Bilingual – inappropriate evaluation	5.95		
Monolingual – suggestions provided	6.98	–5.758	0.918*
Bilingual – suggestions provided	10.98		
Monolingual – appropriate suggestions	2.83	–9.9009	0.712*
Bilingual – appropriate suggestions	6.30		
Monolingual – reasons provided	5.18	–6.880	0.621*
Bilingual – reasons provided	9.89		
Monolingual – reasons related to politeness	0.38	–11.942	102.749*
Bilingual – reasons related to politeness	5.05		

*$p < 0.001$ **$p < 0.05$

As illustrated in Table 8.2, all differences reported above between groups (bilingual vs monolingual) are statistically significant. In this sense, we may assume that our fourth hypothesis, which predicted a higher degree of pragmatic awareness on the part of learners of English as a third language, is supported by our findings. This fact may partly confirm Jessner's (1999) assumption about the advantage of bilingual subjects learning a third language in terms of their interactional competence.

In formulating the hypothesis presented in this chapter (see the first subsection), we identified certain research questions that awaited an answer. We have attempted to provide responses to all of these questions. Our results indicate that bilingual learners' awareness differs significantly from that of monolingual subjects in the discourse-evaluation test. Bilingual learners identified appropriate and inappropriate request moves in particular situations more accurately than monolingual subjects. This latter group of subjects did not provide as many suggestions relating to the situation presented as bilingual subjects did. Significant differences were also found in the reasons provided by learners in justifying their evaluation and regarding the connection of such reasons to politeness issues.

After confirming our hypothesis on the advantage of bilingual over monolingual learners in pragmatic awareness, we attempted to discern whether such a difference would also be illustrated in the participants' pragmatic production. We have observed that our learners' use of specific request forms was influenced by the instructional process they were engaged in (see Chapter 5), their proficiency level (see Chapter 6), and the task type they were required to perform (see Chapter 7). One factor we have not considered so far is that of the effects of bilingualism on pragmatic production. In examining the effect of knowing two languages on using a third one (i.e. English in this particular case), we considered the global use of request acts and the use of specific strategy types (conventionally indirect, direct and indirect) on the part of bilingual and monolingual subjects.

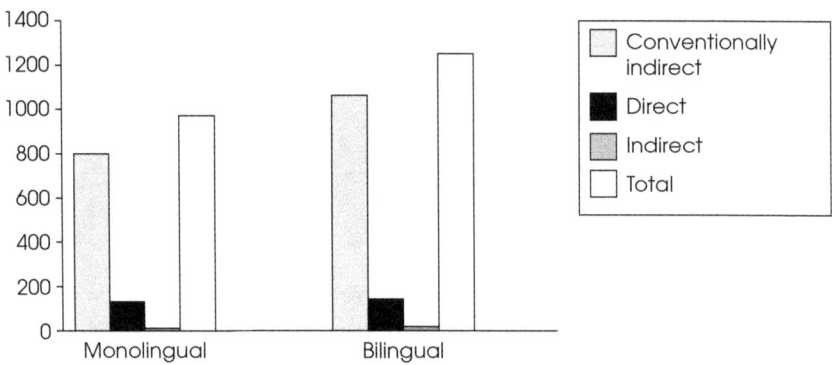

Figure 8.2 Effects of bilingualism on pragmatic production

As shown in Figure 8.2, the global use of request formulations was higher on the part of bilingual than monolingual subjects. Regarding the strategy types used, we observe that bilingual learners used conventionally indirect requests more frequently than their monolingual partners. The former also seemed to employ direct and indirect formulations more often than monolingual subjects, although the difference in the use of these two strategy types might not be as significant as in the case of conventionally indirect formulations. In order to ascertain the divergence in bilingual and monolingual learners' pragmatic production, we made use of a *t*-test for independent samples.

Table 8.2 Effects of bilingualism on pragmatic production

	Mean	t	F
Monolingual – conventionally indirect	10.40	−4.363	1.912*
Bilingual – conventionally indirect	14.00		
Monolingual – direct	1.89	−0.607	0.375
Bilingual – direct	2.06		
Monolingual – indirect	3.75E–02	−2.730	34.339**
Bilingual – indirect	0.19		
Monolingual – global strategy use	12.33	−4.270	0.251*
Bilingual – global strategy use	16.25		

*$p < 0.001$ **$p < 0.05$

According to Table 8.2, we might say that significant differences were found between bilingual and monolingual subjects' global use of request forms. Conventionally indirect forms were also employed more often by bilingual than by monolingual learners, these differences being statistically significant. The level of probability related to differences in indirect strategy use on the part of bilingual and monolingual participants was lower ($p < 0.05$) than significance levels in conventionally indirect use ($p < 0.001$), though still statistically significant. Both bilingual and monolingual subjects resorted to direct request forms and no significant differences were found. These findings indicate that bilingual learners also outperformed monolingual subjects in the use of request formulations, with the exception of direct linguistic formulations.

As Jessner (1997) predicted, interactional competence seems to be further developed in bilingual than in monolingual subjects. Confirmation of that fact comes from the subjects of the present study, who were learning English as a third language and whose performance in the use and identification of appropriate request formulations was examined. We have reported a global advantage of bilingual over monolingual learners of English as a foreign language regarding both pragmatic production and pragmatic awareness. We believe that our findings might relate to the dynamic view of multilingualism suggested by scholars such as Herdina and Jessner (2000) and Cenoz (2000) (see the section on 'Third Language Acquisition' in Chapter 1 for a further description). According to these authors, learning a third language does not posit quantitative but qualitative changes in the overall linguistic system of the learner. New skills and techniques thus arise from learners' previous learning experiences and also from their using more than one language. This might also have been the case for our bilingual learners, who reported a higher degree of pragmatic competence than monolingual subjects.

Furthermore, previous research (Lambert, 1999; Oskaar, 1990) has pointed out the advantage of bilingual over monolingual learners of an additional language in communication skills. As reported in the section entitled 'Learning a Third Language' in Chapter 1, bilingualism has been defined as providing subjects with a deeper insight into language (Lambert, 1999), a highly developed ability to communicate and interpret communication (Jessner, 1997) and a wider amount of pragmatic knowledge (Fouser 1997). Our results seem to support previous studies and they also point to the advantage of third language learners over monolingual learners of English in using linguistic request routines and in their degree of pragmatic awareness relating to such use.

The data analysis relating to this fourth hypothesis aimed at providing a bridge between research in two applied linguistics subfields, namely interlanguage pragmatics and third language acquisition. We predicted an advantage of bilingual over monolingual subjects in terms of pragmatic awareness. Not only was this hypothesis supported by our findings, but our data also showed better performance by bilingual subjects in using request formulations. The assumed arousal of new skills deriving from Herdina and Jessner's (1999) suggested dynamic model of multilingualism was confirmed by our findings, since pragmatic awareness seemed to be more developed in bilingual than in monolingual learners. This issue also corroborates Fouser's (1997) results, which suggested a higher degree of pragmatic awareness on the part of learners of English as a third language. Furthermore, as mentioned before, results confirmed Oskaar's (1990) and Jessner's (1999) statements on the advantage of bilingual learners in terms of their interactional competence.

Given the significant differences of our results and the ascertained advantage of bilingual subjects, which also seemed to confirm some of the existing theories in the third language acquisition subfield, we may state that further research on that subfield is needed for different reasons. On the one hand, the fact that bilingualism or multilingualism is the norm in many European countries, as in the case of Spain, points to the need for studies investigating the actual sociolinguistic characteristics of language learners. On the other hand, results presenting a better performance on the part of bilingual or multilingual subjects seem to call for a deeper focus of studies from acquisitional perspectives on the effect of knowing more than one language in acquiring an additional one. If the connection between results from the interlanguage pragmatics and third language acquisition studies provides us with interesting findings, these should be further considered in focusing on other aspects of real-life interaction. In this way, we could better understand both our learners' development of pragmatic competence and the actual processes involved in third language acquisition. A deeper knowledge in this area would help us foster language learning development in different sociolinguistic and sociocultural settings. In doing this, we would provide reasons for the variety that underlies current linguistic and pragmatic behaviour.

Conclusions

In testing our fourth hypothesis we entered the realm of a different applied linguistics field, namely that of third language acquisition. This hypothesis predicted that bilingual subjects would show a clear advantage over monolingual learners in their degree of pragmatic awareness. To test this hypothesis we analysed results obtained from a discourse-evaluation test, where learners justified their evaluation by providing reasons and suggestions for those request formulas they found inappropriate. We carried out a quantitative and qualitative analysis of the data on the basis of the appropriate and inappropriate evaluations conducted, the appropriateness of the suggestions provided, the number of reasons presented for the participants' evaluations and the reasons that led to politeness issues. Thus, we took into account reasons which included references to sociolinguistic features, the social distance between interlocutors, the degree of imposition in making the request, and the nature of the situation.

Results obtained by means of a t-test statistical procedure demonstrated that bilingual subjects' degree of pragmatic awareness was higher than that of their monolingual counterparts. In the light of these results, we decided to further examine the role of bilingualism in pragmatic production by comparing the bilingual and monolingual subjects' performance in the oral and written tasks (i.e. role-play and discourse-completion test). Findings not only showed that was our hypothesis supported, but they also denoted better performance of bilingual subjects in using request formulations.

The stimulation of new skills deriving from Herdina and Jessner's (2002) suggested model of multilingualism was confirmed by our findings, since pragmatic awareness was proved to be highly developed in bilingual subjects compared to monolingual ones. Furthermore, our results also confirmed Fouser's (1996), Oskaar's (1990) and Jessner's (1999) studies, which pointed to a higher degree of pragmatic awareness on the part of third language learners of English and to the advantage of bilingual learners in terms of their interactional competence.

Chapter 9
Pragmatic Production and Awareness of Third Language Learners: Summarising the Findings

This last chapter focuses on summarising the main findings of the research described in previous chapters of this second part of the book. The aim of the study described was to analyse the degree of pragmatic competence and pragmatic awareness of bilingual and monolingual learners of English in a foreign language context, namely that of the Valencian Community. Bearing in mind findings in the applied linguistics subfields of third language acquisition and interlanguage, our study was guided by four working hypotheses, which were tackled in different chapters.

> Chapter 5: *Pragmatic instruction will affect the learners' degree of pragmatic competence.* (Kasper, 1997; Kasper and Rose, 1999)

> Chapter 6: *There will be a mismatch between beginner and intermediate learners in those developmental stages concerning grammatical and pragmatic competence.* (Kasper, 1997; Kasper and Rose, 1999)

> Chapter 7: *The task performed, whether it be an oral or written task (i.e. role-play vs discourse-completion test) will affect the choice and use of request realisations.* (Kasper, 2000; Rose, 1999; Sasaki, 1999)

> Chapter 8: *Bilingual learners studying English as a third language will show a higher degree of pragmatic awareness than monolingual learners.* (Fouser, 1997; Jessner, 1999)

These hypotheses addressed, firstly, the role of explicit instruction in fostering learners' pragmatic competence in Chapter 5; and secondly, corresponding to Chapter 6, the role of the learners' proficiency level in producing pragmatic items in the target language, particularly those of linguistic request-act realisations and peripheral modification devices. Chapter 7 dealt with the influence of the task type that subjects were required to perform (those of an open discourse-completion test, an open role-play and a discourse-evaluation test) in the production of request acts. Finally, Hypothesis 4 in Chapter 8 predicted that bilingualism would positively affect the learners' degree of pragmatic awareness. In Chapter 8 we predicted that bilingual speakers would show a clear advantage over monolingual learners of English in evaluating the use of linguistic request formulations in particular situations.

Tutoring sessions were held during a semester and they followed Kasper's (1996) suggested stages, those of description, explanation and discussion of pragmatic features. In Chapter 5, we first contrasted the subjects' use of linguistic request-act formulations and peripheral modification devices in the pre-test with routines employed in the post-test. Thus analysis was both quantitative and qualitative. We took into account the total number of strategies employed, on the one hand, and the differences in strategy type used in these two tests, on the other.

Results from the paired t-test pointed to a significant increase in both the number and type of strategies employed in the post-test compared to their use in the pre-test. Subjects resorted more often to conventionally indirect and direct request forms in the post-test. Additionally, we also reported subjects' tendency to use a wider range of peripheral modification devices after the study. In this sense, the hypothesis in this chapter was supported by our findings, and it also confirmed previous studies that attributed a positive role to the explicit teaching of pragmatic items in the target language (Norris and Ortega, 2000; Olshtain and Cohen, 1990).

In the light of the positive results obtained, we decided to further examine the role of instruction in our subjects' performance. We compared the use of request formulas in the first tasks (Role-play 1 and Discourse-completion Test 1), distributed before the instructional process had begun, and in tasks administered immediately after tutoring sessions had finished (Role-play 2 and Discourse-completion Test 2). Results from the paired t-test did not show important dissimilarities in the global number of strategies employed. However, the use of particular strategy types and peripheral modification items differed significantly in both sets of tasks. Thus, there were qualitative (though not quantitative) differences during the training period, as participants resorted to certain strategy types in completing Role-play 1 and Discourse-completion Test 1, and showed a preference for other linguistic request realisations in Role-play 2 and Discourse-completion Test 2. In addition to that, they also denoted a clear preference for resorting to a particular strategy type, that of the conventionally indirect subgroup. Coinciding with Ellis' (1992) study, our subjects' performance varied as instruction progressed, thus indicating the positive role of tutoring sessions in foreign language learners' use of particular formulae in request acts.

In an attempt to address the role of bilingualism in our subjects' production and to further analyse the effects of instruction, we contrasted bilingual and monolingual learners' performance before and after being engaged in instructional sessions. Results from such analysis showed that bilingual learners employed more conventionally indirect strategies than the monolingual group both before and after instruction had taken place. Differences between the two learner groups were statistically significant, and they pointed to the advantage of third language learners regarding their use of conventionally indirect request strategies. However, learners' use of direct strategies did not seem to differ significantly, and for that reason we have argued for the need for further research on the potential interaction between the effects of instruction and bilingualism in the pragmatic production of language learners.

Chapter 6 dealt with proficiency-level effects and pragmatic production. In testing the hypothesis of this chapter we contrasted the use of request-act formulations by subjects at beginner and intermediate proficiency levels in the oral production (Role-plays 1 and 2) and written production tasks (Discourse-completion Tests 1 and 2). Findings showed that intermediate learners outperformed beginners in both quantity and quality in using request forms. Nevertheless, we should also point out that no differences between these two learner groups were found regarding the use of specific request formulations, namely those of the desire (conventionally indirect) and performative (direct) subgroups. This means that our second hypothesis was only partially confirmed.

In interpreting these findings we have highlighted two main concerns. On the one hand, previous studies reporting no differences in their subjects' pragmatic production dealt with intermediate and advanced learners, which was not the case for us. In fact, according to Kasper and Rose (2002), none of those studies had focused on learners at a beginner proficiency level, and that was the reason why we dealt with a beginner group in our study. On the other hand, although no clear mismatch between our subjects' linguistic and pragmatic competence was reported by our findings, they bore certain similarities to longitudinal studies involving beginner learners (Ellis, 1992, 1997). Like Ellis' subjects (1992), ours showed a tendency to use more mitigation items and request realisations in line with their proficiency level.

Besides this, learners' characteristics might also have affected our results, since after contrasting bilingual and monolingual learners' performance with that of subjects at both a beginner and an intermediate proficiency level, we found that conventionally indirect strategies were more frequently employed by the bilingual than by the monolingual subgroups. Hence these findings might have confirmed results reported before on the advantage of bilingual learners even after being engaged in an instructional period (see Chapter 5). Nevertheless, another study drawing a link between the role of bilingualism and the learners' proficiency level might provide us with further clues about variables affecting pragmatic development in learners of English. Given our interest in ascertaining the influence of specific variables in our learners' pragmatic production, we also considered task effects, as displayed in Chapter 7 of the book.

Chapter 7 dealt with the influence of the task type on the subjects' use of request formulations and modification items, as predicted by previous studies (Kasper and Dahl, 1991; Sasaki, 1998). In testing the hypothesis presented in this chapter we compared learners' production in the role-play with their use of requests in the discourse-completion test. The oral task involved pair work and the subjects' performance was recorded, while the written task was done individually. In contrasting task effects on the participants' use of request strategies, we included situations that were identical in terms of social parameters and degree of imposition involved, and we focused our analysis on the formulas elicited by these situations.

Results from applying a paired *t*-test showed significant differences in our subjects' requestive behaviour, with such behaviour being task-dependent. We attributed this divergence to the fact that the written task was carried out individually and no perceived time constraints were involved. In our opinion, the presence of an interlocutor and the fact that our subjects' oral production was tape-recorded might have prompted a decrease in the use of request formulations compared to the number employed in the discourse-completion test.

In line with Beebe and Cumming's (1996) study, our subjects presented longer responses involving more than one turn in the open role-play task, whereas the written task involved the use of one-turn request moves. The use of peripheral modification devices also appeared to be task-dependent. The particle *please,* attention-getters and grounders were frequently employed in the written task, while softeners, disarmers and hesitators were more often used in the role-play task. In this sense, and considering the above-quoted findings, the hypothesis of Chapter 7 was supported by our findings, which further confirm previous studies in the field of interlanguage pragmatics (those of Beebe and Cummings, 1996; Kasper and Dahl, 1991 and Sasaki, 1998).

As it was a case of procedures testing those hypotheses included in Chapters 5 and 6 described above, we further analysed participants' performance by taking into account their linguistic background, that is, the effects of bilingualism. Chapter 7 dealt with the influence of the task type, so we examined bilinguals' and monolinguals' request production in the oral and written task. Results were in line with those relating to previous hypotheses, as bilingual learners employed more conventionally indirect requests than monolingual learners did, both in the oral and written task. Additionally, these findings also confirmed results from the paired *t*-test reported before, which signalled out the fact that learners produced more request strategies in the written than in the oral task.

As has been previously mentioned, bilingualism affected learners' pragmatic production as far as request strategies were involved. We analysed bilingualism effects on two different occasions – i.e. before and after being engaged in explicit instruction sessions – (Chapter 5), on learners of different proficiency levels (Chapter 6) and in different task types (Chapter 7). Yet, at that stage, we focused merely on contrasting bilingual and monolingual learners' production, and we understand pragmatic competence as being made up of both pragmalinguistic and sociopragmatic components (see Chapter 2). In an attempt to deal with this last aspect, we asked our learners to evaluate the appropriateness of particular request realisations to specific contexts in testing the hypothesis of Chapter 8.

Results from the study described in this second part of the book suggest a research agenda for the future in the field of both interlanguage pragmatics and third language acquisition, and they also have important pedagogical implications for foreign language learning settings. One of our aims was to ascertain the role of instruction in the development of pragmatic competence in foreign language learning. According to our findings, and in line with those of previous research, we may say that by teaching pragmatic items explicitly, we can improve our learners' degree of pragmatic competence in the target language. We find this issue of utmost importance in foreign language settings, as learners do not have the chance of using or being exposed to input in the target language outside the classroom setting. Owing to this, it seems advisable to provide learners with relevant input and with opportunities for practice. Additionally, focusing on awareness-raising tasks in understanding pragmatic behaviour may also encourage pragmatic development in foreign language learners, an issue which should be further researched.

The fact that intermediate learners outperformed beginner learners in the use of linguistic request realisations seems to suggest that fostering learners' linguistic competence in the target language may promote pragmatic competence, particularly at lower levels. This idea might be connected to current studies (Alcón, 1999; Fotos, 1998; García Mayo, 2001) that deal with issues of form and also to Bardovi-Harlig's (2000) proposal, which suggests examining the interlanguage part of interlanguage pragmatics. This last author argues in favour of analysing those linguistic formulae involved in the realisation of pragmatic items.

Additionally, one needs to focus on those task types that learners might be required to perform both when participating in research and in the language classroom, in two senses. On the one hand, we may analyse those tasks that better elicit pragmatic behaviour or account for more realistic language use. On the other hand, we should also consider tasks that enable learners to reflect on pragmatic issues and which might promote their pragmatic competence at the same time. We have singled out task effects in eliciting requestive behaviour; however we have not dealt with the pedagogical value of these tasks, as learners did not receive feedback on their performance in those tasks carried out after the instructional process. The inclusion of rejoinder devices in tasks eliciting pragmatic production has been considered, as they might be better fosterers of the acquisition of certain pragmatic items than those tasks not including them. Besides, tasks that do not contain rejoinder or adjoining devices have been acknowledged as providing researchers with more authentic language use and as presenting learners with further opportunities for practising pragmatic aspects of the target language in a setting resembling real life (Kasper and Dahl, 1991). For these reasons, different task types, oral and written, with and without rejoining devices should be employed in the foreign language classroom.

These tasks may be graded so that learners at different proficiency levels can perform them. In our study we have made use of a discourse-completion test, a role-play and a discourse-evaluation task, but other task types such as cartoon oral-production tasks or video evaluation comments can be employed. Research into the extent to which these tasks elicit pragmatic behaviour or metapragmatic awareness is also needed in order to understand processes underlying the pragmatic development of foreign language learners.

Further research on individual factors affecting pragmatic development is needed (Kasper, 2000; Kasper and Rose, 2002). Our research indicates that knowing more than two languages benefits the development of pragmatic competence (see Chapters 5, 6 and 7) and the degree of pragmatic awareness (see Chapter 8). Therefore, existing bilingual or multilingual syllabi in primary or secondary education might be assumed as fostering the acquisition and use of an additional language. In the university setting, we have observed advantages of bilingual over monolingual students belonging to the Valencian Community, but further studies in this and other multilingual contexts are needed to confirm the findings of the present study. Bilingual subjects of the present study were educated within an old bilingual programme in primary school. We wonder whether research on existing bilingual programmes in the Valencian Community would provide us with similar results. Special attention could be paid to all existing educational programmes aimed at fostering multilingualism, as presented in Chapter 3, namely PIP, PIL, PEV and Enriched Bilingualism, recently incorporated into primary schools in the Valencian Community. By comparing subjects from these programmes, we could find out which curriculum and educational conditions best promote the acquisition of English as a foreign language.

To sum up, our study has proved the benefits of bilingualism in promoting pragmatic competence and pragmatic awareness among learners of English as a foreign language. In addition to that, we have ascertained the positive role of explicit instruction, the influence of resorting to various task types and the effect of the learners' proficiency level on producing particular linguistic formulations for request acts and peripheral modification devices. The results obtained have led us to suggest the possible advantages of including pragmatic aspects of the target language in current curricula at different educational levels, those of primary school, secondary school and university, thereby including learners at different proficiency levels and resorting to various task types in eliciting pragmatic behaviour. The following suggestions for further research derive from our findings:

(1) In order to further test the role of instruction in the development of learners' pragmatic competence, further contrastive analyses are needed on subjects who have, and those who have not, received explicit instruction on pragmatic issues. We have particularly focused on request acts, but other speech acts and pragmatic aspects could also be analysed.
(2) The extent to which different task types elicit pragmatic behaviour could be further examined by focusing on learners of different proficiency levels (i.e. beginner, intermediate and advanced) in the target language.
(3) By comparing the pragmatic performance of learners engaged in the different bilingual programmes that now coexist in the Valencian Community, we could better account for those factors enhancing pragmatic development in multilingual settings.
(4) The results obtained in the Valencian Community should be compared with those obtained from studies carried out in other

bilingual communities that include similar bilingual programmes (i.e. Catalonia or the Basque Country). Such a comparison might help us identify those factors that best facilitate the acquisition and use of a third language.

Although our study is subject to limitations (i.e. it addressed only female participants of a similar age group and it focused on one particular bilingual community and one specific pragmatic item, that of request acts), we understand that the results we obtained have contributed to broadening the scope of investigation in the fields of interlanguage pragmatics and third language acquisition, while opening research avenues to be explored in the future.

We have attempted to make a connection between research from the areas of third language acquisition and interlanguage pragmatics. In our opinion, by examining pragmatic issues from a multilingual framework, it should be possible to meet the needs for identifying the pragmatic development of foreign language learners, on the one hand, and for discovering those factors affecting the acquisition and use of a third language, on the other. This would allow us to address two facts that have been traditionally denied or only partially tackled: those of (1) pragmatic competence from an acquisitional perspective with a focus on individual variables (i.e. multilingualism); and (2) multilingualism in foreign language learning and use with a focus on pragmatic competence. A shift is then needed from first language pragmatics to the acquisition of pragmatics in foreign language contexts, and also from second to third language acquisition perspectives. Only in this way might we address the reality in most European communities, as seen in the case of the Valencian Community tackled in the present study.

References

Albanèse, J.F. (1985) Language lateralisation in English – French bilinguals. *Brain and Language* 24, 284–96.
Albert, M.L. and Obler, L.K. (1978) *The Bilingual Brain: Neuropsychological and Neurolinguistic Aspects of Bilingualism*. New York: Academic Press.
Alcón, E. (1994) Negotiation, foreign language awareness and acquisition in the Spanish secondary context. *International Journal of Psycholinguistics* 10, 83–96.
Alcón, E. (1997) Cognitive approaches for explaining the phenomena of second language acquisition and second language use in communication. *Communication and Cognition* 30, 7–28.
Alcón, E. (2000a) Learner-training towards autonomy in the Spanish university context. In R. Ribé (ed.) *Developing Learner Autonomy in Foreign Language Learning*. Barcelona: Promociones y Publicaciones Universitarias.
Alcón, E. (2000b) Desarrollo de la competencia discursiva oral en el aula de lenguas extranjeras: Perspectives metodológicas y de investigación. In C. Muñoz (ed.) *La Adquisición de Segundas Lenguas en el Medio Escolar*. Madrid: Ariel.
Alcón, E. and Codina, V. (1996) The impact of gender on negotiation and vocabulary learning in a situation of interaction. *International Journal of Applied Psycholinguistics* 12, 21–35.
Alcón, E. and Guzmán J.R. (1995) Interlanguage modifications in NS–NNS oral interactions: A study in an English and Catalan language learning context. *Paper presented at the International Conference of Languages in Contact*. Valencia (Spain).
Alcón, E. and Tricker, D. (2000) The use of *well* in spoken interaction: An example of what language teachers and learners can get from analysing spoken discourse. In P. Gallardo and E. Llurdà (eds) *Proceedings of the 22nd International Conference of Aedean*. Lleida: Servei de Publicacions Universitat de Lleida.
Álvarez, P.A. (1984) The relationship between bilingualism and nonverbal creative behaviour among limited-English proficient and Spanish-English proficient hispanic girls of primary school age. *Dissertation Abstracts International* 45, 121–A. University Microfilms No. 84–109, 494.
Andersen, R. (1983) Introduction: A language acquisition interpretation of pidginization and creolization. In R. Andersen (ed.) *Pidginization and Creolization as Language Acquisition*. Rowley, MA: Newbury House.
Andrews, R. (1977) Aspects of language lateralization correlated with familial handedness. *Neuropsychologia* 15, 769–78.
Auer, P. (1997) *Code-Switching in Conversation: Language, Interaction and Identity*. London: Routledge.
Austin, J.L. (1962) *How to Do Things with Words*. Harvard University, William James Lectures 1955. Oxford: Oxford University Press.

Bachman, L.F. (1990) *Fundamental Considerations in Language Testing.* Oxford: Oxford University Press.
Bain, B. and Yu, A. (1980) Cognitive consequences of raising children bilingually: One parent, one language. *Canadian Journal of Psychology* 34, 304–13.
Baker, C. (1996) *Foundations of Bilingual Education and Bilingualism.* Clevedon: Multilingual Matters.
Bardovi-Harlig, K. (1999) Exploring the interlanguage of interlanguage pragmatics: A research agenda for acquisitional pragmatics. *Language Learning* 49, 677–713.
Bardovi-Harlig, K. (2001) Evaluating the empirical evidence: Grounds for instruction in pragmatics? In K. Rose and G. Kasper (eds) *Pragmatics and Language Teaching.* Cambridge: Cambridge University Press.
Bardovi-Harlig, K. and Dörnyei, Z. (1998) Do language learners recognise pragmatic violations? Pragmatic versus grammatical awareness in instructed L2 learning. *TESOL Quarterly* 32, 233–62.
Bardovi-Harlig, K. and Hartford, B.S. (1990) Congruence in native and nonnative conversations: Status balance in the academic advising session. *Language Learning* 40, 467–501.
Bardovi-Harlig, K. and Hartford, B.S. (1993) Learning the rules of academic talk. A longitudinal study of pragmatic change. *Studies in Second Language Acquisition* 15, 279–304.
Barraja-Rohan, A. and Pritchard, C.R. (1997) *Beyond Talk.* Melbourne: Western Melbourne Institute of TAFE.
Barron, A. (2003) *Acquisition in Interlanguage Pragmatics.* Amsterdam: John Benjamins.
Beebe, L.M. and Cummings, M.C. (1996) Natural speech act data versus written questionnaire data: How data collection method affects speech act performance. In S. Gass and J. Neu (eds) *Speech Acts across Cultures. Challenges to Communication in a Second Language.* Berlin: Mouton de Gruyter.
Ben-Zeev, S. (1977) The influence of bilingualism on cognitive strategy and cognitive development. *Child Development* 48, 1009–18.
Bergman, C.R. (1976) Interference vs independent development in infant bilingualism. In G.D. Keller, R.V. Taeschner and S. Viera (eds) *Bilingualism in the Bicentennial and Beyond.* New York: Bilingual Press.
Bergman, M.L. and Kasper, G. (1993) Perception and performance in native and nonative apologizing. In G. Kasper and S. Blum-Kulka (eds) *Interlanguage Pragmatics.* New York: Oxford University Press.
Berns, M. (1990) 'Second' and 'foreign' in second language acquisition/foreign language learning: A sociolinguistic perspective. In B. van Patten and J.F. Lee (eds) *Second Language Acquisition – Foreign Language Learning.* Clevedon: Multilingual Matters.
Bialystok, E. (1982) On the relationship between knowing and using forms. *Applied Linguistics* 3, 181–206.
Bialystok, E. (1984) Strategies in interlanguages learning and performance. In A. Davies, C. Criper and A.P.R. Howatt (eds) *Interlanguage: Proceedings of the Seminar in Honour of Pit Corder.* Edinburgh: Edinburgh University Press.
Bialystok, E. (1988) Levels of bilingualism and levels of linguistic awareness. *Developmental Psychology* 24, 560–67.
Bialystok, E. (1991) *Language Processing in Bilingual Children.* Cambridge: Cambridge University Press.

Bialystok, E. (2001) *Bilingualism in Development. Language, Literacy and Cognition*. Cambridge: Cambridge University Press.
Bild, E.R. and Swain, M. (1989) Minority language students in a French immersion programme. Their French proficiency. *Journal of Multilingual and Multicultural Development* 10, 255–74.
Björklund, S. and Suni, I. (2000) The role of English as a L3 in a Swedish immersion programme in Finland: Impacts on language teaching and language relations. In J. Cenoz and U. Jessner (eds) *English in Europe. The Acquisition of a Third Language*. Clevedon: Multilingual Matters.
Bloomfield, L. (1933) *Language*. New York: Holt.
Blum-Kulka, S. (1983) Interpreting and performing speech acts in a second language: A cross-cultural study of Hebrew and English. In N. Wolfson and E. Judd (eds) *Sociolinguistics and Language Acquisition*. Rowley, MA: Newbury House.
Blum-Kulka, S. (1991) Interlanguage pragmatics: The case of requests. In R. Phillipson, E. Kellerman, L. Selinker, M. Sharwood Smith and M. Swain (eds) *Foreign/Second Language Pedagogy Research*. Clevedon: Multilingual Matters.
Blum-Kulka, S. (1996) Introducción a la pragmática del interlenguaje. In J. Cenoz and J.F. Valencia (eds) *La Competencia Pragmática: Elementos Lingüísticos y Psicosociales*. Bilbao: Servicio Editorial de la Universidad del País Vasco.
Blum-Kulka, S. and Olshtain, E. (1984) Requests and apologies. A cross-cultural study of speech act realisation patterns (CCSARP). *Applied Linguistics* 5, 196–212.
Blum-Kulka, S. and Sheffer, H. (1993) The metapragmatic discourse of American–Israeli families. In G. Kasper and S. Blum-Kulka (eds) *Interlanguage Pragmatics*. New York: Oxford University Press.
Blum-Kulka, S., House, J. and Kasper, G. (1989) *Cross-cultural Pragmatics: Requests and Apologies*. Norwood: Ablex Publishing Corporation.
Borkin, A. and Reinhart, M. (1978) Excuse me and I'm sorry. *TESOL Quarterly* 2, 57–79.
Bou, P. (1993) *Estrategias de comunicación y secuencias tópicas en el discurso conversacional de estudiantes españoles de inglés*. Valencia: Servei de Publicacions Universitat de València.
Bouvy, C. (2000) Towards the construction of a theory of cross-linguistic transfer. In J. Cenoz and U. Jessner (eds) *English in Europe. The Acquisition of a Third Language*. Clevedon: Multilingual Matters.
Boxer, D. and Pickering, L. (1995) Problems in the presentation of speech acts in ELT materials: The case of complaints. *ELT Journal* 49, 44–58.
Breiner-Sanders, K.E., Lowe, P., Miles, J. and Swender, E. (1999) ACTFL Proficiency Guidelines – Speaking 1999. *Foreign Language Annals* 33, 13–17.
Brown, P. and Levinson, S.C. (1987) *Politeness. Some Universals in Language Usage*. Cambridge: Cambridge University Press.
Byram, M. and Leman, J. (1990) *Bicultural and Trilingual Education: The Foyer Model in Brussels*. Clevedon: Multilingual Matters.
Byrnes, H., Child, H., Patrizio, N., Lowe, P., Makino, S., Thompson, I. and Walton, R. (1986) *ACTFL Proficiency Guidelines*. American Council on Teaching of Foreign Languages.
Canale, M. (1983) From communicative competence to communicative language pedagogy. In J. Richards and R.W. Smith (eds) *Language and Communication*. New York: Longman.

Canale, M. and Swain, M. (1980) Theoretical bases of communicative approaches to second language teaching and testing. *Applied Linguistics* 1, 1–47.
Carroll, S. (1995) The irrelevance of verbal feedback to language learning. In L. Eubank, L. Selinker and M. Sharwood Smith (eds) *The Current State of Interlanguage*. Amsterdam: John Benjamins.
Celce-Murcia, M. Dörnyei, Z. and Thurrell, S. (1995) Communicative competence: A pedagogically motivated model with content specifications. *Issues in Applied Linguistics* 6, 5–35.
Cenoz, J. (1991) Enseñanza-aprendizaje del inglés como L2 o L3. Doctoral dissertation. Donostia: Universidad del País Vasco.
Cenoz, J. (1996) La competencia comunicativa: Su origen y componentes. In J. Cenoz and J. F. Valencia (eds) *La Competencia Pragmática. Elementos Lingüísticos y Psicosociales*. Bilbao: Servicio Editorial de la Universidad del País Vasco.
Cenoz, J. (2000) Research on multilingual acquisition. In J. Cenoz and U. Jessner (eds) *English in Europe. The Acquisition of a Third Language*. Clevedon: Multilingual Matters.
Cenoz, J. (2003) The additive effect of bilingualism on third language acquisition: A review. *The International Journal of Bilingualism* 7, 71–89.
Cenoz, J. and Genesee, F. (1998) Psycholinguistic perspectives on multilingualism and multilingual education. In J. Cenoz and F. Genesee (eds) *Beyond Bilingualism. Multilingualism and Multilingual Education*. Clevedon: Multilingual Matters.
Cenoz, J. and Hoffmann, C. (2003) The effect of bilingualism on third language acquisition. Special issue: *The International Journal of Bilingualism* 7 (1).
Cenoz, J., Hufeisen, B. and Jessner, U. (2001a) Towards trilingual education. Special issue: Third language acquisition in the school context. *International Journal of Bilingual Education and Bilingualism*. January.
Cenoz, J., Hufeisen, B. and Jessner, U. (2001b) *Cross-linguistic Influence in Third Language Acquisition: Psycholinguistic Perspectives*. Clevedon: Multilingual Matters.
Cenoz, J. and Jessner, U. (2000) *English in Europe. The Acquisition of a Third Language*. Clevedon: Multilingual Matters.
Cenoz, J. and Valencia, J.F. (1994) Additive trilingualism: Evidence from the Basque Country. *Applied Linguistics* 15, 195–207.
Chomsky, N. (1965) *Aspects of the Theory of Syntax*. Cambridge, MA: MIT Press.
Clyne, M. (1987) Constraints on code-switching: How universal are they? *Linguistics* 25, 739–64.
Clyne, M. (1997) Some of the things trilinguals do. *International Journal of Bilingualism* 1, 95–116.
Cohen, A. (1996) Developing the ability to perform speech acts. *Studies in Second Language Acquisition* 18, 253–67.
Cohen, A. (1997) Developing pragmatic ability: Insights from accelerated study of Japanese. In H. Cook, K. Hijirida and M. Tahara (eds) *New Trends and Issues in Teaching Japanese Language and Culture*. Technical Report No. 15. Honolulu: University of Hawaii, Second Language Teaching and Curriculum Center.
Cohen, A. and Olshtain, E. (1993) The production of speech acts by ESL learners. *TESOL Quarterly* 27, 33–56.
Corder, S. (1978) Language-learner language. In J. Richards (ed.) *Understanding Second and Foreign Language Learning*. Rowley, MA: Newbury House.

Crookall, D. and Oxford, R. (1988) Review essay of/on *Social Psychology and Second Language Learning: The Role of Attitudes and Motivation* by Robert C. Gardner. *Language Learning* 38, 127–40.

Cruse, A. (2000) *Meaning in Language. An Introduction to Semantics and Pragmatics.* Oxford: Oxford University Press.

Cummins, J. (1991) Interdependence between first and second language proficiency. In E. Bialystok (ed.) *Language Processing in Bilingual Children.* Cambridge: Cambridge University Press.

De Bot, K. (1992) A bilingual production model: Levelt's 'speaking' model adapted. *Applied Linguistics* 13, 1–24.

De Bot, K. and Schreuder, R. (1993) Word production and the bilingual lexicon. In R. Schreuder and B. Weltens (eds) *The Bilingual Lexicon.* Philadelphia: John Benjamins.

De Houwer, A. (1990) *The Acquisition of Two Languages from Birth: A Case Study.* Cambridge: Cambridge University Press.

Dell, G. (1986) A spreading activation theory of retrieval in sentence production. *Psychological Review* 93, 283–321.

Dewaele, J. (1998) Lexical inventions: French interlanguage as L2 versus L3. *Applied Linguistics* 19, 471–90.

Dörnyei, Z. (1994) Motivation and motivating in the foreign language classroom. *Modern Language Journal* 78, 515–23.

Dörnyei, Z. and Csizér, K. (1998) Ten commandments for motivating language learners: Results of an empirical study. *Language Teaching Research* 23, 203–29.

Doughty, C. and Williams, J. (1998) *Focus on Form.* Cambridge: Cambridge University Press.

Edmondson, W. (1981) *Spoken Discourse: A Model for Analysis.* London: Longman.

Edwards, J. (1994) *Multilingualism.* London: Routledge.

Eisenstein, M. (1980) Childhood bilingualism and adult language learning aptitude. *International Review of Applied Psychology* 29, 159–72.

Eisenstein, M. and Bodman, J. (1993) Expressing gratitude in American English. In G. Kasper and S. Blum-Kulka (eds) *Interlanguage Pragmatics.* New York: Oxford University Press.

Eisenstein, M., Bodman, J.W. and Carpenter, M. (1996) Cross-cultural realization of greetings in American English. In S. Gass and J. Neu (eds) *Speech Acts across Cultures.* Berlin: Mouton de Gruyter.

Ellis, R. (1984) *Classroom Second Language Development.* Oxford: Pergamon.

Ellis, R. (1985) *Understanding Second Language Acquisition.* Oxford: Oxford University Press.

Ellis, R. (1991) Grammaticality judgements and second language acquisition. *Studies in Second Language Acquisition* 13, 161–86.

Ellis, R. (1992) Learning to communicate in the classroom. A study of two language learners' requests. *Studies in Second Language Acquisition* 14, 1–23.

Ellis, R. (1994) *The Study of Second Language Acquisition.* Oxford: Oxford University Press.

Ellis, R. (1997) *SLA Research and Language Teaching.* Oxford: Oxford University Press.

Ervin-Tripp, S. (1976) Is Sybil there? The structure of some American English directives. *Language in Society* 5, 25–66.

Faerch, K. and Kasper, G. (1983) *Strategies in Interlanguage Communication.* London: Longman.

Faerch, K. and Kasper, G. (1989) Internal and external modification in interlanguage request realization. In S. Blum-Kulka, J. House and G. Kasper (eds) *Cross-cultural Pragmatics*. Norwood, NT: Ablex.

Foster-Cohen, S. (1994) Exploring the boundary between syntax and pragmatics: Relevance and the binding of pronouns. *Journal of Child Language* 21, 237–55.

Foster-Cohen, S. (2000) Review article of Sperber, D. and Wilson, D. (2nd edn: 1995) *Relevance: Communication and Cognition. Second Language Research* 16, 77–92.

Fotos, S. (1997) Communicative task performance and second language acquisition: Do task features determine learner output? *Revista Canaria de Estudios Ingleses* 34, 51–65.

Foulds, G.A. and Raven, J.C. (1950) An experimental survey with progressive matrices. *British Journal of Educational Psychology* 20, 104–10.

Fouser, R. (1995) Problems and prospects in third language acquisition research. *Language Research* 31, 387–414.

Fouser, R. (1997) Pragmatic transfer in highly advanced learners: Some preliminary findings. Dublin: Centre for Language and Communication Studies Occasional Papers No. 50.

Franceschini, R. (1999) Code-switching and the notion of code in linguistics: Proposals for a dual focus model. In P. Auer (ed.) *Code-switching in Conversation. Language, Interaction and Identity*. London: Routledge.

Fuyuka, Y. and Clark, M. (2001) Input enhancement of mitigators. In L. Bouton (ed.) *Pragmatics and Language Learning Monograph Series* (Vol. 10). Division of English as an International Language, University of Illinois at Urbana-Champaign.

Fuyuka, Y., Reeve, M., Gisi, J. and Christianson, M. (1998) Does focus on form work for sociopragmatics? Paper presented at the 12th Annual International Conference on Pragmatics and Language Learning, University of Illinois at Urbana-Champaign.

Galloway, L. (1980) Towards a neuropsychological model of bilingualism and second language performance: A theoretical article with a critical review of current research and some new hypotheses. In M. Long, S. Peck and K. Bailey (eds) *Research in Second Language Acquisition*. Rowley, MA: Newbury House.

Galloway, L. and Krashen, S. (1980) Cerebral organisation in bilingualism and second language. In R. Scarcella and S. Krashen (eds) *Research in Second Language Acquisition*. Rowley, MA: Newbury House.

García Mayo, M.P. (2001) Repair and completion strategies in the interlanguage of advanced EFL learners. *ITL Review of Applied Linguistics* 131–32; 139–68.

García Mayo, M.P. and García Lecumberri, M.L. (2003) *Age and the Acquisition of English as a Foreign Language*. Clevedon: Multilingual Matters.

Gardner, R.C. (1985) *Social Psychology and Second Language Learning*. London: Edward Arnold.

Garrett, M. (1975) The analysis of sentence production. In G. Bower (ed.) *Psychology of Learning and Motivation* (Vol. 9). New York: Academic Press.

Gass, S. and Madden, C. (1985) *Input in Second Language Acquisition*. Rowley, MA: Newbury House.

Genesee, F. (1989) Early bilingual language development: One language or two? *Journal of Child Language* 16, 161–79.

Genesee, F., Hamers, J., Lambert, W.E., Mononen, L., Seitz, M. and Starck, R. (1978) Language processing in bilinguals. *Brain and Language* 5, 1–12.

Genesee, F., Tucker, R. and Lambert, W. (1975) Communication skills in bilingual children. *Child Development* 46, 1010–14.
Giles, H. and Byrne, J.L. (1982) An intergroup approach to second language acquisition. *Journal of Multilingual and Multicultural Development* 3, 17–40.
Goldschmidt, M. (1996) From the addressee's perspective: Imposition in favor-asking. In S. Gass and J. Neu (eds) *Speech Acts across Cultures*. Berlin: Mouton de Gruyter
González, A. (1998) Teaching in two or more languages in the Philippine context. In J. Cenoz and F. Genesee (eds) *Beyond Bilingualism. Multilingualism and Multilingual Education*. Clevedon: Multilingual Matters.
Gordon, H.W. and Weide, R. (1983) La contribution de certaines fonctions cognitives au tratement du langage, à son acquisition et à l'apprentissage d'une langue seconde. *Langages* 73, 45–56.
Green, D.W. (1986) Control, activation and resource: A framework and a model for the control of speech in bilinguals. *Brain and Language* 27, 210–23.
Green, G. (1975) How to get people to do things with words. In P. Cole and J.L. Morgan (eds) *Syntax and Semantics, 3*. New York: Academic Press.
Grice, H.P. (1975) Logic and conversation. In P. Cole and J.L. Morgan (eds) *Syntax and Semantics, 3*. New York: Academic Press.
Grosjean, F. (1982) *Life with Two Languages: An Introduction to Bilingualism*. Cambridge, MA: Harvard University Press.
Grosjean, F. (1985) The bilingual as a competent but specific speaker-hearer. *Journal of Multilingual and Multicultural Development* 6, 467–77.
Gumperz, J.J. (1971) *Language in Social Groups: Essays by J.J. Gumperz*, selected by A.S. Dil. Stanford, CA: Stanford University Press.
Hackman, D.J. (1977) Patterns in purported speech acts. *Journal of Pragmatics* 1, 143–54.
Halliday, M. (1973) *Explorations in the Functions of Language*. London: Edward Arnold.
Hamers, J.F. and Blanc, N. (1989) *Bilinguality and Bilingualism*. Cambridge: Cambridge University Press.
Hammarberg, B. and Hammarberg, B. (1993) Articulatory re-setting in the acquisition of new languages. Reports from the Department of Phonetics, University of Umea, *PHONUM* 2, 61–67.
Harding, E. and Riley, P. (1986) *The Bilingual Family*. Cambridge: Cambridge University Press.
Harris, D.P. and Palmer, L.A. (1970) *CELT Technical Manual*. New York: McGraw-Hill.
Hartford, B.S. and Bardovi-Harlig, K. (1992) Experimental and observational data in the study of interlanguage pragmatics. In L. Bouton and Y. Kachru (eds) *Pragmatics and Language Learning* (Vol. 3). Urbana: DEIL, University of Illinois.
Hassall, T.J. (1997) Requests by Australian learners of Indonesian. Unpublished doctoral dissertation. Canberra: Australian National University.
Hatch, E. (1983) *Psycholinguistics: A Second Language Perspective*. Rowley, MA: Newbury House.
Hatch, E. and Lazaraton, A. (1991) *The Research Manual. Design and Statistics for Applied Linguistics*. Boston: Heinle and Heinle.
Haverkate, H. (1984) *Speech Acts, Speakers and Hearers. Pragmatics and Beyond 4*. Amsterdam: John Benjamin Publishing Company.
Herdina, P. and Jessner, U. (2000) The dynamics of third language acquisition. In J. Cenoz and U. Jessner (eds) *English in Europe. The Acquisition of a Third Language*. Clevedon: Multilingual Matters.

Herdina, P. and Jessner, U. (2002) *A Dynamic Model of Multilingualism. Perspectives of Change in Psycholinguistics*. Clevedon: Multilingual Matters.

Heredia, R. and McLaughlin, B. (1992) Bilingual memory revisited. In R.J. Harris (ed.) *Cognitive Processing in Bilinguals*. Amsterdam: North-Holland.

Hill, T. (1997) The development of pragmatic competence in an EFL context. Unpublished doctoral dissertation. Tokyo: Temple University Japan.

Hoffman, C. (1991) *An Introduction to Bilingualism*. New York: Longman.

Hoffman, C. (1998) Luxembourg and the European schools. In J. Cenoz and F. Genesee (eds) *Beyond Bilingualism. Multilingualism and Multilingual Education*. Clevedon: Multilingual Matters.

Holmes, J. (1989) Sex differences and apologies: One aspect of communicative competence. *Applied Linguistics* 10, 194–213.

Houck, N. and Gass, S. (1996) Non-native refusal: A methodological perspective. In S. Gass and J. Neu (eds) *Speech Acts across Cultures*. Berlin: Mouton de Gruyter.

House, J. (1989) Politeness in English and German: The function of Please and Bitte. In S. Blum-Kulka, J. House and G. Kasper (eds) *Cross-cultural Pragmatics: Requests and Apologies*. Norwood, NJ: Ablex.

House, J. (1996) Developing pragmatic fluency in English as a foreign language: Routines and metapragmatic awareness. *Studies in Second Language Acquisition* 18, 225–52.

House, J. and Kasper, G. (1981) Zur Rolle der Kognition in Kommunikationskursen. *Die Neueren Sprachen* 80, 42–55.

House, J. and Kasper, G. (1987) Interlanguage pragmatics: Requesting in a foreign language. In W. Lorscher and R. Schulze (eds) *Perspectives on Language Performance: Festschrift for Werner Hullen*. Tübingen: Gunter Narr.

Hudson, T., Detmer, E. and Brown, J. (1995) Developing prototypic measures of cross-cultural pragmatics. Technical Report, 7. Honolulu: University of Hawaii, Second Language Teaching and Curriculum Center.

Hufeisen, B. (1991) *Englisch als erste und Deutsch as zweite Fremdsprache. Empirische Untersuchung zur fremdsprachlichen Interaktion*. Frankfurt: Peter Lang.

Hufeisen, B. (1998) L3 – Stand der Forschung – Was bleibt zu tun? In B. Hufeisen and B. Lindemann (eds) *Tertiärsprachen. Theorien, Modelle, Methoden*. Tübingen: Stauffenburg.

Hufeisen, B. and Lindemann, B. (1998) *Tertiärsprachen. Theorien, Modelle, Methoden*. Tübingen: Stauffenburg.

Hummel, K.M. (1993) Bilingual memory research: From storage to processing issues. *Applied Psycholinguistics* 14, 267–84.

Hymes, D. (1972) On communicative competence. In B.J. Pride and J. Holmes (eds) *Sociolinguistics*. Harmondsworth: Penguin.

Ianco-Worrall, A. (1972) Bilingualism and cognitive development. *Child Development* 23, 1390–1400.

James, A.R. (2000) English as a European lingua franca. Current realities and existing dichotomies. In J. Cenoz and U. Jessner (eds) *English in Europe. The Acquisition of a Third Language*. Clevedon: Multilingual Matters.

Jary, M. (1998) Relevance theory and the communication of politeness. *Journal of Pragmatics* 30, 1–19.

Jessner, U. (1997) Towards a dynamic view of multilingualism. In M. Pütz (ed.) *Language Choices. Conditions, Constraints and Consequences*. Amsterdam: John Benjamins Publishing Co.

Jessner, U. (1999) Metalinguistic awareness in multilinguals: Cognitive aspects of third language acquisition. *Language Awareness* 8, 201–09.

Johnston, B., Kasper, G. and Ross, S. (1998) Effect of rejoinders in production questionnaires. *Applied Linguistics* 19, 157–82.

Kasper, G. (1996) Interlanguage pragmatics in SLA. *Studies in Second Language Acquisition* 18, 145–49.

Kasper, G. (1997) Can pragmatic competence be taught? *Network* 6. Second Language Teaching and Curriculum Center. University of Hawaii.

Kasper, G. (2000) Four perspectives on L2 pragmatic development. *Network* 9. Second Language Teaching and Curriculum Center. University of Hawaii.

Kasper, G. and Blum-Kulka, S. (1993) *Interlanguage Pragmatics*. New York: Oxford University Press.

Kasper, G. and Dahl, M. (1991) Research methods in interlanguage pragmatics. *Studies in Second Language Acquisition* 13, 215–47.

Kasper, G. and Kellerman, E. (1997) *Communication Strategies. Psycholinguistic and Sociolinguistic Perspectives*. New York: Longman.

Kasper, G. and Rose, K.R. (1999) Pragmatics and SLA. *Annual Review of Applied Linguistics* 19, 81–104.

Kasper, G. and Rose, K.R. (2002) *Pragmatic Development in a Second Language*. Malden: Blackwell Publishers.

Kasper, G. and Schmidt, R. (1996) Developmental issues in interlanguage pragmatics. *Studies in Second Language Acquisition* 18, 149–69.

Kecskés, I. and Papp, T. (2000) Metaphorical competence in trilingual language production. In J. Cenoz and U. Jessner (eds) *English in Europe. The Acquisition of a Third Language*. Clevedon: Multilingual Matters.

Kellerman, E. (1977) Towards a characterisation of the strategy of transfer in second language learning. *Interlanguage Studies Bulletin* 2, 58–154.

Kellerman, E. (1991) Compensatory strategies in a second language: A critique, a revision, and some (non-) implications for the classroom. In R. Phillipson, E. Kellerman, L. Selinker, M. Sharwood Smith and M. Swain (eds) *Foreign/Second Language Pedagogy Research*. Clevedon: Multilingual Matters.

Kellerman, E. and Sharwood Smith, M. (1986) *Cross-linguistic Influence in Second Language Learning*. Oxford: Pergamon Press.

Kempen, G. and Hoenkamp, G. (1987) An incremental procedural grammar for sentence formulation. *Cognitive Science* 11, 201–58.

Koike, D. (1996) Transfer of pragmatic competence and suggestions in Spanish foreign language learning. In S. Gass and J. Neu (eds) *Speech Acts Across Cultures. Challenges to Communication in a Second Language*. Berlin: Mouton de Gruyter.

Koulos, F. (1986) Bilingualism, sex differences and creativity. Unpublished honors thesis, University of Adulate.

Krashen, S. (1981) *Second Language Acquisition and Second Language Learning*. Oxford: Pergamon Press.

Krashen, S. (1982) *Principles and Practices of Second Language Acquisition*. Oxford: Pergamon Press.

Lambert, W.E. (1977) The effects of bilingualism on the individual. Cognitive and socio-cultural consequences. In P.A. Hornby (ed.) *Bilingualism: Psychological, Social and Educational Implications*. New York: Academic Press.

Lambert, W.E. (1990) Persistent issues in bilingualism. In B. Harley, A. Patrick, J. Cummins and M. Swain (eds) *The Development of Second Language Proficiency*. Cambridge: Cambridge University Press.

Larse-Freeman, D. (1997) Chaos/complexity science and second language acquisition. *Applied Linguistics* 18, 141–65.

Lasagabaster, D. (1997) *Creatividad y Conciencia Metalingüística: Incidencia en el Aprendizaje del Inglés como L3*. Published doctoral dissertation. Servicio Editorial de la Universidad del País Vasco.

Lasagabaster, D. (1998) La conciencia metalingüística en alumnos y alumnas monolingües y bilingües del País Vasco. In I. Vázquez and I. Guillén (eds) *Perspectivas Pragmáticas en Lingüística Aplicada*. Zaragoza: Universidad de Zaragoza.

Lasagabaster, D. (2000) The effects of three bilingual education models on linguistic creativity. *International Review of Applied Linguistics* 38, 213–28.

Leech, G. (1980) *Explorations in Semantics and Pragmatics*. Amsterdam: John Benjamins.

Leech, G. (1983) *Principles of Pragmatics*. London: Longman.

Levelt, W. (1989) *Speaking: From Intention to Articulation*. Cambridge, MA: MIT Press.

Lyster, R. (1998) Immersion pedagogy and implications for language teaching. In J. Cenoz and F. Genesee (eds) *Beyond Bilingualism. Multilingualism and Multilingual Education*. Clevedon: Multiligual Matters.

Mackey, W.F. (1967) *Bilingualism as a World Problem*. Montreal: Harvest House.

Mackey, W.F. (1970) The description of bilingualism. In J. Fishman (ed.) *Readings in the Sociology of Language*. The Hague: Mouton.

Maeshiba, N., Yoshinaga, N., Kasper, G. and Ross, S. (1996) Transfer and proficiency in interlanguage apologizing. In S. Gass and J. Neu (eds) *Speech Acts across Cultures*. Berlin: Mouton de Gruyter.

Mägiste, E. (1984) Learning a third language. *Journal of Multilingual and Multicultural Development* 5, 415–21.

Malakoff, M.E. (1992) Translation ability: A natural bilingual and metalinguistic skill. In J. Harris (ed.) *Cognitive Processing in Bilinguals*. Amsterdam: Elsevier.

Manchón, R. (2001) Un acercamiento psicolingüístico al fenómeno de la transferencia en el aprendizaje y uso de segundas lenguas. *Estudios de Lingüística*.

Matsumi, N. (1994) Process of words memory in second language acquisition: A test of bilingual dual coding model. *Japanese Journal of Psychology* 64, 460–68.

McClure, E. (1977) Aspects of code-switching in the discourse of bilingual Mexican–American children. In M. Saville-Troike (ed.) *Linguistics and Anthropology*. Washington.

McGlone, J. (1978) Sex differences in functional brain asymmetry. *Cortex* 14, 122–28.

McLaughlin, B. (1978) The monitor model: Some methodological considerations. *Language Learning* 28, 309–32.

Meier, A. (1997) Teaching the universals of politeness. *ELT Journal* 51, 21–28.

Meisel, J.M. (1986) Word order and case marking in early child language: Evidence from simultaneous acquisition of two languages. *Linguistics* 24, 123–83.

Muñoz, C. (2000) Bilingualism and trilingualism in school students in Catalonia. In J. Cenoz and U. Jessner (eds) *English in Europe. The Acquisition of a Third Language*. Clevedon: Multilingual Matters.

Murphy, B. and Neu, J. (1996) My grade's too low: The speech act set of complaining. In S. Gass and J. Neu (eds) *Speech Acts across Cultures*. Berlin: Mouton de Gruyter.

Nayak, N., Hansen, N., Krueger, N. and McLaughlin, B. (1990) Language-learning strategies in monolingual and multilingual adults. *Language Learning* 40, 221–44.

Nelson, G.L., Al-batal, M. and Echols, E. (1996) Arabic and English compliment responses: Potential for pragmatic failure. *Applied Linguistics* 17, 411–32.

Norris, J. and Ortega, L. (2000). Effectiveness of L2 instruction: A research synthesis and quantitative meta-analysis. *Language Learning*, 50, 3.

Nunan, D. (1996) Issues in second language acquisition research: Examining substance and procedure. In W. Ritchie and T.K. Bathia (eds) *Handbook of Second Language Acquisition*. San Diego: Academic Press.

Nunan, D. and Lam, A. (1998) Teacher education for multilingual contexts: Models and issues. In J. Cenoz and F. Genesee (eds) *Beyond Bilingualism. Multilingualism and Multilingual Education*. Clevedon: Multilingual Matters.

Obler, L. (1989) Exceptional second language learners. In S. Gass, C. Madden, D. Preston and L. Selinker (eds) *Variation in Second Language Acquisition: Psycholinguistic Issues*. Clevedon: Multilingual Matters.

Obler, L.K., Zatorre, R.J., Galloway, L. and Vaid, J. (2000) Cerebral lateralization in bilinguals: Methodological issues. In L. Wei (ed.) *The Bilingualism Reader*. London: Routledge.

Olshtain, E. and Cohen, A. (1983) Apology: A speech act set. In N. Wolfson and E. Judd (eds) *Sociolinguistics and Language Acquisition*. Rowley, MA: Newbury House Publishers.

Olshtain, E. and Cohen, A. (1990) The learning of complex speech act behaviour. *TESL Canada Journal* 7, 45–65.

Olshtain, E. and Weinbach, L. (1993) Interlanguage features of the speech act of complaining. In G. Kasper and S. Blum-Kulka (eds) *Interlanguage Pragmatics*. New York: Oxford University Press.

Omar, A.S. (1991) How learners greet in Kiswahili. In L. Bouton and Y. Kachru (eds) *Pragmatics and Language Learning* (Vol. 2). Urbana: DEIL, University of Illinois.

Oskaar, E. (1990) Language contact and culture contact: Towards an integrative approach in second language acquisition research. In H. Dechert (ed.) *Current Trends in European Second Language Acquisition Research*. Clevedon: Multilingual Matters.

Padilla, A.M. and Liebman, E. (1975) Language acquisition in the bilingual child. *Bilingual Review* 2, 34–55.

Paivio, A. (1991) Mental representations in bilinguals. In A.G. Reynolds (ed.) *Bilingualism, Multiculturalism and Second Language Learning*. Hillsdale, NJ: Lawrence Erlbaum.

Paivio, A. and Desrochers, A. (1980) A dual-coding approach to bilingual memory. *Canadian Journal of Psychology* 34, 390–401.

Palmer, J.C. and Posteguillo, S. (1996) Autonomous learning in ESP: The self-access centre at Universitat Jaume I. In S. Barrueco, L. Sierra and E. Hernández (eds) *Lengua para Fines Específicos IV*. Alcala: Universidad de Alcalá de Henares.

Paradis, M. (1977) Bilingualism and aphasia. In H. Whitaker and H. Whitaker (eds) *Studies in Neurolinguistics* (Vol. 13). New York: Academic Press.

Paradis, M. (1980) The language switch in bilinguals: Psycholinguistic and neurolinguistic perspectives. In P. Nelde (ed.) *Languages in Contact and Conflict*. Wiesbaden, Germany: Franz Steiner Verlag.

Paradis, M. (1990) Language lateralization in bilinguals. *Brain and Language* 39, 570–86.
Paradis, M. and Lecours, A.R. (1979) L'Aphasie chez les bilingues et les polyglottes. In A.R. Lecours and F. Lhermitte (eds) *L'Aphasie*. Paris: Flammarion.
Poulisse, N. (1993) Theories of communication strategy use: Some recent proposals. In N. Poulisse (ed.) *Learning Strategies in Second Language Use*. Amsterdam: John Benjamins.
Poulisse, N. (1997) Language production in bilinguals. In A.M. de Groot and J.F. Kroll (eds) *Tutorials in Bilingualism*. Mahwah, NJ: Lawrence Erlbaum.
Poulisse, N. and Bongaerts, T. (1994) First language use in second language production. *Applied Linguistics* 15, 36–57.
Poulisse, N. and Schils, E. (1989) The influence of task- and proficiency-related factors on the use of compensatory strategies: A quantitative analysis. *Language Learning* 39, 15–48.
Rampton, B. (1999) Language crossing and the redefinition of reality. In P. Auer (ed.) *Code-switching in Conversation. Language, Interaction and Identity*. London: Routledge.
Ricciardelli, L.A. (1992) Creativity and bilingualism. *Journal of Creative Behaviour* 26, 242–54.
Ringbom, H. (1987) *The Role of the First Language in Foreign Language Learning*. Clevedon: Multilingual Matters.
Robinson, M.A. (1992) Introspective methodology in interlanguage pragmatics research. In G. Kasper (ed.) *Pragmatics of Japanese as Native and Target Language*. Technical Report No. 3. Honolulu, HI: University of Hawaii at Manoa, Second Language Teaching and Curriculum Center.
Rose, K.R. (1992) Speech acts and questionnaires: The effect of hearer response. *Journal of Pragmatics* 17, 49–62.
Rose, K.R. (1994) On the validity of DCTs in non-Western contexts. *Applied Linguistics* 15, 1–14.
Rose, K.R. (1998) An exploratory cross-sectional study of interlanguage pragmatic development. Unpublished ms.
Rose, K.R. (2000) An exploratory cross-sectional study of interlanguage pragmatic development. *Studies in Second Language Acquisition* 22, 27–67.
Rose, K.R. and Kasper, G. (2001) *Pragmatics in Language Teaching*. New York: Cambridge University Press.
Rose, K.R. and Ng, C. (2001) Inductive and deductive approaches to the teaching of compliments and compliment responses. In K. Rose and G. Kasper (eds) *Pragmatics in Language Teaching*. New York: Cambridge University Press.
Rose, K.R. and Ono, R. (1995) Eliciting speech act data in Japanese: The effect of questionnaire type. *Language Learning* 45, 191–223.
Ross, S. (1997) An introspective analysis of listener inferencing on a second language listening task. In G. Kasper and E. Kellerman (eds) *Communication Strategies. Psycholinguistic and Sociolinguistic Perspectives*. New York: Longman.
Rost, M. (1990) *Listening in Language Learning*. London: Longman.
Sanz, C. (2000) Bilingual education enhances third language acquisition: Evidence from Catalonia. *Applied Psycholinguistics* 21, 23–44.
Sasaki, M. (1998) Investigating EFL students' production of speech acts: A comparison of production questionnaires and role plays. *Journal of Pragmatics* 30, 457–84.

Schmidt, R. (1983) Interaction, acculturation and the acquisition of communicative competence: A case study of an adult. In E. Judd and N. Wolfson (eds) *Sociolinguistics and Language Acquisition*. Rowley, MA: Newbury House.

Schönpflug, U. (2000) Word-fragment completions in the second (German) and third (English) language: A contribution to the organisation of the trilingual speaker's lexicon. In J. Cenoz and U. Jessner (eds) *English in Europe. The Acquisition of a Third Language*. Clevedon: Multilingual Matters.

Schumann, J. (1978) *The Pidginization Process: A Model for Second Language Acquisition*. Rowley, MA: Newbury House.

Searle, J.R. (1969) *Speech Acts: An Essay in the Philosophy of Language*. Cambridge: Cambridge University Press.

Searle, J.R. (1975) Indirect speech acts. In P. Cole and J.L. Morgan (eds) *Syntax and Semantics 3: Speech Acts*. New York: Academic Press.

Searle, J.R. (1976) The classification of illocutionary acts. *Language in Society* 5, 1–24.

Searle, J.R. (1979) *Expression and Meaning: Studies in the Theory of Speech Acts*. Cambridge: Cambridge University Press.

Sharwood Smith, M. (1981) Consciousness-raising and the second language learner. *Applied Linguistics* 2, 159–69.

Sharwood Smith, M. (1994) *Second Language Learning: Theoretical Foundations*. London: Longman.

Sifianou, M. (1999) *Politeness Phenomena in England and Greece. A Cross-cultural Perspective*. Oxford: Oxford University Press.

Skehan, P. (1988) Language testing. *Language Teaching* 21, 1–13.

Skutnabb-Kangas, T. (1984) *Bilingualism or Not*. Clevedon: Multilingual Matters.

Slugoski, B.R. and Turnbull, W. (1988) Cruel to be kind and kind to be cruel: Sarcasm, banter and social relations. *Journal of Language and Social Psychology* 7, 101–21.

Sperber, D. and Wilson, D. (1986) *Relevance: Communication and Cognition*. Oxford: Blackwell.

Sperber, D. and Wilson, D. (1995) *Relevance: Communication and Cognition* (2nd edn). Oxford: Blackwell.

Sussman, H.M., Franklin, P. and Simon, T. (1982) Bilingual speech: Bilateral control? *Brain and Language* 15, 125–42.

Swain, M. (1985) Communicative competence: Some roles of comprehensive input and comprehensible output in its development. In S. Gass and C. Madden (eds) *Input in Second Language Acquisition*. Rowley, MA: Newbury House.

Swain, M. (1995) Three functions of output in second language learning. In G. Cook and B. Seidlhofer (eds) *Principle and Practice in Applied Linguistics: Studies in Honour of H.G. Widdowson*. Oxford: Oxford University Press.

Takahashi, T. (1996) Pragmatic transferability. *Studies in Second Language Acquisition* 18, 189–223.

Takahashi, T. (2001) Explicit and implicit teaching of pragmatic routines: Japanese *sumimasen*. In K. Rose and G. Kasper (eds) *Pragmatics in Language Teaching*. New York: Cambridge University Press.

Takahashi, T. and Beebe, L.M. (1987) The development of pragmatic competence by Japanese learners of English. *JALT Journal* 8, 131–55.

Takahashi, S. and DuFon, M.A. (1989) Cross-linguistic influence in indirectness: The case of English directives performed by native Japanese speakers. Unpublished manuscript, Department of English as a Second Language, University of Hawaii at Manoa.

Tarone, E. (1980) Communication strategies, foreigner talk, and repair in interlanguage. *Language Learning* 30, 417–31.

Tarone, E. (1983) On the variability of interlanguage systems. *Applied Linguistics* 4, 143–63.

Tateyama, Y., Kasper, G., Mui, L., Tay, H. and Thananart, O. (1997) Explicit and implicit teaching of pragmatic routines. In L. Bouton (ed.) *Pragmatics and Language Learning* Vol. 8. Urbana IL: University of Illinois at Urbana-Champaign.

Thomas, J. (1995) *Meaning in Interaction. An Introduction to Pragmatics*. New York: Longman.

Torrance, E.P. (1966) *Rewarding Creative Behaviour*. Englewood Cliffs, NJ: Prentice Hall.

Trosborg, A. (1987) Apology strategies in natives/non-natives. *Journal of Pragmatics* 11, 147–67.

Trosborg, A. (1995) *Interlanguage Pragmatics. Requests, Complaints and Apologies*. New York: Mouton de Gruyter.

Turner, K. (1996) The principal principles of pragmatic inference: Politeness. *Language Teaching* 29, 1–13.

Turrell, T. (2000) *Multilingualism in Spain. Sociolinguistic and Psycholinguistic Aspects of Linguistic Minority Groups*. Clevedon: Multilingual Matters.

Vaid, J. (1983) Biligualism and brain lateralization. In S. Segalowitz (ed.) *Language Function and Brain Organization*. New York: Academic Press.

Van Dijk, T. (1977) *Text and Context*. London: Longman.

Van Geert, P. (1994) *Dynamic Systems of Development. Change between Complexity and Chaos*. New York: Harvester Wheatsheaf.

Viereck, W. (1996) English in Europe: Its nativisation and use as a *lingua franca*, with special reference to German-speaking countries. In R. Hartmann (ed.) *The English Language in Europe*. Oxford: Intellect.

Volterra, V. and Taeschner, T. (1978) The acquisition of language by bilingual children. *Journal of Child Language* 5, 311–26.

Waddington, C.H. (1977) *Tools for Thought*. Paladin: Frogmore.

Wagner, D.A., Spratt, J.E. and Ezzaki, A. (1989) Does learning to read in a second language always put the child at a disadvantage? Some counter-evidence from Morocco. *Applied Psycholinguistics* 10, 31–48.

Watts, R.J., Ide, S. and Ehlich, K. (1992) *Politeness in Language*. Berlin: Mouton.

Wei, L. (2000) *The Bilingualism Reader*. London: Routledge.

Weinreich, U. (1968) *Languages in Contact: Findings and Problems*. The Hague: Mouton.

Williams, S. and Hammarberg, B. (1998) Language switches in L3 production: Implications for a polyglot speaking model. *Applied Linguistics* 19, 295–333.

Wolfson, N. (1989) *Perspectives: Sociolinguistics and TESOL*. New York: Newbury House.

Wunderlich, D. (1980) Methodological remarks on speech act theory. In J.R. Searle, F. Kiefer and M. Bierwisch (eds) *Speech Act Theory and Pragmatics*. Dordrecht: Reidel Publishing Company.

Yoshimi, D.R. (2001) Explicit instruction and JFL learners' use of interactional discourse markers. In K. Rose and G. Kasper (eds) *Pragmatics and Language Teaching*. Cambridge: Cambridge University Press.

Ystma, J. (2000) Trilingual primary education in Friesland. In J. Cenoz and U. Jessner (eds) *English in Europe. The Acquisition of a Third Language*. Clevedon: Multilingual Matters.

For Product Safety Concerns and Information please contact our EU Authorised Representative:

Easy Access System Europe

Mustamäe tee 50

10621 Tallinn

Estonia

gpsr.requests@easproject.com